SEWARD'S LAW

SEWARD'S LAW

COUNTRY LAWYERING, RELATIONAL RIGHTS, AND SLAVERY

PETER CHARLES HOFFER

CORNELL UNIVERSITY PRESS
Ithaca and London

First published 2022 by Cornell University Press

Library of Congress Cataloging-in-Publication Data

Names: Hoffer, Peter Charles, 1944– author.
Title: Seward's law : country lawyering, relational rights, and slavery / Peter Charles Hoffer.
Description: Ithaca [New York] : Cornell University Press, 2022. | Includes bibliographical references and index.
Identifiers: LCCN 2022010576 (print) | LCCN 2022010577 (ebook) | ISBN 9781501767333 (hardcover) | ISBN 9781501767340 (pdf) | ISBN 9781501767357 (epub)
Subjects: LCSH: Seward, William H. (William Henry), 1801–1872. | Seward, William H. (William Henry), 1801–1872—Political and social views. | Seward, William H. (William Henry), 1801–1872—Influence. | Country lawyers—New York (State)—Biography. | Practice of law—Political aspects—New York (State)—History—19th century. | Slavery—Political aspects—United States—History—19th century. | Antislavery movements—United States—History—19th century.
Classification: LCC E415.9.S4 H64 2022 (print) | LCC E415.9.S4 (ebook) | DDC 973.7092—dc23/eng/20220805
LC record available at https://lccn.loc.gov/2022010576
LC ebook record available at https://lccn.loc.gov/2022010577

Contents

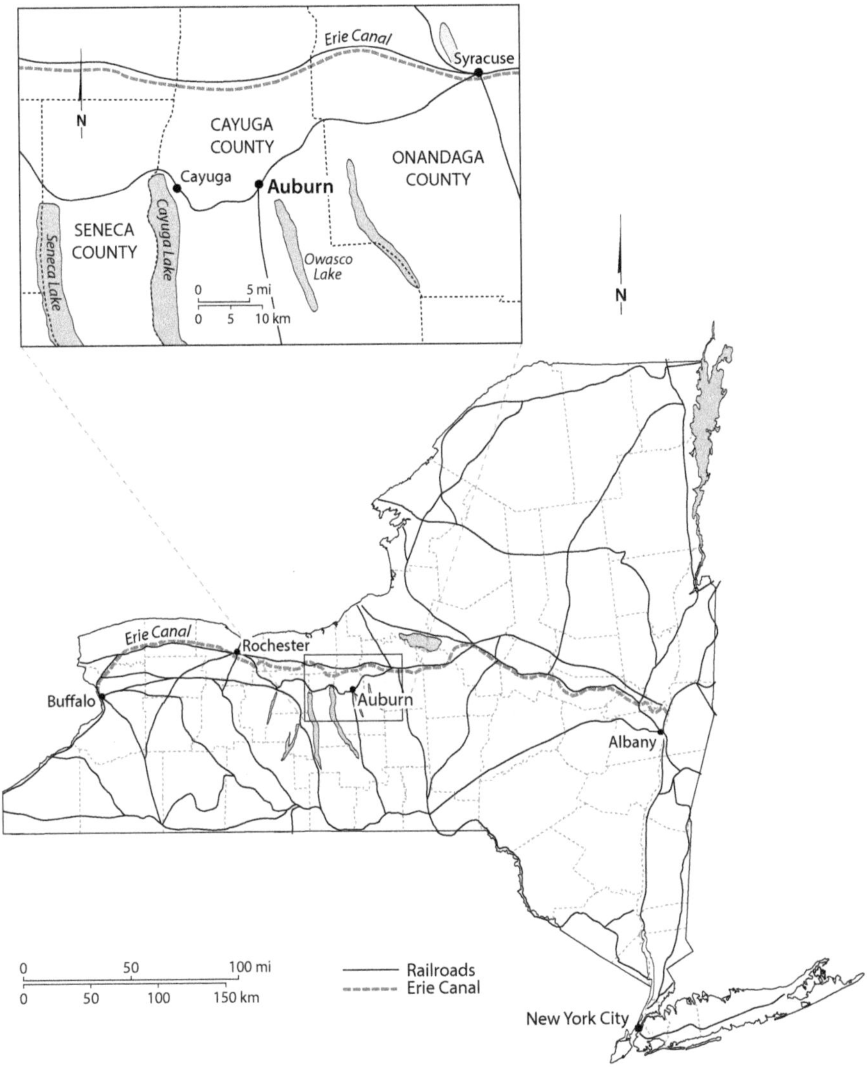

Seward's legal world, ca 1855. Map by Bill Nelson.

SEWARD'S LAW

Introduction
The Country Lawyer

The William Henry Seward (1801–1872) of the history books is an antebellum and Civil War politician who almost won the Republican presidential nomination in 1860. He is the secretary of state who enabled the purchase of Alaska from tsarist Russia. Not so well known is that Seward was one of the era's most successful litigators, anointed the "king" of the patent law bar by one newspaper. Even more important, though largely ignored, is Seward's effort to frame a jurisprudence based on "relational rights" in a democratic society. These rights were communal and reciprocal, what everyone owed to every other member of the community. Though limited by the Victorian mores and the racialist presumptions of the day, relational rights was a platform for the end of slavery. Slave law was the antithesis of this liberal jurisprudence, for in the legal regime of the peculiar institution masters owed nothing to their bondmen and women, while those enslaved owed life and labor to their masters.

Seward, decried in his time variously as an ambitious trimmer, a rabid abolitionist, and a tool of political operator Thurlow Weed, was not wholly any of those. Aligning his legal practice with his politics reveals a man who wanted more and better law through reasoned and progressive politics. Neither conservative nor radical, Seward's relational jurisprudence infused his arguments in court, his ideas of good laws, his public orations, his speeches in Congress, and his view of political parties. He believed that public law should evolve toward freedom of enterprise and equality of persons before the law and that the Constitution incorporated a standard of relational duty and dignity. His union, as he said in his most famous public address, was a "democracy of property and persons," a bond created by "a fair approximation of universal education" and "operating by means of universal suffrage," sadly, a vision that he would not live to see fulfilled and even more sadly, one that he did not fully understand, for he could not and would not see everyone as fitting his ideal of equality.[1]

My assumption here, as in my other works, is that a lifetime spent as a lawyer influences how one responds to the challenges of everyday life, including those of public life. Even when he entered the highest realms of national politics, Seward remained a "country lawyer" at heart. His habits of mind, his jurisprudential instincts, if one can call them such, arose out of his practice of law in upstate New York. He professed to hate the day-to-day strife of litigation, but he loved winning in the cockpit of the courtroom.

Once upon a time in the first half of the nineteenth century, the vast majority of legal practitioners in America were country lawyers. As the country lawyer began to vanish from the landscape, Justice William O. Douglas, who had briefly opened a law practice in his Yakima, Washington, hometown, told the American Bar Association that the country lawyer would always be an "integral part of the community in which he lived," for "his position in town and country exacted responsibilities." Soon to be Justice Louis D. Brandeis was even more effusive in his praise. The country lawyer "secured breadth of view largely through wide professional experience. Being a general practitioner, he was brought into contact with all phases of contemporary life . . . The relative smallness of the communities tended to make his practice diversified not only in the character of matters dealt with, but also in the character or standing of his clients. For the same lawyer was apt to serve at one time or another both rich and poor, both employer and employee. Furthermore—nearly every lawyer of ability took some part in political life."[2]

Supreme Court Justice Robert H. Jackson had been a country lawyer. He recalled what the job's responsibilities were. "The county-seat lawyer, counsellor to railroads and to Negroes, to bankers and to poor whites . . . always gave to each the best there was in him-and was willing to admit that his best was good." Jackson concluded that the country lawyer "has been an American institution . . . Such a man understands the structure of society and how its groups interlock and interact, because he lives in a community so small that he can keep it all in view." The country lawyer was the person to whom one went with problems, who would listen and advise—at no cost (at first). He was trusted. He settled disputes among neighbors long before the profession of mediator appeared. He did not specialize, nor did he pick and choose clients. He rarely declined service to worthy ones because of inability to pay. Once enlisted for a client, he took his obligation seriously. Douglas agreed: "country lawyers very often are closer to the hearts and dreams of America than the prominent big-name lawyers."[3]

The country lawyer was not easily bluffed or confused. He saw issues and people for what they were. His adoption of the country manner was as much a pose as the antebellum urban gentry's adoption of European sophistication. A country lawyer himself, Illinois's Abraham Lincoln's penchant for telling stories during legal consultation or in court was a prime example of this calculated behavior. "As a practicing lawyer, traveling from one county seat to another, Lincoln discovered the effectiveness, power, and usefulness of the well-placed anecdote." Though hardly in Lincoln's league as a raconteur, New York's William Henry Seward was also "a superb master of ceremonies" and an "inveterate storyteller," enjoying (and later recording in detail) his conversations with anyone who came to his door in Auburn.[4]

It may be too easy to oversimplify the country lawyer as if there were but one type. The use of the term should not obscure the variety in country law practices and practitioners. Some country lawyers did not aspire to more than their rural practices and their local lives. Some were unsuccessful in practice and uprooted themselves over and over. Others eagerly left the countryside and journeyed to the city and (sometimes) fame. But their traits were general ones, and they would have recognized one another in town, in the courtroom, and on the country roads they once traveled. True, many of the most prominent lawyers of the years before the Civil War were determined not to be country lawyers. One thinks of the early national New York bar's stars like James Duane, Alexander Hamilton, and Aaron Burr, none of whom can be called country lawyers. Or Daniel Webster and William Pinkney, who began their careers in the country and left as soon as they could to live and work in Boston and Baltimore, respectively.[5]

The practice of law in the small towns and rural areas that dominated the countryside in the years before the Civil War had both an elevating and humbling character. Law was a profession, subject to codes of conduct, requiring specialized study and admission to local and state bars based on examinations. For the most part, lawyers and judges enjoyed elite status in antebellum middle-class America. At the same time, lawyering was a competitive, exhausting, and often frustrating occupation in a world of rapid change. Losing a case was a humbling experience. As Seward wrote during his battle to save Henry Wyatt from the gallows, "in this court I am fighting a battle in which I ask no sympathy or support." He got none, and his client was convicted.[6]

The country lawyer grew up surrounded by farms and small-town businesses. The most common lawsuit involved some form of debt, and the most common prize was ownership of land. Outside of court, the collection of debts was a mainstay of country practice. Though written about a contemporary of Seward's, this country lawyer "is just a bit more animated, a bit more cheerful when the client is a creditor. He likes entrepreneurs, and . . . is naturally drawn to men who have money and loan it out. . . . On the other hand, perhaps he assumes a slight air of sympathy with the debtor . . . and so tries to strike a balance between compassion and a coolly rational unemotional appraisal of the case." Sales and purchases, mortgages, and other "real property" also filled the docket. Disputes sent the lawyer to the local courthouse to find deed and mortgage papers.[7]

The country lawyer knew something that those who teach law from the top down—black letter law, lawbook law, appellate case law—may have forgotten. As the legal historian Laura Edwards explains, ordinary people in the nineteenth century, people without much formal power or official standing, routinely used law "to advance their own interests." In local courts, "disadvantaged" people of color, Native Americans, the working poor, and women defined law in terms of social custom and personal identity, a law of reciprocity and dignity that existed alongside the law that "legitimized a hierarchical order" of property and power. The country lawyer aided and abetted these individuals, sometimes simply interceding for them, sometimes bringing a suit in their name, sometimes simply lending his voice to theirs.[8]

Antebellum country lawyers came in all shapes and sizes, from the willowy, sandy-haired, blue-eyed, five-foot six-inch Seward to the six-foot-four rawboned "Honest Abe" Lincoln. Some dressed like dandies. Others, like Lincoln and Seward, preferred plain clothing. All of these lawyers shared one trait, or they would not have been successful. They were hard workers, putting in more hours than the farmer and the grocer whose suits they represented in court. One manual of practice for lawyers, David Hoffman's *A Course of Study* (1836), explained their credo: "to my clients, I will be faithful, and in their causes zealous and industrious." Lawyers read more than the average American. State case reporters, newspapers, and legal documents required close attention. Seward's personal library included many works of literature and history, but like most lawyers, Seward read quickly rather than deeply. (The list of books in his library runs to the hundreds; he simply could not have read all of them closely and still carried on the rest of his career. The law books were largely those of his father-in-law's purchase.) The country lawyers traveled more than most Americans, too, riding the circuit from county seat to county seat, staying in the capital when the state supreme courts were in session. As Seward wrote to his wife Frances, when he was traveling the circuit, "I have only one regret—your inability to enjoy the excursion with me. But I should not have the boldness to ask you to share a country lawyer's lodging. . . . I fear, abhor, detest, despise and loathe litigation. The irascible, the headstrong, and the obstinate pity my peaceful disposition; yet they solicit my aid to extricate them." Back from the hustings, the country lawyers kept their offices open from dawn to dusk, and whether, like Seward and Lincoln, they were avid advice-givers to all and sundry or preferred to listen, they were accustomed to dealing with all sorts of people. Lawyering was adversarial. That meant that lawyers vied with other lawyers in written briefs and in court. The adversarial system put a premium on winning suits. At the same time, country lawyers would prove themselves able mediators, a tradition of alternative dispute resolution that went back to England. Natural rivalries among these lawyers developed. That was law practice, and it left its marks on all of them.[9]

Last but hardly least, the country lawyer did not see all rights as abstract or absolute. Some, of course, were—the black letter law of the case reporters and the treatises. The country lawyer also saw obligations and duties that surrounded legal strictures. His practice included matters personal and public, familiar and distant. These were relational, tying members of the community to one another. They were the sort of rights that one's neighbors understood (or would be expected to understand) when they disputed with one another or sat as jurors resolving disputes. As one modern country law firm explains on its website, it represents a client's personal life, business affairs, and reputation. Then as now, sorting these out case by case required skill, forbearance, and toleration. In sum, relational rights were not rights mandated by the state. They could exist in the absence of state legislation, though they might become part of it, for example, in domestic relations law.

Relational rights, as understood by Seward, did not exclude other sources of rights. For example, when he served as governor of New York State, from 1839 to 1843, Seward advocated a wide variety of public program reforms. These included prisoners' rights, educational rights, and the rights of immigrants and Indians. Such rights rested in part on an expansive (if somewhat inchoate) vision of the ideal community but also on far more conventional ideas of republican inclusiveness. The good state saw to the welfare of its inhabitants. These were Whig Party aims, focused on "improvement" through state action, but then, Seward was a Whig Party luminary at that time.[10]

There was one important element of reform rights in Seward's time that did not play a major role in his idea of rights. He belonged to a church, took his pew and paid his assessments, was baptized as an adult, and wondered whether he was a good Christian but was tolerant in matters of religion, having ties to many sects' leaders. His relative uninterest was striking, for the antebellum years in upstate New York were rich in religious fervor. One historian called Seward's home country a region "burned over" by evangelic preaching. Out of this ferment came movements as diverse as the Church of Jesus Christ of Latter Days Saints, the drive for women's right to vote, the Oneida Movement, and the Second Great Awakening. But little of that pietism appeared in Seward's speeches, and although his library contained books about religion, he did not incorporate much text from them in his writings, save in the "Higher Law" speech of 1850.[11]

Not every country lawyer did or would have been able to formulate this notion as a species of jurisprudence, for it resisted formulas. The country lawyer did not deal in such theoretical discourse in any case. Like the variety and intricacy of fact patterns in his caseload, relational rights grew out of community understandings and misunderstandings about what each member owed to other member. Seward was exceptional in his effort to flesh out the doctrine and apply relational rights jurisprudence in public discourse. As he told an audience at the dedication of Capital University in Columbus, Ohio, on September 14, 1853, "one nation, race, or individual, may not oppress or injure another because the safety and welfare of each is essential to the common safety and welfare of all."[12]

As governor in the "Virginia Affair," as co-counsel in *Jones v. Van Zandt* (1847), in speeches on the hustings and on the Senate floor, from 1848 through 1861, and in his role as US secretary of state, Seward's notion of relational rights law confronted the most vexing issue of his day—slavery. Because he applied relational rights jurisprudence to slavery, Seward had to think, write, and speak in ways somewhat unfamiliar to the country lawyer, which in turn made Seward's contribution to American jurisprudence more significant.

CHAPTER 1

"There Is No Law of This State Which Recognizes Slavery"

Governor of New York

In an 1871 autobiography, written a year before his passing and published in 1877, William Henry Seward recalled the day that Daniel Webster came to Rochester, New York. Webster was not really a country lawyer. He preferred the city, with its big-pocket clients and its complex commercial litigation. Rochester was the center of wheat milling in the state, and the state fair was the main attraction that 1843 afternoon. Webster was once again running for the presidency, and the crowd had swelled with the promise of one of Webster's storied addresses. Webster did not miss opportunities like this to sway voters, but he was indisposed that day, likely inebriated, and Seward agreed to speak in "Divine Daniel's" place. Seward was in Rochester in the course of his law practice, having the previous year left his gubernatorial office. The moment was one of far greater significance than the crowd understood, for Webster's generation, the successors to the founders, was passing, and Seward's generation would lead the nation through its next and most trying years.[1]

By 1842, Seward was fast becoming one of the most important politicians of this generation. He had served as a state senator (1831–1835); and two-term governor (1839–1843). He would become a two-term senator (1849–1861) and US secretary of state (1861–1869). Able, ambitious, and hardworking, Seward earned a national reputation. Welcoming to immigrants, Roman Catholics, Native Americans, and supportive of advancements in technology and commerce, he was recognized as a reformer. Yet there was something puzzling about Seward. He denounced unthinking fidelity to political parties, but come election time he traveled around the state giving rousing speeches for his party's candidates. On the hustings, personal contact was his elixir, and he returned friendship with affection, but he seemed to rub some people the wrong way. Visiting in England in 1859, Seward was greeted by Queen Victoria and Lord Russell, two people who would, in years to come keep England from aiding the Confederacy. However, behind his back, critics called Seward "vaporing and blustering." Newspaper editors whose politics did not match Seward's were even more acerbic. "He is a cunning, crafty man, full of plots, and incapable of a plain single meaning," according to the editors of the Baltimore *American and Commercial*. Though welcomed when he appeared in public to speak, newspaper reports invariably noted his slouching and unkempt deportment. Abraham Lincoln's Secretary of the Navy Gideon Welles found Seward "versatile and prolific," but not "persistent and reliable." Welles denounced how Seward's "restless activity, unceasing labors, showy manifestations, and sometimes incautious exercise of questionable authority" made life for those around him impossible. Appointed commander of the Army of the Potomac during the Civil War, George McClellan (an engineer by trade and Democratic politician by choice), described Secretary of State Seward as "meddling, officious, incompetent little puppy." As he wrote to friend and confidant Thurlow Weed, on December 31, 1842, as his second term as governor was ending, "I am a mystery to myself. What am I? What is there belongs to me that has entitled me or secured to me, without a claim, such friend and affection" as Weed's.[2]

Some later historians have accepted all of these faults in Seward, along with general dismissal (or simple omission) of his jurisprudence. As the biographer Glyndon Van Deusen summed them up, "He talked too much, and in so doing made statements and took attitudes that hurt him in public life. He underestimated the potential of the black man for standing as a peer with whites. His cockiness, his self-assurance, disgusted many of his contemporaries. Too often he gave the impression of moving from calculation rather than from the heart. He was fascinating, able, often impressive, but altogether lacking in that great quality, humility." Other historians have found Seward a useful representative of others' thoughts and motives, but not an original thinker or a deep one.[3]

Looking back from 1871, Seward could have been proud of his many achievements, but he had not gained his great goal—the White House. There was something else missing in a life filled with momentous events and great deeds. There is a time when great crises call for something more audacious than a country lawyer's sense of simple justice to one's neighbors. He spoke and wrote of the evils of slavery, but he drew back from accusing the masters of the slaveocracy by name. No one, certainly not historians many years after their subjects have passed, can see into their subjects' inner sanctum of desire, will, and self-image. Seward's otherwise effusive body of writings often concealed as much as it revealed about his motives. Personality aside (if the historian can ever assay their subject's inner motives), perhaps the country lawyer was not a perfect fit for the national leader.

Seward's autobiography was published by his son Frederick, along with a selection of his early letters, in 1877. Frederick edited the letters to elide sensitive personal matters, which the archival collection reveals, but the selection offers indispensable evidence of Seward's thinking on public matters. Seward had paused his reminiscences in 1834, during his term in the New York State Senate, intending to resume them after another writing project, but death took him before he could finish the former. By the time he began the autobiography, he had retired from public life, enjoyed a final trip abroad, and sensed that death was near. He offered frank insights into how he saw himself as well as the details of his life. His writing in the autobiography and the letters was detailed and conversational, often so rich in anecdote that one could imagine oneself sitting by his side as he puffed his cigar and listening to him tell stories and share opinions. The letters allow us to sit virtually in his company, swathed in aged and fermented cigar smoke, and listen as he spoke, nonstop.[4]

Seward's background was solidly upper middle class, his grandparents owning land, his father, Samuel Sweezy Seward, a Columbia College trained physician, then a merchant, magistrate, and judge. At the time of his death he was worth 300,000 dollars (about 10 million in 2020's money—hardly a mogul, but very well off). His father owned slaves, as did many wealthy men in central New York, although the relative proportion of slaves to free persons was small. William (called Henry by his family) was born in 1801, in Florida, New York, a village west of the Hudson River and north of New York City. One of six children, a third son, in a family whose size was typical for the area's English / Welsh population, his own prospects were good, and he diligently pursued them. Bookish, delicate, slender, of medium height and reddish complexion, he did not relish school but proved himself a fine young orator in his father's store. His father told him that advancement depended on pleasing others, but even as a schoolboy, Seward's ambition to get ahead was tempered by a strain of moralism that sometimes was off-putting to others.[5]

Nineteenth-century autobiographies were often self-conscious literary displays, scripted performances of emotion and adventure. Family, friends, and mentors all had prominent places. In Seward's one senses a tension between aspiration and achievement, first in fulfilling his father's expectations, then in reaching his goals. The first crisis was his relative (compared with his schoolmates') inability to translate Latin. It brought an anxiety that was, one might conclude, out of proportion to the failure, but politics—public life, appearances in both senses of the word—brought relief from the inner doubts. He learned to observe others' conduct, not just in relation to his own advancement, but with a kind of clinical detachment, and that characteristic he carried with him his entire life. This combination of personality (or psychology if one wishes) and the experience of a country lawyer in upstate New York that shaped Seward's view of the world, of politics, and of his prospects.[6]

Seward recalled that the War of 1812, fought in and around New York's northern border, left a profound impression on him. He was thereafter a patriot, a Unionist, and later, proud to be an officer of the state militia. He also found the company of African Americans amenable. There were slaves in the neighborhood, but Seward did not accept the notion that slavery was natural. Slavery was dishonorable to everyone connected with it, he concluded. From a young age, he recalled, I was "determined to be an abolitionist." This sentiment, expressed in old age, was not entirely forthcoming. Seward disliked slavery intensely, thought it morally wrong, and a bar to progress, and did not want it to expand north or west, but he did not demand government action to end slavery nor aid slaves to escape their masters until the Civil War made such actions essential to victory.[7]

Other traits and views came early—admiration of cities, commerce, technology, learning, and a certain stiff-necked resistance to admitting error. He excelled at the business of learning at Union College and put it to good use in later years. He loved travel—to the South, to Canada, to Europe—often impulsively leaving his duties behind, his spirit entranced by the prospect of novelty. It was a restlessness characteristic of many Americans, a nation compulsively, if not voluntarily, on the move. He learned more about slavery during a sojourn teaching in Georgia, along with the hatred of Yankees among the common people of the South. The planter class was more gracious but just as suspicious of him as he was of them. He was less a sojourner than a visitor. He saw and moved on, a nonparticipant observer before that term became fashionable.[8]

At college, debates among the students over slavery during the Missouri statehood crisis severed prior harmony among northern and southern men. It was a harbinger of the sectional schism in national politics. After the semester in Georgia, he returned to Union College and graduated with honors. His experience at college warned him that even in this "era of good feelings" politics and social attitudes were an explosive mix. "Society was irreconcilably divided on the subject of politics and religion."[9]

Seward first read law in the summer of 1819, in the Goshen, New York, law office of John Duer, at the start of what would be a gap year in his studies at

Union College. After his graduation from Union in 1820, he returned to his legal studies in Goshen for a year, then turned to John Anthon's New York City office for further studies. New York City was the seat of the federal circuit trial court for the southern district of New York (the court for the northern district met in Albany), and country lawyers had to know both state and federal law. In 1821, once more Seward moved his studies, this time to the law office of Ogden Hoffman in Orange County, and in 1822 passed the bar exam the state required of practitioners. His mentors were the cream of the crop. Anthon had an extensive practice in the city and something of a reputation "of being the best practitioner at the New York bar. Although somewhat brusque in manner and possessed of a displeasing voice, he showed great skill in marshaling facts and in legal exposition and analysis." Duer read law in the office of Alexander Hamilton and would establish a practice in Orange County and then New York City. In 1828, President John Quincy Adams appointed Duer US attorney for the Southern District of New York, and he later served on the state's superior court. Hoffman came from a leading New York family and would shortly be elected to the state assembly and then to the US Congress.[10]

It also helped the country lawyer with ambitions to marry well. He settled in Auburn, New York, at the head of Owasco Lake, literally in the center of the upstate region, to begin his practice. There Seward looked for a suitable mate—loyal, well educated, and presentable. He found one in Frances Miller, Judge Elijah Miller's daughter, and they wed in 1824. Her father was a lawyer and judge of means, and she was more than Seward could have asked for—a reform-minded gentlewoman who loved and respected him and bore him five children—Augustus (1826–1876); Frederick (1830–1915); Cornelia (1836–1837), William H. Jr. (1839–1920); and Frances (Fanny) (1844–1866). The married couple moved into Seward's father-in-law's house, giving Seward the opportunity to travel for legal and later political matters, knowing that the growing family he left behind was safe and secure. Daughter Fanny Seward's diary recorded a happy family life. It was not always so. Frances resented William's long absences, and Judge Miller would sometimes chide Seward about failing to attend to legal business (actually, failing to dun his debtors for payment and to drum up new business), but the household was a busy and copasetic one, at least seen from the outside.[11]

Reading law was something of a misnomer, for the primary occupation (and the reason why lawyers took on student clerks) was the drudgery of lawyering—writing or copying legal documents. Going to court with one's mentor was required, but more important was the proper and on-time preparation of paperwork. The writ pleading system still dominated the county and superior courts, and failure to provide the court clerk with the proper writ (the paper stating the action with its strange mixture of Latin, law French, old English, and modern terminology) for each party in each suit doomed the litigant. Exceptions were criminal practice, practice in equity (where the alleged harm was described in plain English and the relief sought was spelled out in the claim), and domestic law. Seward also used his law clerks as stenographers; for example, young Samuel Blatchford was tasked with turning Governor Seward's dictation into a written introduction to the state's geological survey.[12]

For both the country lawyer and his students, the world of law and lawyers was rapidly changing between 1815 and 1860. Disputes over trespass, water rights, promissory notes, and land conveyances did not go away, but the rise of multi-state insurance, transportation, and manufacturing operations provided new and lucrative opportunities for the legal profession. Railroad lawyering led the way, and both Seward and Lincoln had rail lines as clients. New inventions made railroads profitable, and Seward would become a leading patent lawyer. The *Louisville Daily Journal*, in politics no friend to Seward, described him as "the best patent lawyer perhaps in the United states."[13]

Single practice remained the norm, but busier lawyers formed partnerships. The partnership was a legal construct, a kind of contract among individuals. They owned and managed the business. Often contentious and rarely long-lasting, legal partnerships were hardly anything like the corporate partnerships of today. Nevertheless, working with a law partner was an ongoing experience in a cooperative endeavor. Seward was fortunate in his choice of partners, first his father-in-law, then Auburn's own Samuel Blatchford Jr., son of a wealthy Whig politician Richard Blatchford, who started as a secretary and became a partner. Samuel Blatchford would, in 1882, become an associate justice of the US Supreme Court. Nelson Beardsley was added to the team in 1833, and then John Porter joined them in 1836. Beardsley and Porter would go on after the partnership with Seward ended to form the forerunner of the Cravath firm in New York City. They were replaced by Christopher Morgan, a former member of Congress who had clerked with Seward, and in 1844 Seward formed the partnership of Morgan, Blatchford, and Seward. Morgan went on to become the New York secretary of state in 1847, mayor of Auburn, and a Republican stalwart. In addition, Seward hired on William Beach and George Underwood as junior partners after he left the governor's office. Seward's mix and match of partners was not unusual. Lincoln had three law partners, a similar mix and match of mentors and rivals, finally finding one, William Herndon, who understood and appreciated Lincoln's folksy approach to lawyering.[14]

Although his practice largely remained local, Seward appeared in the state's highest courts. When he lost in the Cayuga courts, he appealed to the state Supreme Court of Judicature. His record was mixed. From 1830 to 1834, he also sat on the Court for the Correction of Errors with the other senators, the chancellor of the state, and the members of the state's supreme court, the former a court to which his cases might be appealed. The Court for the Correction of Errors had the final say on cases, often overturning the decisions of the Supreme Court, whose members sat with the senators and the chancellor. It was a small circle of men who managed the litigation. The justices of the Supreme Court and the chancellor did not have private practices, but their close relatives did, and the same names reappear as counsel and judge over and over. On the Court for the Correction of Errors Seward did not take part in any case in which he had an interest, so far as one can tell from the records of the two courts.[15]

On the Court for Correction of Errors, he was not shy about offering his opinions in cases. He wrote in eight cases, some of his opinions quite long. What was especially striking about his participation in those hearings where he was present was his confidence in his own judgment. He did not hesitate to disagree with the chancellor or the members of the state supreme court who sat with him on the Court for Correction of Errors and whose Supreme Court decisions he sought to reverse. *Parks v. Jackson* (1833) was one such case. It involved a series of land transactions, portions of which were consummated while litigation about the parcels involved was ongoing. A jury had asked the trial judge for a legal ruling and he turned to the Supreme Court of Judicature. That court, in an opinion by Justice Samuel Nelson, found the contested sale void. Seward disagreed. His grounds were only partly legal:

> In my judgment, the application of the rule in a case like the present would be unjust, and could be sustained upon no grounds of necessity or general convenience. It is but a few years since the greater part of the whole territory of this state was in a wild and uncultivated condition, and of comparatively very small value. Large Tracts of land still remain in the same condition. The history of the state and of the whole country shows that the only manner in which this wilderness was thus far reclaimed, was by the purchase of small quantities of land by contracts preliminary and conditional; by virtue of which the purchaser entered into possession, proceeded to erect his dwelling, gradually removed the forest, and derived from the soil itself the means of paying the purchase money. Thus, by performing his contract, he secured to himself the legal title of the land.[16]

Seward spoke for a community largely composed of people who sold, bought, and improved land. Their contracts were legal bonds that bound the community together. Loosen these by allowing litigants' interests to outweigh the interests of those who lived on the land would physically and socially destroy the community. One sees here the seeds of Seward's evolving relational rights jurisprudence. As it happened, Seward's opinion carried the day. Although Chancellor Reuben Walworth voted to affirm Nelson's opinion, Seward and the other nineteen senators voting overturned Nelson's ruling.[17]

Seward also practiced in Walworth's chancery court in matters of equity until the law docket and the equity dockets were merged in the state's courts, in 1848. The court of equity, like the Senate, met in Albany, and the Supreme Court of Judicature held circuit in New York City, Albany, and Utica. In the 1830s a trek from the Syracuse region, where Seward's practice largely lay, to Utica or Albany was a strenuous matter. The Erie Canal connected Syracuse to Schenectady, west and north of Albany. Utica was along the way. Passenger travel on the canal was common. In 1836 one passenger left a description of the passage from Schenectady, the next stop after Albany to Buffalo, aboard a packet boat.

> These boats are about 70 feet long, and with the exception of the Kitchen and bar, is occupied as a Cabin. The forward part being the ladies' Cabin, is separated by a curtain, but at meal times this obstruction is removed, and the table is set the whole length of the boat. . . . On finding we had so many passengers, I was at a loss to know how we should be accommodated with berths, as I saw no convenience for anything of the kind, but the Yankees, ever awake to contrivances, have managed to stow more in so small a space than I thought them capable of doing. . . . The berths are allotted according to the way bill, the first on the list having his first choice, and in changing boats the old passengers have the preference. . . . These Boats have *three* Horses, go at a quicker rate, and have the preference in going through the locks, carry no freight, are built extremely light, and have quite Genteel Men for their Captains, and use *silver* plate.

The cost was about four dollars per 100 miles in 1836 for this less than luxurious travel, and using it took days to get from Syracuse to Albany. A rail line from Albany to Schenectady opened in 1831. The line between Utica and Syracuse RR began service in 1839, the same year as the Auburn and Syracuse RR. Connections to Rochester and then Buffalo the west followed in the 1840s. When the various sections of the railroad from Buffalo to Albany were finished, during Seward's governorship, travel between the state capital and his home became far easier. The entire line was consolidated as the New York Central in 1867.[18]

Lawyers had been drawn to public service from the founding of the republic, but as sectional conflict loomed larger in the decades before the war, lawyers seemed to play a more visible role in the nation's guidance. Sectional conflict was one of the reasons why men like Seward and Lincoln thought law and politics were so closely intertwined. Part of the transformation from private counsel to public official for lawyers like Seward and Lincoln required self-promotion, which lawyers seeking higher office willingly provided. Seward would attach himself to Thurlow Weed and Horace Greeley, editors of leading Albany and New York City newspapers, respectively. Two of Lincoln's law partners had important political careers in Illinois. Lincoln himself professed that lawyering could not be separated from the public good. As one scholar has summarized these attitudes, "For lawyers turned politicians / statesmen, the keys were twofold, constitution and the common law, both envisaged as foundations for institutions that would restrain or limit the power of the state and ensure liberty." Lawyers / politicians cast themselves as the guardians of public liberty just as in their practices they promoted private rights. "Or so they believed."[19]

Those lawyers who succeeded in gaining public office proved that practicing law could be what the law professor Henry St. George Tucker of Virginia called "the most successful path, not only to affluence and comfort, but to all the distinguished and elevated stations in a free government." The nation exhibited a "widely shared preoccupation with law and politics," according to one student of the first antebellum law schools, and success in politics required the same appearance of virtue as success in the other. True, there were winners and losers in most every case, but losing well might burnish a reputation when winning through guile might cost one the trust of future clients—and future voters. Lincoln urged lawyers to be honest, to discourage rather than stir up litigation, and to honor the law rather than abuse it. Joseph Story summed up the prevailing ideology of lawyering at the apex of practice: the lawyer was "the public sentinel" of virtue.[20]

In turn, the rising lawyers / politicians gained from legal practice a surer sense of themselves as advocates of political causes; legal practice in the antebellum era was as much about advocacy of ideas as about "black letter" (formal lawbook) learning. The leaders of the profession, like Maryland lawyer / politician Roger B. Taney, were distinguished for their skill at untangling issues, not particularly for their mastery of arcane knowledge, and for their representation of all kinds of clients. Such men were lucid and even passionate in oral argument. Future leaders of the bar like North Carolina's Thomas Ruffin developed their own styles of courtroom combat. Ruffin was "hardly ever courteous and not always respectful and frequently abusive." By contrast, Georgia lawyer and future congressman Alexander Stephens relied on his learning and eloquence to win cases. Virginia's Jubal Early, later a corps commander in the Confederate Army, admitted that "I had in a very limited degree the capacity for public speaking . . . and it was regarded that my forte at the law was not before a jury as an advocate, but on questions of law before the court." Early went on to political service when he was not volunteering for military service. Both sets of qualities abetted lawyers/politicians' political advancement, for in many cases the very impulse that led them to practice law had fueled their ambition for public office. After which, their political energies could be devoted to legal subjects. Law practice and political office were like the coupling rods that propelled old-fashioned locomotive wheels: the action of one driving the motion of the other.[21]

As a political figure, often in the public eye, Seward did not present an imposing presence. Cartoonists caricatured his slight, stooped, long-nosed, large-eared, plain-faced figure—a "slouching, slender figure, a head like a wise macaw," with a "hoarse voice, [and] offhand manner," Henry Adams recalled when they met. Though pedantic and long-winded, dressed modestly and never without his cigar, he was a compelling orator and a gracious host to audiences large and small. He loved travel and company, and his home was often filled with visitors and friends. He was always courteous, though often the victim of scandalous defamation. Seward obliquely admitted as much, for "in the earnest canvassing suspicion often follows the magistrate, and scandal follows in the footsteps of the statesman."[22]

In his autobiography Seward recollected that political party affiliation and religious sect membership did not mean so much to him as his own idea of benefit to the community. He chose the Episcopal Church and the Jeffersonian Republican Party as much out of social convention as any conviction. Then, he recalled, he started to worry about the "bold and dangerous theories" of the Republicans, which "were to culminate in nullification and secession," though perhaps that was hindsight. He turned next to the Anti-Masonic Party, a brief flirtation, and then in 1834 announced himself a Whig—the party in opposition to President Andrew Jackson. His admiration for John Quincy Adams had also influenced his choice of party, although Adams was not really a party man himself. There was something almost Quixotic about these affiliations, as if Seward were searching for something in party politics that was not there—something beyond local affiliations and sloganeering. As the parties became less ideological and more pragmatic, his attachment to the Whig faction's reform program (and its more reform-minded wing) made increasing sense.[23]

The autobiography documented Seward's connection with the newspaper mogul and master politician Thurlow Weed, a connection that would persist throughout both men's careers. Seward recalled his first impression of Weed in 1824. Traveling in Rochester, an axle of the wagon in which Seward rode broke, and his traveling companions fell into the mud. "Among a crowd, which quickly assembled, one taller and more distinctive, while more deferential and sympathizing, than the rest, lent the party some assistance." This was Weed. He wrote at the time to his wife, Frances, "Weed is very much with me, and I enjoy his warmth of feeling. A politician, skillful in understanding and persevering in execution, whose exacting principle is personal friendship or opposition, and not self-interest—that is Just Thurlow Weed." For the next fifty years, Weed continued to help Seward out of the mud into which he would fall.[24]

At the same time, Seward had (remember he is writing in 1871, so the insight is actually hindsight) a revelation—the future of the nation lay to the west; "that the vast material sources of the country are in the region laying westward of the Alleghany Mounts." To gain the commerce and allegiance of that region, the "best efforts" of the older parts of the country, and of Seward himself, would be required. "The road of progress" lay in freedom, but to travel that road, one must go in company with others. Thus the true purposes of political party were not self-aggrandizement, but community and national interest. For that, Seward would tell the Senate, in 1850, "I know nothing, I care nothing—I never did, I never shall, for party." When political parties obstructed the way forward, that is.[25]

In the autobiography, Seward next turned to the contests of political parties in New York, principally those around the choice of governors (a natural topic given his prior service in that office). Aware, as he wrote in 1871, that he too would become governor, he focused on particular issues and events that would affect his own rise to that office. Here were freemasons, the border wars with Canada, the schisms of the major parties, and the rise and fall of local associations. In his dealings with fellow party members, Seward worked for unity, usually to no avail. Attempts to work across party lines also stalled the result of which he saw as a "loss" of the enterprising spirit, the aim of improvements, and a cause of "future disunion of the states" (a shot at the Democratic Party's role in the crisis of 1860–1861 before there was a Democratic Party).[26]

As to his own politics, well, politics was the subject of the bulk of Seward's recollections. As a Jeffersonian Republican, an Anti-Masonic candidate, and then a Whig, his politics were more local than national. He campaigned in the Albany to Rochester corridor on local issues and won a seat in the state senate. Elected in 1830, after withdrawing his name for a spot in the state assembly, he was aware of his relative youth. "For the first ten days I sat like a stone in my seat" he wrote to Frances. Then the real Seward began to emerge. "I said to myself, 'Henry Seward, you are a fool to be afraid of your shadow. Show yourself a man.'" In speeches and letters thereafter, he revealed his lodestars: public free education, internal improvements, enterprise, support for the rights of immigrants in general and Roman Catholics in particular, and abhorrence of slavery. In later years, he was not an immediatist, though often wrongly viewed that way, nor, on the other side, merely a Free Soiler, though he seemed to oscillate between the two poles of antislavery opinion, depending on the audience for his remarks. Immediatists wanted an end to slavery everywhere as soon as possible. They opposed compensated colonization of slaves back to Africa and deplored gradualism's attempt to persuade slaveholders to manumit their bondsmen and women. Free Soilers wanted to prevent the expansion of slavery from the South to the North and West. Though he was called inconsistent and hard to track in his politics, the latter was much like his personality: gregariousness and energy, on the one hand, and his introspection and caution, on the other. The exception was when his dander was up, as in the Virginia Affair discussed below. Then his biographers saw how he planted his feet and swung with both fists.[27]

Seward was aware that Supreme Court Justice Samuel Nelson was a Democrat, a party that Seward had abandoned. But reading Seward's objections to Nelson's opinions one does not find partisan animus. These men—Seward, Nelson, Walworth, and the other members of the elite bar—were part of a fraternity of lawyers and judges whose professionalism, at least in their legal roles, trumped partisanship. Although he had little use for Andrew Jackson, the leader of the Democrats, Seward supported Jackson's forceful response to Nullification in 1832 and 1833. Political affiliation did not dominate his thinking; for Seward and Jackson, both lawyers, South Carolina's unlawful response to the tariff was simply unacceptable. On February 16, 1833, Senator Seward addressed that body in support of a resolution that Jackson's actions represented the "true Principles" of the Constitution. Seward told his colleagues that if they did not support the president, they would have "waived" the Constitution and nullification would become the law of the land.[28]

Although Seward was now a Whig and had his eye on higher office, there were other prospects more attractive, and these, rather than grubbing for office, influenced his thinking. His love of travel took him to Europe in 1833 and convinced him that the United States would prove that an enlightened people were capable of self-government. It also whetted his taste for diplomacy. Later, son Frederick wrote that Seward's favorite avocation was travel. Wherever he went South, he found slavery. As he wrote in 1835 from the Shenandoah Valley to Beardsley, "I had thought that this part of Virginia, by reason of its being less oppressed under the curse of slavery was exempted, in a great degree, from the evils suffered in that part of the state lying east of the Blue Ridge." But that part of the Old Dominion was sunk "too deeply in the infatuation, not to say the guilt, or purchasing slaves" and the land was "reduced to the humiliating condition of a breeder of slaves for the southern and western markets, and the staple of her commerce is young slaves of both sexes." Seward and Frances saw a coffle of slave children being brought to market to be auctioned off, like cattle. Young Frederick, traveling with them, never forgot the scene.[29]

Seward ran for the governorship in 1834 as a Whig. He lost. He returned to his law practice and found that political activity had not hurt business. In 1836 he added a new partner, John Porter, an older lawyer with a local practice. Seward, not surprisingly given his opinion in *Parks v. Jackson*, became entangled in the gambling spirit of the age: land speculation. One popular form of speculation was writing loan notes with land not yet developed as collateral, assuming that settlers would improve the land and the notes could be renegotiated or would increase in value. The opportunity came in the shape of the Holland Land Company, formed to sell lands to settlers in western New York. Seward agreed to act as an agent for company, not selling but settling disputes. He opened a law office in Westfield, in Chautauqua Country, and traveled from Auburn to Buffalo, doing business with various land jobbers (and making political contacts), until the Panic of 1837 threw the land speculators' prospects into disarray. Settlers could not or would not pay what they had owed, and the ripple effect imperiled the entire state economy. Seward was able to right the ship of the failing Holland Land Company, at least for a time. With the collapse of President Martin Van Buren's Democratic administration, based in part on the Panic of 1837 (requiring the purchase of lands in specie), Whigs swept the state elections in 1838. In that year, Seward won the governorship in the first of two terms.[30]

By progressing from a purely local law practice, the fifty or so miles around Auburn, to the entire Erie Canal corridor, Seward had not only grown his legal reputation; he had made himself into a familiar political figure upstate. He still had to win over the New York City voters, but his tolerant views toward Roman Catholic immigrants and his support of parochial education won him the backing of important Catholic leaders. Always an exuberant supporter of internal improvements, fiscal stringency was not his favorite policy. He was a consistent proponent of government spending on internal improvements. Here the experience of the country lawyer may have been crucial, for the replacement of the rutted, muddy country road by the railroad tracks made it far easier for the country lawyer to expand his practice.[31]

In addition to the fiscal problems of the state, Seward's gubernatorial terms from 1839 to 1843 were disquieted by legal troubles, notably the "Virginia

Affair." In it, his relational rights doctrine found a cause to champion. In 1839, three free Black merchant seamen on the crew of the New York ship *Robert Carter* concealed Isaac, a Virginia slave carpenter brought aboard the ship to make repairs and smuggled him to the port of New York. Slave catchers retrieved the runaway, and Lieutenant Governor Henry Hopkins of Virginia requested the extradition of the three free sailors for trial in his state: "an offense peculiarly and deeply affecting the general interest of the good people of this Commonwealth, recognized as felony and severely punished by our laws." After studying the request for some time, Seward declined. "There is no law of this state which recognizes slavery." The runaway they tried to assist was recaptured and returned to his owner. But because the act of the three sailors was committed in New York harbor, it would not have "contravened any statute." Seward then added his own view that "in my opinion the offense is not within the meaning of the constitution of the United States."[32]

On their face, the questions the exchange of letters between Seward and Hopkins raised were both interstate and federal. As a matter of common law, no state was required to use the laws of another state. This doctrine was part of what was called choice of law or conflict of laws, and Justice Joseph highly Story had written a treatise on it in 1834. A state might, if it wished to do so, adopt the laws of another state, which was what Hopkins demanded of Seward. In penal (criminal) cases the general rule was that a suspect held in one state could not expect it to enforce the laws of another state. Neither could the other state expect its foreign laws to be enforced in the state in which the alleged perpetrator was found. Sending anyone back to stand trial for an act that was not a crime in the state where the person had found refuge was entirely a matter of discretion on the part of the latter state. Seward was perfectly within the law, as Story understood it, in declining.[33]

There was also a federal question involved. The Full Faith and Credit Clause of the Constitution (Article IV, Section 1) said that "Full Faith and Credit shall be given in each State to the public Acts, Records, and judicial Proceedings of every other State." If this were read literally, it would mean that the law of slavery would be national, not sectional, and New York must comply with Virginia's request. It would also mean that Virginia law must comply with New York's. In short, the clause was self-contradictory when applied to slavery. In *Pacific Employers Ins. Co. v. Industrial Accident Commission* (1939), the Supreme Court limited the application of the clause to the authenticating of records of courts, excluding the operation of state statutes—the position that Seward took a century earlier. But was the offense not within the scope of the rendition for crime clause of Article IV, Section 2? No. The three sailors were not fugitives from Virginia justice, as they had not been indicted for any offense there yet.

In any case, Hopkins and his fellow Virginian officials were furious with Seward. When New York later requested the extradition of a forger, they refused, giving Seward the opportunity to expand on his previous replay. "I must insist, with perfect respect, that the general principle of civilized communities is in harmony with that which prevails in this state, that men are not the subjects of property." In short, the law of nations, which New York obeyed according to Seward, had no place for slavery, a barbaric (that is, uncivilized) institution. Seward being Seward then added, "I do not intend here to draw in question the wisdom or that virtue of those states which establish an opposite principle." This disclaimer would become a feature of his later US Senate addresses, blasting slavery, then civilly (and patronizingly) forgiving its managers. Bear in mind that Seward was already running for reelection for governor, and the support of antislavery forces in New York was vital to that cause. The two missives to Hopkins were widely reprinted in pro-Seward newspapers.[34]

But there was a lot more to the Virginia controversy of 1839–1843, as it was later called. It was the first occasion for the then-governor Seward to show how relational rights, hitherto applied to private lawsuits, also applied to the public law of slavery. It made the country lawyer into a public law jurisprudent. The first letter to Hopkins was short and terse. It sounded like a judge rejecting a motion because it was defective—in this case, because it lacked details of the alleged offense. The entirety of the correspondence bore a different character, expanding into a lesson on constitutional jurisprudence. The federal Constitution allowed states to fashion their own municipal laws, under which Virginia had protected the property rights of slaveowners, but the Constitution did not impose Virginia law on New York, or New York law would then be valid in Virginia. This would have been the wrong kind of reciprocity, for it would force New York to adopt Virginia's antirelational rights laws. Abetting of slave-stealing cut into the very heart of communal reciprocity, and so could not be enforced with respect to residents, even temporary ones, of the state. The crucial and fundamental legal point was that Seward considered the three men citizens of New York, a status that Virginia would not have accorded them under its laws. He concluded that "Our constitution and our laws interdict slavery in every form." This was somewhat ingenuous, as New York had adopted a gradual emancipation plan for slaves, and there were still slaves in New York when Seward was growing up. The last slave was freed by state law on July 4, 1827.[35]

Seward's decision still did not please Virginia authorities, and Seward wrote Hopkins once more in reply to Virginia's repeated request that Seward return the three sailors to Virginia. The second letter, dated October 24, 1839 was pure Seward—learned and chatty by turns, respectful but unyielding, and perhaps as a matter of plain constitutional text (the Full Faith and Credit Clause again) unsound, but as an expression of his own political/legal philosophy, rather revealing.

The second letter was a point-by-point refutation of Hopkins's arguments. One can imagine Seward sitting with the same books of authority on the law of nations and the federal Constitution as Hopkins. Hopkins was a lawyer and for a time the state's attorney general. Seward, always courteous, had "high respect" for Hopkins's credentials and took his reply seriously. Seward then shifted his role from judging Hopkins's affidavit insufficient in the first letter to a counsel preparing a legal brief on states' rights, conflict (or choice) of law doctrines, and the Constitution. Hopkins had cited the eighteenth-century Swiss jurist Emmerich de Vattel on the obligation, in the law of nations, for a sovereign state to seek the return of fugitives from justice from another sovereign state. But the Constitution spoke only of rendition for treason, felony, and other crimes, whereas the three fugitives had not committed any crimes under New York law. Why would New York then surrender its sovereignty over "citizens of this state" at the undefined whim of another state? Seward noted that such demands might be permitted if the persons sought were accused of treason or a serious felony, but he did not regard helping a slave to find refuge in a free state such a crime. In any case, Vattel's definition of the obligation was far too broad and was not incorporated in the federal Constitution. While citing Vattel, a Swiss international lawyer who wrote a century earlier, was something of a reach for Hopkins (according to Seward, Hopkins had even misread Vattel), Hopkins had also pointed to a similar passage in Chancellor James Kent's works. Kent was New York's greatest jurist, and Seward knew it. But Hopkins had not cited the full passage from Kent. Kent continued that in New York law deciding those crimes for which rendition was required belonged to the "discretion" of the chief executive of the state to which application for rendition was made—in this case Seward.[36]

A third letter followed on November 9, 1840, when one would have assumed that the tempest would have quieted. Instead, Virginia's cause had become the cause of the slave South, and against that phalanx stood a resolute Seward. Thomas Gilmer, governor of Virginia, had enclosed a resolution of the state legislature, which Seward had referred to his own legislature. They found that the matter was not in their jurisdiction, and so he had to report that he was without advice from his own legislative branch. He wrote, thus, for himself a reply that was even longer than its predecessor.[37]

The essence of Seward's responses was "it seems to me that [New York's stance] not only involves the essential principles of civil liberty, and the federal relations of the states, but their sovereign and reserved rights." The most important of these was their ability to protect "their own citizens." Seward proposed that the relation between New York and the three Black sailors was the same as the relation between the state and any other of its citizens. The state was a community whose members shared rights, and whose members owed to one another what they claimed for themselves. It was thus not states' rights per se that Seward defended, but the concept of relational rights of the body of citizens that the state housed. For the three men sought by Virginia were not citizens under its laws but were citizens under the laws of the state of New York. If they did not have all the rights and privileges of white male New Yorkers, that was an incident of defective state legislation (that Seward opposed), but that did not make them any less deserving of the protections of the state. New immigrants, children, women, and Native peoples also lacked the full panoply of rights, but they too were citizens. Seward's robust definition of citizenship was thus part of his program for reciprocal legal protections. As he concluded, "there is a law of our nature (a higher law) which would forbid the execution of any statute hostile to all our habits, opinions, and policy." That higher law was what the Constitution incorporated when it began with a Preamble "to form a more perfect Union, establish Justice, insure domestic Tranquility, provide for the common defense, promote the general Welfare, and secure the Blessings of Liberty to ourselves and our Posterity."[38]

The rest of the letter was thus a fulsome (and somewhat overbroad) defense of relational rights applied to criminal extradition. On the one hand, if Seward anticipated how this same argument might apply to resistance to national Fugitive Slave Act going far beyond the 1793 Act (that is, to personal freedom laws in the 1850s), he did not discuss it. On the other hand, he did not show any awareness of how his arguments might be linked to John C. Calhoun's compact theory of the Constitution, with its logical application to Nullification. In those versions of states' rights, a state could resist not only the incursive demands of another state but the improper introduction of federal authority.[39]

Taking the three letters together, a loose constructionist of the Constitution favoring a strong central government might well find Seward's lawyering deficient with the result that Virginia had the better of the exchange. But as Seward repeated according to New York law, the decision to return the three men to Virginia was his. The alternative, to try them in New York, was impossible because they had not committed any crime in New York or while at sea under New York law. Their act of helping a slave to evade capture may have been a crime under Virginia law, but New York was not bound to aid the enforcement of an obnoxious Virginia law. Again, this may have been a defective reading of the Comity or Full Faith and Credit Clause of the Constitution, but the three men had not yet been tried and found guilty of anything in Virginia, and would not until they were returned. Additional letters followed on November 10, 1840, March 25, June 8, October 8, and November 8, 1841, the last of which protested a Virginia law directed at New York. All shipping bound for the latter state was to be inspected carefully to ensure that no slave hid on the outbound ship.[40]

The country lawyer is indefatigable in pursuing his client's interests, filing every paper with the court, so Seward dutifully answered every letter from Virginia, politely, going over every point, repeating himself as if each letter were the first. Country law practice often required that counsel return to the courts over and over, filing new briefs and rearguing cases. Seward was merely doing as governor what he was accustomed to doing as a lawyer in Auburn.

Seward's letters did not reveal that he had long held a grievance against Virginia's slave laws. As he wrote to fellow lawyer Jarvis Lake, in 1844, "ten years ago in Virginia, I slept under the same roof, unknowingly with a man-merchant who was driving ten children . . . to the capital of that ancient commonwealth, whose motto was *sic semper tyrannis,* there and then to be sold in Texas, or other new slaveholding territories." Opponents of slavery holding office in New York had been "muzzled" by political considerations from speaking out against the atrocities of human bondage. In 1844, free of the civil niceties of the governorship, Seward could "testify to what we know." The tight-faced good manners of his letters to the Virginia authorities at that time had concealed his true feelings. He had hammered away on technical points in those exhaustive, exhausting letters because he felt constrained by his high office, in a public example of passive aggression.[41]

As chief executive of the state of New York, Seward was required (though he hardly needed the invitation) to promote various projects to the legislature. Into these proposals he inserted other bits and pieces of an evolving jurisprudence of governance. Again and again, he rejected the idea that democracy would improve the commonweal by itself. The machine of popular opinion must be governed by law. Consider the essay he contributed as an introduction to the *Natural History of New York* (1842). As governor, it was expected he would survey the law of the state, in the course of which he added, "the constitution guarantees the franchises of citizenship to every member of the state." On its face, this was a little misleading, as women could not vote, and people of color had to have more property than whites to exercise their franchise. His comment was thus aspirational rather than descriptive. But as in

Seward's replies to Virginia lieutenant governor Hopkins, it assumed that the three Black sailors were citizens of New York by New York law. Seward continued, "Among these franchises are trial by jury, the writ of habeas corpus, freedom of speech and of the press," all answers to Virginia, Mississippi, Georgia, and any of the slave states who wanted the return of alleged enablers of the runaway without due process of law. Seward modestly forbore to add that legislation on trial by jury of alleged slave runaways was his own project.[42]

The emanations of the Virginia Affair were far-reaching. The exchange between the two states' governments continued into 1841, with the legislature of New York providing for jury trial for suspected runaways and Virginia responding by passing laws to inspect ships of New York registry, supposedly for runaway slaves. For a time, Virginia refused to accede to New York's request for the return of a convicted forger, a clear case for rendition. Other slave states joined in the controversy, showing support for Virginia. Mississippi, for example, found Seward's conduct "an outrage upon the chartered rights of Virginia, and a precedent full of danger to all the slaveholding states." Seward was not impressed. As he wrote to the World Anti-Slavery Convention in June 1840, "I have not the slightest hesitation in assuring you that at no time, nor under any circumstances, shall I fail to do whatever may be within the scope of my lawful power and rightful influence, and calculated to my judgement to promote, in the most effectual manner, the great and philanthropic work of universal emancipation." One notes many qualifications in the promise. Characteristically, Seward reminded the delegates that he would not step outside the law nor act precipitously nor substitute their judgment for his when it came to abolition.[43]

In these writings, one sees how law, rightly construed as reciprocal (that is, as construed by Seward) enlarged the bounds of democracy and contracted those of slavery. For example, the laws governing public schools and libraries contributed to democracy by enlightening every citizen, and that enlightenment, in turn, guided future elections and lawmaking. The system did not govern itself. It required the state to contribute funds and support. One answer to the conundrum of slavery in a democratic society lay in universal public education. Educate everyone and, in time, the former master and the former slave could sit at the same table and enjoy the same fruits of progress. So too, he wrote that the law in New York, beginning with the acquittal of John Peter Zenger in 1745, freed the press from prior restraint. Thus the flowering of the newspapers in the state allowed a free press, even with its occasional violations of fair play and decency, to inform a democratic people. The press, at its best, was an engine of free minds, and thus an enemy to slavery. By contrast, as he told the Chautauqua Convention in 1846, "slavery has impoverished the states where it exists so much that they are incapable of endowing schools, maintaining mails, constructing roads, or supporting armies." The sharing of information through public education and a free press extended and brought together a community, a necessary precondition of relational rights.[44]

In the election of 1841, after the sudden death of President William Henry Harrison and Vice President John Tyler's support for the state's Democratic Party, the Whig majority in the New York State legislature vanished. Democrats more closely tied to southern commercial interests made their presence felt in state governance. Once again, the relative merits of Governor Seward's reform projects were overshadowed by criticism of Seward for being an abolitionist. Unmoved, Seward upped the ante. He opened the 1842 session of the state legislature with proposals for aiding the Six Nations population of the state, quartered largely on reservations, pressed for public libraries, public assistance to parochial schools, and the reform of prisons. When South Carolina proposed to search all vessels going from Charleston to New York for runaway slaves in retaliation for Seward's response to Virginia, he again refused to surrender the "persons claimed by Virginia." Seward wryly mentioned South Carolina's states' right objections to the tariffs during the Nullification Crisis. He added, "happily it is not necessary to decide between these certainly very incongruous interpretations" by South Carolina, as New York intended to uphold its own trial by jury law.[45]

With the state legislature dominated by Democrats after the 1842 elections, Seward's refusal to accede to Virginia's demands came under attack. He did not back down. Replying to a Senate (i.e., Democratic majority) resolution, he demurred, "I cannot do so when a request conflicts with constitutional duties. . . . Cherished principles of civil liberty forbid me equally from recognizing such a natural inequality of men as the solution of the legislature seems to assume, and from contributing in any way to perpetuate the inequalities of political condition, from which result a large portion of the evils of human life." Seward did not rely on his Whig Party credentials to deny the Democrats' proposal; he had held these views before there was a Whig Party, and would continue to hold them when the Whig Party was no more.[46]

Seward's proposed technical legal reforms did not win legislative approval. These were, first, the abolition of debtors' prisons, and second, the reduction of legal fees. He was acquainted with both as a country lawyer. With the state involved in so many speculative ventures, debtors abounded. The former reform had come slowly, thus, over the course of the first three decades of the nineteenth century. Finally, in 1831, an act of the legislature allowed imprisonment only when the creditor could prove the debtor had engaged in fraud. The federal bankruptcy law of 1841, although a short-lived measure, aided

Seward's initiative, but the state did not pass appropriate supporting legislation. Far more controversial was the revision of the old legal fee system. This cumbersome and duplicative way of paying lawyers actually increased the amount of litigation and slowed the settlement of suits. Seward tried and failed to get a reform bill through the legislature. Lawyers in and out of government protested. The system was not finally abolished until 1847–1848.[47]

One could say, with some justice, that Seward the country lawyer saw himself as the chief legal officer of the state as well as its chief executive, although the state had an attorney general, Willis Hall, a Whig legislator named by his colleagues to that office in 1839, who served for much of Seward's terms. Seward involved himself in legislation, promoting and even drafting bills for the legislature. He pressed for reform in a wide variety of legal forums, including city judicial offices, the professionalization of the bar, internal improvements, and penal law. He patiently heard appeals for pardons in capital cases, and ordered them in lesser crimes when he thought that the convict could rehabilitate. Even when he declined, as in the murder conviction of John Colt, in 1842, he studied the case carefully before deciding. He acted as a mediator when he could, even when the "rent wars" erupted in Albany County during the first year of his gubernatorial term. At first, he threatened, cajoled, and readied the militia, then "probed" beneath the surface of the riots to find some common ground between the landowners and the renters. In a time when the impact of the Panic of 1837 still hammered the state's economy, Seward's executive program of internal improvements seemed unrealistic to his opponents; today they seem obvious. Like his reforms, his role in the rent wars, and his handling of the three prisoners case, he saw relational rights as the ground for good law, fairly administered. What was more, the country lawyer could be an able chief executive; the skills gained in practice were transferable. But political opposition limited what he could do—a lesson that Seward took with him into his temporary retirement office.[48]

Chapter 2

"Harboring and Concealing a Weary and Fainting Slave"

Antislavery Litigator

Seward did not run for a third gubernatorial term, and 1843 found him temporarily out of public office. He needed to resuscitate his legal practice. He could not, as governor, engage in active practice (unlike his state senatorial terms). At least the burden of replying to applicants for patronage was lifted from his shoulders, as was the handling of appeals for pardons in criminal cases and the many extradition requests, including frequent repetitions, over 700). He tried to minimize the setback to his political ambitions. As he wrote to Christopher Morgan, a fellow Auburn attorney who had lost his seat in the House of Representatives at the same time as Seward left the executive office, "defeats are bad for the end of a political life, but not bad in the beginning." Seward returned to the full-time practice of law. At first, "by advising parties to compromise unfortunate suits, I have kept out of court, and am trying to do so." In the next years, he was back in circuit court in Auburn, the Supreme Court of Judicature and the Chancellor's Court in Albany, and federal court in Albany and New York City. Trains relieved some of the burdens of travel, but a carriage accident in 1844 left Seward incapacitated for a time, and Frances was beside herself with worry.[1]

At first, even friendly observers worried that he was not as well prepared to argue cases as he had been before his gubernatorial terms. As Whig politician and fellow lawyer Erastus Root, a senior member of the bar, wrote to Thurlow Weed, "[Seward] was evidently embarrassed" when he opened an argument for a case that had already been defaulted; He had "returned to the bar far less fit for its duties," than when he had left. The printed records of the Court of Appeals (the new highest court of the state) from 1847 to 1860 do not show his appearance as counsel of record. His legal papers from the period similarly show little business. At the same time, his son Frederick recalled that in Auburn, Seward was "indefatigable at his toils at the little one-storied law-office on South Street, where he prepared his papers and received his clients." Days spent in his office studying precedent and treatises were invariably broken by friends and supporters dropping by. Then "he would cheerfully throw aside books and papers, and stroll out into the garden" to "discuss the political outlook, or the social problems uppermost in the public mind."[2]

Seward adopted the pose of disliking the practice of law. His biographers took this at face value, with the logical consequence of assuming that he was unhappy in his work. True, he wrote wryly of having "no ambition for the honors" of legal advancement (meaning a judgeship), and compared everyday dealings with clients like walking a dreary "treadmill." He hated delay, waiting for trials to begin and juries to return from their deliberations, and drew a disparaging comparison to a canal boat waiting for a toll gate on the Erie Canal. "I would take a turnpike gate rather than linger at the bar." Yet he reveled in the cut and thrust of good argument and traveled all over the Northeast representing clients and causes. As he wrote to Frances from Albany, in his last days as governor, "I now think that I shall be content to go into my old office at Auburn, and take direct hold of such law-business as shall come to me." He represented clients while he sat in the US Senate.[3]

In court, Seward's energy served him well. Arriving at opening day of court in Rochester, New York, he outwitted his legal opponents. As he wrote to Frances, "I have been at Rochester, went up on Sunday night and returned today. Being on the ground at the opening of the court, I defaulted my adversaries [they were not there to respond to the court's summons], and saved myself the necessity of longer tarrying there." By the end of 1846, whatever reservations he had once held about law practice were receding. "Every day since my retreat from public life, the profession [of law], which I once so ungratefully despised, has been increasing its rewards." At the same time, the toll of working long hours weighed on him. On October 16, 1847, he wrote to Frances: "I am weary, weary to death, of this eternal pressure of occupation which leaves me no leisure for the society of my family and for enjoyment of books. I look upon my life, busy as it is, as a waste." Seward was a man of many moods.[4]

He had to continue to practice law because the debts accumulated in the Panic of 1837 loomed. When he departed the governorship in 1843, he wrote to Weed in elegiac tones: "All excesses leave a train of penance. Sad as the times are, and huge undertaking, I will try to meet all debts . . . my success will depend on how well I prepare myself." He had loaned money to relatives that the subsequent uncertainties of investment (the downside of enterprise) had dissipated. His country practice of law, unlike Daniel Webster's national practice at the Supreme Court, "left me without an assurance of the pecuniary independence which I had already found indispensable to the social and political independence at which I aimed." The interest on the Chautauqua notes he had cosigned amounted to nearly half a million dollars. His son Frederick later recalled that "the amount of work in any case rather seemed to stimulate than to discourage him." Until this time somewhat indifferent to his expenses and slow to dun his debtors, he now began to look more carefully at the bottom line. Still, he needed a benefactor. Fortunately, Richard Blatchford and Weed would help, and so, later, would the inheritance of his father's fortune. By the end of the decade, he expected a yearly income of about 5,000 dollars, and his fees exceeded his expectations.[5]

He took on junior partners, William Beach and George Underwood, who helped with the research for cases. Blatchford's contribution to the practice was still a treasure. Students, too, were employed for a term—jammed together in a new two-room office in Auburn. The students did what their predecessors did a hundred years before—copied papers, listened, and read. "People come to a lawyer," one of the students recalled Seward saying, "because they have reason to believe that he understands affairs better than they do." Apparently Seward the country lawyer was loved more than Seward the governor. He kept busy, although the causes he argued were a little less momentous than those he championed as governor. Nevertheless, Seward's in-box was filled, which pleased him. "I was employed in every cause of importance after my arrival. Popular feeling was with my clients, and there was a kindness toward me, so I succeeded in all my causes"; the good feeling of the jurors was far more important to the country lawyer than the niceties of the law itself. Or rather, local law and local politics (that is, popularity of client and counsel) would usually carry the day. Lesson learned.[6]

Even out of office, for the country lawyer like Seward politics remained a compelling interest. His clients were potential voters. His students were potential officeholders. He knew that some of them would look for elected posts. At the sessions of the courts, he mingled with elected officials. He took on voluntary public duties and, in the process, gained support from his neighbors. The former lawmaker remained a politician; the present lawyer might yet again be chosen for high office. But out of office, his world was one of hard choices. The lawyer/politician had to choose his close friends and his public speech carefully.

He had to cultivate like-minded newspapers editors and learn to withstand the attacks of his opponents' journalism. He could not be tender-minded, as the philosopher William James would later depict those intellectuals for whom rationality, idealism, and optimism guided their steps. James might well have had Seward in mind when he conceived that categorization.[7]

The habits of the country lawyer—gregariousness, the willingness to listen, the ability to see both sides of issues (for today's opponent might be tomorrow's client)—Seward had absorbed into his politics. By turns, he was a mediator and a litigator. He understood political relations the way that he understood relational rights of clients and opposing parties. "He would fight the adverse party and fight his counsel, fight every hostile witness, and fight the court, fight public sentiment, fight any obstacle to his client's success. He never quit. He could think of motions for every purpose under the sun, and he made them all. He moved for new trials, he appealed." Then he would join opponents' counsel and the judges at the local tavern for convivial after trial conversation. Fierce in defense of clients but always civil to opponents, he loved the law as a profession and a way of life. But the country lawyer was also something of a prisoner of his time and place, rarely rising above the limitations time and place imposed on him, hence the frequent complaints about law practice.[8]

Seward proved a staunch friend when an old political supporter came looking for legal help—defending his political ally, the newspaper publisher Horace Greeley, from a slander suit waged by the author James Fenimore Cooper. In future days, Greeley would turn against Seward, but in the 1840 reelection campaign, a narrow victory for the governor, Greeley had been a genuine friend: "but at least in one earnest, ardent, indignant heart [Greeley's] he will henceforth be honored more the three thousand votes he has lost [from his first term margin of victory], considering the causes, than for all he has received in his life." As early as 1843, Seward knew that Greeley's travails in court over his war of words with Cooper would bring him to Seward's door.[9]

In 1845, the defamation suit became a proxy for the Whig Party's contest against Cooper's ascendant democracy. Cooper had sued Weed, among others, for printing negative reviews of his books, a total of eighteen cases in all, and won all but two. Greeley had commented unfavorably on Cooper's character in an account of the suits in the *New York Tribune*. Cooper then sued Greeley. Greeley engaged Seward to appeal from the jury trial verdict. Greeley's paper reprinted the defense that Cooper had acquired in Otsego County—the reputation of a proud, captious, censorious, arbitrary, dogmatical, capricious, illiberal, revengeful, and litigious man. The defense was that the depiction was true, and thus not libelous, and in the alternative, that it was an opinion generally held; and the third was that the freedom of the press must be protected against such suits. In his address to the court, Seward was saddened that "encroachments on personal rights in the law of libel have at length brought a conflict between the judiciary and the press." A free press was necessary "in our democratic system," and it was unfair and unreasonable to impose on democratic journals "the rules of libel establish in the worst of times in England." A fair opinion should be free from tests of absolute and total truth. Had everyone forgotten the lesson of the seditious libel law of 1798?[10]

The formulary opening passages of the case report hinted at the personal and the political animus. Cooper told the court that "The declaration, after the usual introductory matter, alleged, in the first count, the publication by the defendants in the 'N. Y. Tribune,' of a certain false and malicious libel of and concerning the plaintiff," to which Cooper objected, "as a matter of intelligence" rather than opinion "without any sort of feeling towards Mr. Cooper." Greeley had allegedly refused to recant or even modify his stance. Seward's reply was that the newspaper article merely reported what had already been published, along with a legitimate (that is, permissible) editorial comment. What was more, "This is not a censorious or a ridiculing writing. It reflects upon the plaintiff certainly, but not severely, or censoriously, and it does not convey any sentiment of ridicule." Under the common law of libel, some injury to reputation must be shown, but "In the case before the court, the publication complained of charges no act criminal or immoral, or which tends to degrade the plaintiff or to exclude him from society. It is not alleged that the plaintiff lives in Otsego Co., or that he has any friends or connections residing there. How, then, can it be held to impair his fame to be esteemed disreputable in that county?" Swallow that. Remember that Cooper was a leading figure in the state Democratic Party, and Seward was a Whig. Seward also argued that truth was a positive and compelling defense. "This is to be proved, not by showing specific acts or conduct, but by showing what his reputation really was." That reputation was a matter of fact to be found by a jury, as it was in this case. Not least, "Besides, the new rule is inconvenient and impracticable, and calculated to prejudice parties in making their just defense." The chilling impact on newspaper political commentary, so vital at a time when the newspapers were the primary source of popular political information, was palpable. The court agreed. "The *innuendo* in this case, which states the meaning of the publication to be that the plaintiff, in consequence of being known in the County of Otsego, was in bad repute there, and would not for that reason like to bring a suit for a libel in that county, appears to me to express the true meaning of the publication. The question whether the alleged libel was published of and concerning the plaintiff, and whether the true meaning of the words is such as is alleged in the *innuendo* or not, is a question of fact which belongs to the jury and not to the court to determine."[11]

Judge Freeborn Jewett rendered the opinion, and shortly thereafter was elevated from the superior court to the chief judgeship in a newly created Court of Appeals. He came from the nearby town of Skaneateles, not far from Auburn. The entire Cooper—Weed—Greeley affair was, in effect, a dysfunctional family feud. A registered Democrat, Jewett served one term in the US Congress and then returned home to resume his legal practice. Seward and Greeley were Whigs, but Greeley never forgot a friend and campaigned vigorously for the creation of the new courts. His *Tribune* decried the "deplorable state" of the New York courts. They were "clogged with litigation . . . which lingers from year to year and ruins clients by its enormous expensiveness without bringing their suits to a conclusion." Greeley could well cite his own experience as evidence (his case took nearly four years to reach its conclusion). The New York State constitutional convention of 1846 that engaged in wide-ranging legal reform acceded to Greeley's pleas on the reorganization of the court. It was to this court that Jewett was appointed. Thus, once again, law and politics intersected.[12]

In 1846, Seward also involved himself in two criminal trials whose outcome was hotly contested. There was no public defender system, as there is today, and the country lawyer was sometimes called upon by a client or a client's supporters or by the court to step in as counsel. In these cases, Seward sometimes acted pro bono publico, that is, without a fee. In these two cases, of Henry Wyatt and William Freeman, Seward faced public opprobrium as well as unremunerated expense. As governor, Seward had the power to pardon felons, a power he used sparingly, primarily for younger offenders in crimes against property. He showed comparatively less mercy when the offender was well placed or acted in reckless disregard of common decency. Even as the chief executive of the state his sense of community values and common sense justice influenced his granting of pardons. Of course, then he spoke for the state. Now he was on the other side of the issue.[13]

In these cases, Seward assessed whether the idea of relational rights could migrate from civil to criminal cases. Crimes were defined by state statutes. Reciprocal relationships seemed to have no place in defense of alleged crimes, as by definition the accused had violated community norms. But Seward averred that in both the Wyatt and Freeman murder trials, recent advances in the insanity defense affected the outcome. That is, the insanity defense injected a relational quality into crimes—was the perpetrator of the act aware of its criminality, that is, had the mental defect removed the defendant from the community and its obligations? Did he or she understand the nature of his or her act, or of its consequences at the time, in effect meaning that he no longer could share communal ideas of right and wrong? In the English 1843 case of Daniel M'Naghten, a jury acquitted a young assassin who acted insanely without being judged insane. The rule that arose from the case was that in a murder case sanity was a "rebuttable assumption." When a defendant had been deprived of his ability to tell right from wrong, or to understand what he was doing because of mental illness, he was guilty but insane and ordered to an asylum instead of to the gallows. Seward was the first US lawyer to deploy the M'Naghten rule.[14]

It would not be easy to convince the trial judge to allow such an argument, given the traditions of the state criminal courts. When Seward began to practice in 1823, the criminal courts were "little changed—in form and operation—from the colonial court system erected in the 17th Century." Although a supreme court sat above the trial courts, and the court for correction of errors occupied the top of the system, trial judges were few in number and rode circuit from county town to county town. "In effect, each judge was himself an institution with substantial, if not really unlimited, authority to determine the rules of legal practice before his court. Also, each judge generally had the final word in controversies before him as there was little in the way of an appellate court structure." While this system, simple and inexpensive (judges were paid by the county, not by the state), may have suited the largely rural upstate, under the new constitution of 1846 the entire criminal justice system was overhauled. "The Supreme Court was substantially enlarged—with the number of its justices being increased from 3 to a minimum of 32. These justices would be selected from and serve in judicial districts drawn to coincide with county lines. . . . The Supreme Court became a statewide court of complete and original jurisdiction. At the same time, lesser trial courts, with limited subject matter and geographical jurisdiction, were given constitutional status." The 1846 convention also "gave birth to the beginnings of a two-tiered appellate apparatus." Intermediate appellate courts were established, and above them was placed the Court of Appeals as the state's highest court of appellate jurisdiction. Gone was the Court for the Correction of Errors. "Finally, the convention mandated that trial judges be popularly elected for fixed terms of office, and that the Legislature enjoy significant rule—making authority in the formulation of court procedures." But at the trial court level, election of local judges meant that the bench was more than ever amenable to the views of the locality. "Trial courts were virtually autonomous bodies, both administratively and jurisdictionally." It was in this institutional setting that Seward had to argue for Wyatt's and Freeman's lives. For him and his co-counsel it would be a true test of relational rights, and the trials showed that Seward's relational rights jurisprudence, at least in criminal practice, had severe limitations.[15]

Accused of murdering another inmate of Auburn penitentiary, Wyatt reached out to Seward, who agreed to represent him. Blatchford joined him on the case. The willingness of a former governor to argue for the life of a convicted felon was itself remarkable. The argument that Wyatt had been driven to madness by "inhuman treatment" in prison was an attack on a state institution by its former supervisor. The prosecution even teased Seward that the prison officials were his own appointees. He replied that by brutalizing Wyatt, the prison had driven him out of its community, and consequently it could not expect him to honor its rules.[16]

Wyatt had been convicted of burglary and sentenced to the Auburn penitentiary for ten years. He allegedly confessed to the crime of murder of another inmate while incarcerated. At his February 1846 trial in the Cayuga County Courthouse, Seward's cross-examination of witnesses proved that Wyatt was flogged on more than one occasion, and he argued that the abuse drove the defendant mad. His cross-examination focused on the gory details of the punishment, along with the evasiveness of the prosecution witnesses (the jailors), and the suggestion that the prosecution had rehearsed their testimony with the inmates' made an impression on some of the jurors. Seward called these "infamous witnesses." Seward impeached the confession, made, he proposed, under duress, or, in the alternative, fabricated by the jailor to absolve himself of responsibility. The prison had failed in its responsibility to Wyatt and to all its inmates. These facts and allegations, perhaps even more than his summation on the law—it was an early case of irresistible impulse—gained a hung jury for Wyatt. But his attempt to translate relational rights into the rights of a prisoner did not sway popular opinion. Seward was losing the case in the newspapers. Seward later wrote to Weed that the chorus of public condemnation falling on him was furious, but he would persist. Seward had long been a critic of the state prison system, as governor had argued for prison reform, and this gave him the opportunity to restate his concerns.[17]

Blatchford had addressed the jury on the matter of insanity. Note that this was not based on some concept of relational rights. Instead, it was a primer on mental states. There were three kinds of insanity—from imperfect development of the mind (imbecility), madness (mental disease), and a kind of stress disorder (intellectual mania or temporary insanity), all of which were legal defenses to criminal acts. Blatchford then read to the jury the testimony of the expert witnesses to prove that Wright was not in possession of his reasoning faculties when—if—he committed the homicide. The prosecution countered that those in day-to-day contact with Wyatt would know his mental state a lot better than the expert witnesses, and these men—inmates and jailers—thought Wyatt sane. Just the same, the prosecution arrayed its own medical testimony. Still, Seward and Blatchford had sown enough doubt in some jurors' minds to win a hung jury for their client. But a second trial ended in a conviction, and Wyatt was executed.[18]

While Wyatt was awaiting retrial, William Freeman, a Black man just released from the same prison, killed a family of four people, including an infant. Again Seward agreed to defend a killer, and again Seward's defense was that the defendant was insane. Perhaps the state had an absolute right to Freeman's life, but its prosecution strategy was to depict Freeman as a man devout of moral capacity, who was well aware of right and wrong. That July 1846 afternoon, in the same Cayuga County courtroom, in Seward's own Auburn, before the same judge who sentenced Henry Wyatt came Freeman's case. Seward, joined by co-counsel David Wright, presented evidence that Freeman, while in prison, had behaved bizarrely, but the judge instructed the jury that Freeman understood the difference between right and wrong. He was sane enough to stand trial. The trial that followed again featured expert testimony that Freeman was insane, but the prosecution, led by John Van Buren, son of the former president, insisted that he was merely a Black savage.[19]

Seward arranged for his argument for Freeman to be published immediately, having prepared a copy for the printer. Seward conceded that the murder was atrocious, and no one guilty of such an act should go free. Seward did not inveigh against the death penalty, but he did insist that Freeman was mentally incapable of understanding his acts. He was a man, not a beast, and entitled to be treated as a man who had lost his senses. "I am arraigned before you [the jury] for undue manifestations of zeal and excitement," Seward pleaded, shifting the attention of the jury from Freeman to himself, but his only fault was sleepless nights and indefatigable research into the nature of mental defects. He pleaded "not for a murderer," but for "a negro without intellect, sense, or emotion." According to Seward, Freeman did not even know he was on trial and did not understand the proceedings against him. Here, as in the case of the three sailors, Seward was not "the prisoner's lawyer," he was the lawyer for society, for the common decency of all men. Seward pressed his case. Asked to plead, Freeman was "driven to silence and bewilderment," unable to comprehend because he had the mind of a child. It was an ingenious shift of poses, from the criminal as an evil monster to the defendant as a helpless infant, from the adversarial system to one closer to the Continental one, in which defense and prosecution do not joust with one another. Then Seward turned about and insisted that beneath the apparent madness still dwelt a spiritual mind, a soul, and Freeman's color and ancestry should not be held against him. The twists and turns of his defense did not persuade the jury; they were Seward's neighbors and knew well enough his prowess before a jury. Freeman was convicted. Seward and Wright went to Rochester to appeal, and the supreme court there found that the trial judge's instructions to the jury to assume Freeman was sane were faulty. A new trial was ordered, but before it was docketed prison officials decided that Freeman was incompetent to stand trial. He died in prison shortly thereafter.[20]

It was a Pyrrhic victory for Seward. Seward had reached out to his neighbors sitting in the jury box to join him in his explication of relational rights. He said, here was a man like any other among us who had lost his senses, who was not responsible for his acts, as reprehensible as they were. But the jury was not persuaded. Their sense of the enormity of the offense, added to their racialist attitudes, condemned Freeman to death. The prosecution's version of relational wrongs triumphed over Seward's appeal to the better nature of the jurors. Here relational rights—the shared sense of right and wrong of the community—bowed to the racism that ran like a braid through the free North. Did this not prevent any form of relational rights, even one so deeply held as Seward's, so trusting on the innate sense of justice of freemen, from winning out against slavery? Seward had to plead a technical argument to an appellate court to save Freeman for another day. But Seward was not done thinking about and making a case for relational rights in public forums.

Seward's defense of Freeman conceded the local assumption that the Black man was morally and intellectually inferior to his white neighbors. Seward shared something of these assumptions; however, that did not mean any diminution in his dislike of slavery. By the closing years of the decade, politics and law converged on the slavery issue. One might say that all national politics in these years touched slavery. No neutral observer could doubt how entrenched proslavery argument was in law as well as electoral politics. But Seward saw freedom and progress in the nation endangered by the slave power. He had already responded to the threat with his refusal to return the three slaves to Virginia, and during his governorship had pressed the state legislature to mandate trial by jury for suspected runaways. Still, slavery was winning in the federal courts.[21]

The great obstacle to antislavery legalism in federal courts was *Prigg v. Pennsylvania* (1842). When Maryland slave catcher Edward Prigg violated the Pennsylvania law against kidnapping, and the state sought his return from Maryland, the suit between Maryland and Pennsylvania went directly to the US Supreme Court under its original jurisdiction. Maryland challenged the Pennsylvania law for violating the Rendition Clause of the federal Constitution and the Fugitive

Slave Act of 1793 enacted under the clause. So potent was proslavery thinking at the Supreme Court level that even Massachusetts justice Joseph Story, who abhorred slavery, had to concede its place in the fundamental law of the nation in his opinion for the court.[22]

The Constitution's Rendition Clause (Article IV, Section 2: "No person held to Service or Labour in one State, under the Laws thereof, escaping into another, shall, in Consequence of any Law or Regulation therein, be discharged from such Service or Labour, but shall be delivered up on Claim of the Party to whom such Service or Labour may be due") was the basis of the Fugitive Slave Law of 1793. Under the fourth section of that act, "respecting fugitives from justice, and persons escaping from the service of their master, on a charge for harbouring and concealing fugitives from labor, the notice need not be in writing by the claimant or his agent, stating that such person is a fugitive from labor under the third section of the above act, and served on the person harbouring or concealing such fugitive, to make him liable to the penalty of five hundred dollars under the act." The operative effect of the Rendition Clause and the Fugitive Slave Act of 1793 on states' laws offering due process protections to people of color (who might not be runaway slaves) was plain—the states were not to interfere with slave catchers even though the state had, or were (in the case of the Northwest Ordinance), created with the explicit rejection of slavery.

As a justice of the Supreme Court, Story felt bound to obey the letter of the law. "It is historically well known, that the object of the clause in the Constitution of the United States, relating to persons owing service and labour in one state escaping into other states, was to secure to the citizens of the slaveholding states the complete right and title of ownership in their slaves, as property, in every state in the Union, into which they might escape from the state where they were held in servitude." Story then added, in what legal jargon calls a dictum, or statement not strictly necessary to determine the outcome of the case, "The full recognition of this right and title, was indispensable to the security of this species of property in all the slaveholding states; and indeed was so vital to the preservation of their domestic interests and institutions, that it cannot be doubted that it constituted a fundamental article, without the adoption of which the Union could not have been formed." Whether this was good history or sound legal doctrine depended on whose version of history and doctrine contemporaries adopted. The abolitionists certainly did not agree that "Its true design was to guard against the doctrines and principles prevailing in the non-slaveholding states, by preventing them from intermeddling with or obstructing or abolishing the rights of the owners of slaves."[23]

What was the Supreme Court to do with Pennsylvania's insistence on due process for alleged runaways (the same due process that New York had adopted at Seward's urging)? "The clause manifestly contemplates the existence of a positive, unqualified right on the part of the owner of the slave, which no state law or regulation can in any way qualify, regulate, control, or restrain." One can read this as a slap at states' rights, for Story was a staunch nationalist, but then must one read it as "slavery national, freedom sectional"? In any case, Story was adamant, "The slave is not to be discharged from service or labour, in consequence of any state law or regulation of the free states or persons in them."[24]

Story added another dictum that the law of 1793 regarding the recapture of fugitives and the Rendition Clause did not require the state or its officers to abet the recapture, though it might choose to do so (or it might not decide to help). To which dictum Chief Justice Roger Taney of Maryland objected. "And if the officers of the state are not justified in acting under the state laws, and cannot arrest the fugitive, and detain him in prison without having first received an authority from the owner; the territory of the state must soon become an open pathway for the fugitives escaping from other states." Associate Justice Peter Daniel of Virginia offered an even stronger opinion along the lines Taney laid down. "I hold then that the states can establish proceedings which are in their nature calculated to secure the rights of the slaveholder guaranteed to him by the Constitution. Without mandated state assistance, the recapture of runaways would be ineffectual at best and downright dangerous at worst." In other words, antislavery sentiment in the free states had grown so common that recapture was becoming difficult.[25]

Although Justice John McLean of Ohio was an opponent of slavery, he could not directly dispute the authority given the master under the Rendition Clause and the Fugitive Slave Act of 1793. He could and did offer grounds for due process in state courts. There is a hint of relational rights in the concurrence, but the hint was not developed. "The slave, as a sensible and human being, is subject to the local authority into whatsoever jurisdiction he may go. He is answerable under the laws for his acts, and he may claim their protection. The state may protect him against all the world except the claim of his master." Slaves were not "mere" property. They were both persons and chattels. The master had an absolute right to the slave. There was no reciprocity in that relationship. "In a state where slavery is allowed, every coloured person is presumed to be a slave; and on the same principle, in a non-slaveholding state, every person is presumed to be free without regard to colour." McLean chose a states' rights stance—the same as in Seward's contemporaneous response to Virginia. "On this principle, the states, both slaveholding and non-slaveholding, legislate. The latter may prohibit, as Pennsylvania has done under a certain penalty, the forcible removal of a coloured person out of the state."[26]

Sitting in the governor's office at the time, Seward did not participate as counsel or friend of the Court in *Prigg*, but five years later he joined Ohio Free Soil Democrat and abolitionist Salmon Chase as co-counsel counsel for John Van Zandt, the defendant in the next most important slavery case of its day, *Jones v. Van Zandt* (1847). Chase had argued Van Zandt's cause in the lower federal court and had prepared his argument there for publication. His fellow Ohioan, Justice McLean, told Chase that the docket for the February meeting of the US Supreme Court was pretty full already, but he welcomed Chase to present an oral argument if he chose. McLean had heard it all already, as he was one of the two judges (the other was district judge Humphrey Howe Leavitt) in the earlier federal circuit court trial of Van Zandt—allowing the appeal because he and the district court judge agreed to disagree (grounds for an appeal), from the jury verdict for Wharton Jones. Chase sent the printed version of his argument to the Supreme Court anyhow.[27]

In preparing the case for the appeal to the High Court, Chase had sought the aid of fellow Democrat Edwin Stanton, a leading Ohio lawyer and anti-slave politician, but Stanton declined. Chase then reached out to Seward, a Whig in politics but one whose actions as governor of New York and defense of Freeman might prove him Chase's kindred spirit. Seward took the case pro bono, as Van Zandt was impoverished. Seward lauded Chase's printed argument, which Seward said he had studied carefully, as "conclusive on every point." Chase had stressed the villainy of the slave catchers; the vulnerability of the elderly defendant; the errors in the statement of the plaintiff, hence the factual errors in the indictment; the trial court's failure to construe the act strictly, hence technical errors in its instructions to the jury; the inept draftsmanship of the 1793 Fugitive Slave Act (e.g., between seizing the alleged fugitive and holding the alleged fugitive; what kind of notice was required, and to whom delivered); and even hinted that the law lent itself to "the arbitrary caprice of judges" (a coded reference to the predominance of slave state justices on the bench). The brief offered everything that Chase could think of in 107 pages of case law. But Seward decided to add his own brief in the "cause of freedom" because he wanted his views widely disseminated. That argument had "required much labor and study" Seward recalled. He arranged for its printing and submitted the print version to the Court, then appeared before it to present the oral argument. Unlike Chase's, Seward's was based on relational rights.[28]

The supposed facts of the case were these: in 1842, Wharton Jones, a Kentucky slaveholder, hired two slave catchers to pursue his slave Andrew among others who fled into Ohio, a free state. Van Zandt, an old white farmer who formerly lived in Kentucky, known locally as an enemy of slavery, "harbored the alleged slave and transported him in a covered wagon twelve or fourteen miles, so that the boy thereby escaped pursuit, and his services were thereby lost to his master." The master wanted Jones to pay the fines set by the 1793 statute, whether or not the alleged slave was subsequently recaptured. Note that the report of the case referred to the slave as "the boy" and "colored" as well as "Andrew," the remark about color a common basis for the assumption that he was a slave. That made him a fugitive under the law. Had he escaped wrongful confinement, the issue would have been put differently. Could McLean have put it this way? On occasion, jurists in the free states would do exactly that. McLean was an abolitionist. But the letter of the law was strict and left little room for humane discretion. Most joined with Story in adopting an impersonal stance—it is not the judge but the law that speaks. McLean felt constrained not to accede to abolitionist arguments.[29]

Van Zandt had covered the wagon, and the lower court presumed that his act demonstrated his knowledge that the hidden passenger was a runaway slave. But had not Andrew sat with Van Zandt on the bench at the front of the wagon? Did covering Andrew with the blanket prove Van Zandt's knowledge that Andrew was a runaway slave? Was it presumptive evidence that he was "harboring" a fugitive? Surely this did not make Van Zandt liable in the light of relational rights, according to Seward. "Harboring and concealing a weary and fainting slave, though known as a slave, is not injurious, and does not disturb society." Instead, Seward proposed, society was built on another, more fundamental convention than the Constitution: hospitality to the stranger. This was the core of all society, a reciprocal relationship that predated all constitutions. "Under no law can this act be deemed immoral; and in most cases, it would be charitable." Only by the strict application of law rather than a humane act of hospitality, what Seward termed "wisdom and humanity" and we have recast as relational rights, could Van Zandt be guilty of anything.[30]

Seward came to Washington, DC, and argued the case before the court in February 1847. Salmon P. Chase's written argument had been 107 pages; Seward's came to 38 pages when later published. The reporter for the court, former Maryland congressman Benjamin Chew Howard, declined to include both in his report of the case, instead summarizing the points the two men made in defense of Van Zandt. (Perhaps for this reason both counsels had their full briefs printed.)[31]

Seward's arguments were procedural and substantive. The first mirrored Chase's; the second were his own. They remind us of his skill as a lawyer when he cared about a cause: confident, composed, logical, and relentless. He insisted that the prosecution failed "Because, first, neither count sufficiently charges the defendant with notice that Andrew was a fugitive from labor. Secondly. It is not sufficiently averred that Andrew was held to labor or service to the Plaintiff, in Kentucky, by the laws thereof, and escaped and fled from that State into Ohio. Thirdly. It is not sufficiently averred, that the Defendant harbored or concealed the fugitive. . . . It is not charged, in either count, that the Defendant had notice before the alledged harboring or concealment, that Andrew was a fugitive from labor." McLean ruled according to the statute in the lower court. Seward wanted McClean to rule according to the law of nature. "His Honor, the presiding Judge of the Circuit Court, (McLean) held, that positive, direct, and formal notice was not necessary; and that knowledge possessed by the defendant, however obtained, was equivalent to such notice, or a substitute for it. Such a construction of the Statute is obviously necessary, to support this declaration. But this construction relieves this penal Statute against liberty and humanity of a condition, expressly and emphatically declared."[32]

Humanity went hand in hand with the presumption of free status, which only express (written and proved) evidence could overawe. "He [the defendant] may harbor the slave, and conceal him from his pursuers, as the law of nature commands, until after notice. . . . If NOTICE be a condition precedent, then the notice must be explicit, certain, direct and comprehensive. Such notice is capable of being averred. No such notice is averred; or, at least, none such is described." The law of nature was not some abstract natural right. It was relational—the relation between Andrew and Van Zandt created the moment Andrew sought Van Zandt's aid.[33]

McLean had assumed that notice could be constructive; that is, if all parties knew something, then the law was satisfied. Seward disagreed. "We humbly submit, that these general principles, however true, are never applied in construing Penal Statutes. Legal conditions may be dispensed with for equivalents, to promote the ends of justice in civil controversies; but they cannot be waived when they are barriers, erected for the protection of the accused." Alleged slaves were people under the Constitution, and "only the construction of the learned Judge, makes the Congress of the United States interdict protection, hospitality and charity, to the Slave." Here was the hint of a broader relationship—the relationship that everyone under the Constitution bore to everyone else.[34]

But fervid calls for extralegal humanitarianism were not the centerpiece of Seward's argument. Nor was it an argument based on abstract rights. Van Zandt did not have the right to conceal and convey Andrew to freedom, and Andrew did not have the right to seek Van Zandt's aid. Instead, Seward's argument rested on reciprocity. Seward asked the Court to assume, as he did, that every person who lived and worked in the nation was free until proven otherwise. Note that the attack was not aimed at slavery itself, but at the power that the existence of a slave system had to destroy the relationship among all the people. The indictment of Van Zandt averred on the claim of one man that Andrew was a slave. No doubt he was held to labor in Kentucky, and the court below had assumed that being held to labor was the equivalent of slavery. "Facts must be stated in pleading, not argued" or assumed. "The allegation that Andrew was a slave, was property, and was possessed by the Plaintiff, present facts from which the court are required to infer that Andrew was held to labor by law." If he were a slave, let the plaintiff bring written proof to the court, let the question be adjudicated in the same way that any dispute was litigated. Andrew deserved due process because, Seward argued, his freedom must be contested in a court of law before Van Zandt was to be held Andrew's rescuer.[35]

The 1793 law did not require evidence of the sort that Seward demanded because its framers and fifty years later its enforcers assumed that dark skin color was a non-rebuttable presumption of slave status. If one was Black and worked in Kentucky, one was a slave. In any case, according to testimony in the trial court, Van Zandt was neither told nor shown evidence that Andrew was a runaway before the defendant aided in the escape. By contrast, anyone who saw Andrew and tried to capture or detain him was presumed guiltless under the statute. Anyone who aided and abetted his flight was presumed to be a violator. Anyone who claimed to be his owner, or to represent his owner, was assumed to speak the truth, and did not need to provide written evidence of that claim, because color was presumptive evidence. Seward repeated: where was the proof that Andrew was a fugitive, when so many men were traveling over the land to find better circumstances. Just so, "the institution of slavery accustoms us to confound the broadest distinction in nature, not less to subvert the plainest principles of justice." Slavery and the slave regime in law mangled all relationships.[36]

The relationships that Seward celebrated had a history deeply rooted in human progress. "The cause of human liberty, however baffled, never rests," he judged. In the eighteenth century it expressed itself in the abolitionist movement—still small, but irreversible. The first evidence here was the Declaration of Independence, which "bears memorable testimony of the high tone which the American mind had then assumed." Next was abolition in the northern states. Then came the Northwest Ordinance. Ohio was free territory, and then a free state, the inheritor of the long, slow process of the emancipation of men from unfair and unmerited burdens. History worked liberty free from slavery. The founders were "deeply imbued with the sentiment of abolition."[37]

The nation and its laws were built on this relational foundation. It was a capacious community. Ohio was part of it, as was Kentucky, New York, and Pennsylvania. All its people were members of the community. History is often part of an appellate pleading, as all cases before the appellate bench have histories, but Seward's historical essay was broader. As the nation's territory grew, so did the reciprocity owed and offered to all who lived in the country. The Confederation Congress agreed as well that there would not be slavery within the Territory. The Constitution incorporated the ordinance. Ohio was free of slavery. The states formed from the Northwest Territory, including Ohio, agreed to "extend the fundamental principles of civil and religious liberty . . . and to fix and establish these principles as the basis of all laws, constitutions, and governments." These included the writ of habeas corpus. The Act of 1793 contravened these agreements in general and in particular, for no provision was made to extend these to suspected fugitive slaves.[38]

The essence of this argument was not the familiar one of states' rights. True, northern free state leaders readily made such arguments to protect their personal liberty laws. But the law of freedom, in New York for example, did not rest on New York's absolute sovereignty (or the Fugitive Slave Law would have no purchase in New York when Seward was governor). It was organic and grew from the elaboration of mutual obligations among the people of the various states. So Seward supposed. Why was Andrew, an adult male "free to roam the world" and certainly free under Ohio laws, pursued? What law presumed slavery for him and made him on his face a fugitive? The Act of 1793 must have had, unstated but understood, some mechanism for identifying him. The answer was that a certain skin color raised the rebuttable presumption of fugitive status. (It was the same argument that the prosecution made in the Freeman trial; the same presumption of debased manhood that Seward rejected then.) But nothing in the text of the federal law said anything about color. It merely repeated the language of the Fugitive Slave Clause. The Ordinance of 1787 and Ohio's subsequent constitution made the exact opposite assumption. All men were free and equal under the law. Given this logic, Seward could rightly declaim "compromises may be made by compact on the subject of slavery," limiting the constitutional power of the state—not a states' rights argument at all, then.[39]

For Seward it was not state law per se, but the alignment of Ohio State law with relational rights among Ohio's citizenry, the group to which Van Zandt belonged, that gave force to his argument. Slavery was an imposition on all the duties that all men owed one another, whose ill-effects could be seen in assuming that a Black man was a slave. Though Kentucky state law did this, it was an exception to the reciprocity that all good law exhibited. That exception was racism, and slavery ushered it into the law like a thief in the night.

The penultimate Seward argument was hermeneutic. It raised the question of how courts are to interpret legislation. Although the common law rested largely on courts interpreting precedent (that is, prior judicial opinions), legislation had become an increasingly important source of law in the new republic. Law reformers in the early nineteenth century argued that legislation was superior to precedent because it narrowed and made law more precise. As Francis Lieber wrote in his *Legal and Political Hermeneutics* (1839), to find "some firm and solid foundations of right and morality" in the law, one had first to lay down rules for the construction or interpretation of laws. For "civil liberty" law in the "exact administration of the laws," not in the varying impositions of "public power." Any law must "harmonize" with the superior law governing the subject, thus a statute on slavery must conform to the general spirit of the Constitution. Different subjects in a single statute must not be conflated with one another, as their separate and distinct treatment implies that they are not the same. A statute in whole or in part should always be read in light of the purpose and general sense of its governing law—here, the Constitution. Correct "construction" of meaning in law "signifies the discovery of the spirit, principles, and rules which ought to guide us . . . with regard to subjects" in inferior legislation. If the Constitution was meant to supply "the blessings of liberty" to "we the people," then the Rendition Clause and the Fugitive Slave Act passed under it should lean in the direction of freedom.[40]

Although caricatured as an radical abolitionist, Seward was not a member of that circle. He was opposed to slavery but assumed that time and reason would show the wrongs of slavery to those who owned slaves. He owned a copy of Lieber's essays on property and labor. Lieber's rules for construction of statutes were not inherently antislavery (nor was Lieber when he lived and taught in Columbia, South Carolina), but abolitionist jurisprudents like Salmon Chase, Lysander Spooner, Alvan Stewart, and New York's own Gerritt Smith (with whom Seward had a personal relationship) had already insisted that the federal Constitution should be read as an antislavery document. Seward did not join them. Instead, he proposed that the fugitive law should be read narrowly, for the 1793 law was badly drawn. As written, the act was both vague and overbroad. It could apply to all fugitives from labor or none. It did not mandate evidence that the individual who ran was a slave and did not provide due process for an innocent to redeem his freedom. No state intervention was allowed, whatever the protections in that state's law for suspected fugitives or those who aided them. In an ordinary process, courts must allow lawyers for the accused to present exculpatory evidence. Here, courts were invited to ignore those protections. Seward conceded that every benefit of the doubt, in Congress and the courts, had gone in favor of slavery. Seward also admitted that the prior cases created a precedent in favor of the present case. It is not surprising then that Seward's target was the state of Virginia, with whom he had, as governor of New York, carried on an increasingly vituperative exchange about rendition. It was Virginia that had sought the act, and Virginia that refused to comply with other states' requests for the return of felons until its own interests were satisfied.[41]

Finally, Seward complained that the Fugitive Slave Act of 1793 criminalized what was a civil dispute. With the rendition of fugitives from justice, a matter of criminal law, Seward had no complaint, but as slavery rested on contract, a civil matter, and slaves, as property, were not committing a felony by seeking their freedom then by analogy no one assisting them should be treated as criminals. The law analogized the runaway as a fugitive from justice, when in fact, according to Southern slave law, he was no more than missing property. Slaves were not criminals for running away from a contract. Fugitive debtors, for example, were not considered felons. Story's opinion for the Court in *Prigg* upholding the constitutionality of the act mistakenly conflated the two kinds of flight, a mistake, and not the only one that Story made. He thought that the point of the statute was to return the slave to the master, whereas as written, the statute said nothing about returning the slave; instead, it punished all who aided and abetted the runaway. Although the members of the constitutional convention knew all about slavery, they carefully excluded the word from the document. Claimants to labor, rather than master, appeared in the clause, hence in the law. It became "an engine for oppression and slavery" as Southern representatives gained control of Congress. If the Court did not stop the trend, all labor would become slavery, and all free state laws bow to the laws of the slave states. If the Constitution were the work of "we the people" such a construction of the clause and the act had to be erroneous.[42]

Even here, Seward was not arguing from the standpoint of the natural rights of the slave. It was Van Zandt—his client and the defendant—whose rights he sought to preserve. For the same reason, Seward was not equating good law with morality. He did not argue that the opposite of rights was wrongs. Instead, rights derive from relations. Both men's rights lay in obligations they owed one another. These rights were relational. Van Zandt's relation to Andrew, embedded in the concept of hospitality, was so basic that it need not have been mentioned in the positive law. Due process was a pale illumination of relational rights as fundamental as hospitality. But due process demanded the obedience of all courts of law. The Fugitive Slave Act of 1793 violated due process not because it denied rights or dignity, or freedom to the alleged runaway, but because it denied rights to the free person who treated a runaway as a fellow human being.[43]

Changing the context in which we view his words in defending *Van Zandt* from a purely legal one—a brief in a lawsuit—to a political/legal one, that is, placing it in the overlap of the two regimes, permits us to glimpse how Seward was refining his solution to the democracy/slavery problem. He knew that *Prigg* foreclosed the appeal for the old farmer, but he made it anyway in *Van Zandt*. Was he wasting the court's and his time? Was he simply posturing for the abolitionist vote in the state? No, for him a court case conjoining democracy (after all the fugitive slave law was an act of Congress) and slavery was the perfect venue for another, further exploration of how law should promote freedom based on relational rights. Seward was offering far more than a clever attempt to evade the letter of the law. He was proposing an entirely alternative view of the penal law. An act that did not harm society, and a law whose punishment (return to slavery) was entirely out of proportion to the crime (aiding and abetting a runaway), could not be a just law. "If there be no such effort, or design, it is as lawful, and as humane, to harbor the slave, as to entertain a fellow Freeman." Even the master must be sensitive to this, for, if the kind-hearted did not harbor the slave, and the slave perished or was disabled, the master faced a total loss. The relation between master and slave was so asymmetrical that it bent the law out of shape.[44]

Seward dwelt at length on other contradictions that slavery and freedom, side by side, posed in the nation and its laws. The common law, "which abhors slavery," provided the terms and remedies for the act. How could slaves be both property and persons? How could slaves be vigorous and manly, yet under the total control of masters? How could slaves held by force nevertheless escape that yoke? Why did the exceptions and mercies of law regarding slaves elsewhere not apply to the 1793 law? Most important, in a country where democratic equality was the ideal and free will the basis of religion, what had any slave done to burden himself with slavery? Hidden in this, though not explicit, was the end of slavery in the British and French possessions, already over a decade old. What made the United States different?[45]

Seward's answer lay not in a fierce condemnation of slavery, the language of the abolitionists, or the excoriation of the master class but in expanding the law beyond its text. Here reappeared his "habits, opinions, and policy" of the Virginia letters standing above the letter of the law, in this case the 1793 Fugitive Slave Act. He proposed that hospitality was a law of civilized societies as old as time itself. People had a "natural right . . . even in savage life, to give necessary shelter, comfort, and sustenance to the wayfaring men, the stranger, and the fugitive." The act not only forbade this; it made easy the efforts of individual plaintiffs to prevent other individuals from offering hospitality. And the courts, instead of construing the act strictly, read it in the largest, most proplaintiff way. It made the stranger into a fugitive and the needy into a criminal. The child who ran from duress but happened to be Black was presumed to be a slave. The woman who escaped the vilest of labor (and worse) was nevertheless to be returned to the cruel master—these were the dictates of the act. And the good Samaritan was assumed to have knowledge of the flight, and thus to pay the fine and return the man, woman, and child—without any evidence other than the say-so of the pursuers. The best that could be said of it was that the Court was promoting property rights over human rights. The worst—Seward did not risk a contempt of court citation, whatever he may have been thinking of Taney and his fellow jurists. And hospitality (what the guest owed to the host and the host owed to the guest) was the essence of relational rights. Such rights were not written into the law but the rock upon which all good law must rest.[46]

On what basis, of law or fact, could Seward have persuaded a court to agree with him? Not this court, of course, but a court made up of herculean justices? This case clearly had become a cause célèbre for the abolitionist cause, and Seward's co-counsel, Chase, had written long and eloquently in what was clearly an abolitionist brief against slavery itself. Like Chase, who regarded the case as a political one for his own political ambitions in Ohio, Seward knew that his participation would have political repercussions. As he told Chase when the day was done, "I reached out over the Court to the people."[47]

Both Chase and Seward knew that the defense of Van Zandt had no chance of winning. Setting aside the highly charged political climate, in which a majority of the voters were not ready to end slavery, the Court had already spoken in *Prigg*. Although the Court was not bound by precedent, this one was too close in time and unanimous to overturn. Second, the composition of the Court—its majority coming from slave states (Levi Woodbury, Samuel Nelson, and McLean being the exceptions)—made it highly unlikely that the Court would desert *Prigg*.[48]

Woodbury wrote for the entire Court a simple response to Chase's and Seward's eloquence and passion. "Now the act of Congress does not, in terms, require the notice to be in writing, nor does the reason of the provision, nor the evil to be guarded against, nor any sound analogy. The reason of the provision is merely, that the party shall have notice or information sufficient to put him on inquiry, whether he is not intermeddling with what belongs to another. If the information given to him, orally or in writing, is such as ought to satisfy a fair-minded man that he is concealing the property of another, it is his duty under the constitution and laws to cease to do it longer." The Fugitive Slave Act of 1793 was constitutional, and the case came under the clear mandate of the statute. Woodbury added, unnecessarily (that is, as an obiter dicta) that "Any other construction, too, would be suicidal to the law itself, as before a notice in writing could be prepared and served on the defendant, the fugitives would be carried beyond the reach of recovery in many cases, and in others would have passed into unknown hands." The added admonition was precisely what Chase and Seward should have feared—an open defense of slave-catching in the free states.[49]

Seward did not confine what today would be called public defender lawyering to his own state's or the US courts. When Michigan farmers accused of conspiracy to commit vandalism and arson against the Central Michigan Railroad were arrested, and their cause seemed hopeless, their cause became Seward's. The Great Detroit Conspiracy trial of 1851 consumed most of Seward's spring and summer. The much-disputed facts were these: Trying to recoup their investment in a shoddy railroad enterprise that was nearly bankrupt, the owners of the Central Michigan Railroad ran their trains through farmland, at night, with no lights, bells, or whistles, and no fences along the tracks. A predictable result was the loss of farmers' livestock to the speeding locomotives. Farmers, led by one Abel Fitch, organized protests, filed lawsuits, and when these failed (the territorial government in the pocket of the rail line) began a campaign of sabotage. The line hired spies and agents provocateurs, who urged the conspirators to up the ante by burning down the rail station in Detroit. Thirty-seven of the alleged conspirators were rounded up, summarily jailed (with huge bail bond fees), and tried for conspiracy.[50]

Local lawyers (for the farmers' plight had drawn sympathy) reached out to Seward for help. He agreed. The proceedings took three months, and two of the accused died in prison, among them Fitch. On August 10, 1851, Seward wrote home, "This everlasting trial, like revolution, seems to have almost banished Sundays. We have examined more than three hundred witnesses, indeed, nearer four hundred, and the night, adjourned days, and Sundays, have afford too little time to post up the multifarious details of the evidence, and arrange them for use. . . . We have impeached the prosecuting informer, by one hundred and twenty witnesses." By the beginning of September, with the first of the crops harvested, farmers had begun to pour into Detroit to watch the trial. "We are in a vast room, with a vast audience gathering. Public sympathy is doing its work. Public meetings are gathering in the country. The city is moved and the prosecution is alarmed." Seward's closing argument, delivered over the course of two sweltering days at the end of September, attacked the credibility of the prosecution witnesses. He got all but twelve of the defendants off.[51]

In all three of these cases Seward regarded the defendants' rights as relational. That is, he did not base his defense on some abstract or absolute right the defendants had, but that the jury needed to see the deeper relationships the law imposed on all citizens. Van Zandt and Andrew, the farmers and the railroaders, all shared membership in their communities. Consequently, they shared obligation to one another that the law should have recognized, Seward thought. As Seward told the Michigan jury in his defense of Abel Fitch, "the corporation invoked the legal tribunals, and failed . . . the settlers [faced] a corporate police of mercenary spies." The mores of the community were cast aside by the avarice and malice of a business that should have promoted communal harmony, and instead the "employed ten lawyers" to abuse legal procedure to bring secret indictments against the innocent.[52]

Not all of Seward's lawyering advanced the cause of his jurisprudence. He was not a Salmon P. Chase of Ohio or a John P. Hale of New Hampshire, focusing his entire practice on abolitionist cases. Like every country lawyer, he was a generalist and took what came his way. As his national reputation grew, what came his way was more remunerative and took him farther from home than his earlier practice. In 1850, Seward defended one Peter Marigold on a federal charge of counterfeiting coins. The question was whether a federal statute of 1825 defining the offense was constitutional application of the affirmative grant in Article I, giving Congress the exclusive power to mint coins, which in turn would give the federal government exclusive authority over prosecution of counterfeit coining. In this case, his argument went a lot closer to Virginia's states' rights argument: "the court forgets that the Constitution found all the States in possession of jurisdiction over private frauds; and it is to be inferred that it was thought that jurisdiction might best be left there. The question now is, not whether it was wisely left there, but whether it was left there." The argument did not persuade the Court, and it instructed the lower forum to move ahead with the case.[53]

A year later, in representing the owners of the schooner *Cuba*, sunk after a collision with the propeller steamboat *Genesee Chief* on Lake Ontario, Seward carried the day. The district federal court, supported by the circuit court for the northern district of New York, found the *Genesee Chief* at fault for failing to give way to the sailing ship. The owners of the *Genesee Chief* appealed to the US Supreme Court, but an opinion by Chief Justice Taney upheld the lower court decisions. The captain of the propeller should have steered away. The interesting matter in the case was whether the federal courts had jurisdiction in the first place. Lakes, as navigable waters, fell under that category. It does not appear that Seward argued the case before the Court, but his presence gave the appellees greater weight.[54]

Patent law was becoming Seward's specialty. The 1840s and 1850s were especially attractive to patent lawyers, as the incremental and partial invention of so many parts of machines gave rise to "patent thickets" of litigation. Seward favored all manner of internal improvements, many utilizing novel technologies. When he was governor, inventors sent him copies of plans and models of their products seeking his advice. As he wrote to James Renwick, a professor of physics at Columbia College, in October 1839, "among the duties brought upon me by my public relation is that of hearing the explanation of persons engaged in the invention of improvements in mechanism. Although it is not so written in the constitution, I am expected to hear patiently all inventors, encourage the few whose labors seem likely to result beneficially for themselves and the public, and discourage that far greater number whose plans are unphilosophical or absurd." He had become the patent whisperer.[55]

Soon after Seward left the governor's office, he found himself the defender of the "Woodworth patent." Frederick Seward told the story: Seward père was approached by the purchaser of the patent, one James Wilson, when the latter heard Seward arguing a case in Albany. Wilson was so impressed that he insisted Seward take his case. Seward demurred—he was not familiar with patent law, but Wilson persisted, and Seward agreed. The patent on a woodworking machine had been purchased by Wilson from Woodworth's son. Seward first represented Wilson in Albany, and then traveled all over the north helping Wilson ward off alleged patent offenders, not always successfully. The case ultimately ended in the US Supreme Court, before which Seward was admitted to practice on January 7, 1846. Seward, joined by an aged Webster, argued that the mere replacement of one kind of knives by another was not a new invention but an infringement. They lost, but Seward's pay came in installments of 5000 dollars (the same as Webster's). Henceforth patent holders rushed to Seward's door. He was no longer just a country lawyer, but a lawyer who traveled the countryside.[56]

Patent cases of major industries, for example in textiles, toolmaking, and farm equipment, required years of meticulous study and labor. Even suits over how stoves dispersed smoke (and whether patents for one stove were infringed by a different stove) required Seward and his co-counsel to pour over diagrams and detailed descriptions of the stoves. Representing the plaintiff stove designer, Seward won. He excelled in this kind of labor—quick mastery of lots of details. Other patent cases took years to resolve. For example, in the infamous 1843–1854 case of the "hook-headed spike," a patent infringement suit brought by Troy Nail and Iron Factory against Corning and Company of Albany, Seward represented the Albany company and argued that the two companies had entered into an agreement that superseded the patent, in effect allowing the defendant to use the hook bending lever in its production of spikes. Seward lost in the New York court. Corning then appealed to the Circuit Court for the Northern Circuit of New York, a federal trial court, and won. Troy Nail appealed that decision, and the case went to the US Supreme Court, which reversed the circuit court, Seward once again on the losing side. The Court perpetually enjoined appellees from using the patent. The written agreement between appellees and the assignor, which permitted appellees to use a patented bending lever to manufacture brad-headed spikes, was not supported by any consideration. Seward then found himself waiting in the office of New York chancellor Reuben Walworth (the injunction was an equitable remedy) to negotiate the reparations owed by Corning to Burden. With thousands of the spikes sold, "voluminous accounts" and a "cloud of witnesses," the process seemed endless. Seward often practiced in the state's court of chancery, of which he later remarked, "it was nearly a drawn battle for all the belligerents." One is reminded of *Jarndyce v. Jarndyce* in Charles Dickens's *Bleak House*, another case in chancery (albeit a fictional one): "We asked a gentleman by us, if he knew what cause was on? He told us Jarndyce and Jarndyce. We asked him if he knew what was doing in it? He said, really no he did not, nobody ever did." Seward found himself bogged down in chancery on more than one occasion, and when he was governor, Seward asked the assembly to enlarge the membership of the Court of Chancery from one chancellor "as shall be necessary" to avoid the logjams.[57]

Sometimes Seward found himself arguing in court against the patentee himself. Such was the case of his battle with Elisha Foote, Jr., a lawyer, judge, and inventor of a draft regulator for stoves. The cases, under the caption *Foote v. Silsby*, and then *Silsby v. Foote* went from the district trial court in the circuit for the Northern District of New York to the Supreme Court of the United States three times between 1848 and 1858, with Foote representing himself and Seward representing the defendant. The issue was not the award that the jury at trial gave Foote (he won the infringement suit), but whether the lower court had erred in not allowing the certain evidence read in court. In the circuit court hearing the first appeal, Justice Samuel Nelson of New York (the justices rode circuit) refused to order a new trial. The mistake was a harmless error. When the appeal from the other side was heard by the Supreme Court in 1853, Foote and Seward reappeared. This time the issue was whether the illness of a juror should have prevented the verdict from being recorded. The appellant lost. But the parties were not done, and in 1858 the case reappeared on the Supreme Court docket, Foote once again representing himself and Samuel Blatchford replacing Seward for Silsby. Both sides wanted the justices to revise the interest that had accumulated. An exasperated Justice Nelson reported that the Court was divided on how to do this, and there would be no opinions. Instead, the interest calculated by the special master in the equity court below would stand.[58]

Defeats in the Foote and Corning cases did not diminish Seward's reputation in patent cases because he won as many as he lost. He traveled a circuit common to the patent lawyers—from New York City to Washington, DC, and back again, with occasional stops in Albany where the chancellor of New York sat. In the McCormick Reaper cases, Justice Samuel Nelson delivered an opinion in the federal circuit court which McCormick appealed to the Supreme Court in Washington, which sent the case back to the federal circuit court in New York City, Seward dutifully trailing along. The details were these: The case was first heard at the Albany session of the US Circuit Court for the Northern District of New York. Before the federal circuit courts of appeal were created, in 1891, these circuit courts were trial courts, to which, among other matters, patent cases were directed (under 1793 and 1819 judiciary acts). Federal law had made patent a federal matter, and the patent act of 1836 created a patent office for the securing of patents to new and useful inventions. McCormick's patent rights dated to 1834, and by 1848 were done—except that he wanted an extension because he had improved the machine. The improvements were efficacious, but that did not stop competitors from rushing to build machines very similar to his. The case had bounced from Ohio to New York, and there Seward joined his former clerk and junior partner Samuel Blatchford (who would become a Supreme Court justice himself in 1882), arguing that the McCormick reaper was protected by patent against its growing number of competitors. This time Seward's law firm won.[59]

In Seward's day, patent law incorporated doctrines and remedies from equitable practice. Parties stated their claims in plain English, including the alleged violation of the patent and the desired remedy. These included good faith production of accounts and other evidence when the other party asked the court to so order. The parties that sought equitable remedies could gain injunctions barring competition from patent violators. Equity of this type was inherently relational—the parties owed to one another certain obligations that one party had allegedly violated. These were not absolute or abstract rights. Instead, they resided in prior (mis)conduct. The chancellor (and all US judges are chancellors from the time of the Judiciary Act of 1789) had in personam jurisdiction—that is, jurisdiction over the persons rather than over the property. Using this power, the chancellor sought to uncover the prior relationship of the parties to the patent after examining evidence produced by both sides (in depositions, affidavits, or written records). Again, the process (as opposed to the final award) did not rest on absolute property rights, but the relationships of the parties to one another over the course of their dealings. There was no jury. The court might appoint an expert in the field to assist in the ruling.[60]

Seward's appellate practice was now booming. (It was not unusual for senators to represent private clients in federal court suits while the members sat in the national legislature.) For example, the year 1853 brought Seward to the bar of the Supreme Court three times. The first case was *Wiswall v. Sampson*; the second Troy Nail and Iron case (again), and the third was *Huff v. Hutchinson*. In *Wiswall*, the issue was ownership of real estate, to wit a commercial plot in Mobile, Alabama. Appellants wanted the High Court to reverse the finding of the federal circuit court for the southern district of Alabama. A renter had built a store on the plot but then went out of business. The lot was then sold, but appellants, a New York firm, argued that the sale was void for fraud. The sale of the property after the mortgage was foreclosed went forward without consent from the court of equity in Mobile that had appointed a receiver to the property. Was the sale of the property at auction to a third party still binding? Could it be challenged? Yes, the Supreme Court found that the sale was illicit, and the title of the purchasers was not valid. The fact situation was enough to cross Solomon's eyes, as various courts in the state and then the federal court tried to sort out the claims of parties. By the time the suit reached Washington, DC, parties would have paid counsel far more than the lot was worth. Seward did not write the brief, but he argued it for the winning side.[61]

In *Huff*, a case coming to the Court on appeal from the district of Wisconsin, the Court decided a dispute involving a surety. This was a bond or other thing of value put up by one party to pay for a debt or default of another party if that party lost the lawsuit. In this case, the surety holder was a federal marshal. When the defendant in the case lost, the surety refused to pay the bond. The marshal then sued for it and won in the district court. The surety appealed, claiming that the bond was given to the previous holder of the office, and his successor could not sue for it. In effect, the claim was that the bond was a private rather than a public obligation. What was more, the case did not belong in federal court, as all the parties were Wisconsin businessmen. As it happened, the creditors in the suit were a New York firm, and this created a "diversity of jurisdiction," cases of which could be removed to federal court. The New Yorkers wanted Seward to argue the case for them. He won it.[62]

What linked the three cases to Seward was that parties in them were New Yorkers. New York commercial banks, real estate firms, and wealthy individuals all turned to Seward when their interests were at stake. The country lawyer was their lawyer even when the cases went to the Supreme Court in Washington, DC. Still, Seward's rise to prominence in such cases was striking because he was only admitted to practice in the Supreme Court six years earlier.

Arguably, Seward's greatest courtroom triumph came in riverine commerce, once again representing New York claimants. The Hudson River Bridge Company gained a state charter for a bridge across the Hudson at Albany, but the city of Troy objected. Counsel for the city feared that the bridge would privilege Albany commerce over Troy's. The case came in the Circuit Court for the Northern District of New York in 1859, and took Seward, arguing for the bridge, to Albany. Why was the case in federal court to start? Plaintiff, seeking an injunction against the project chartered by the state, argued that the federal government had exclusive regulation of inland waters (the Hudson River), hence the state could not charter the new bridge. Basing the suit on a federal issue allowed the plaintiff to bring the suit in a federal court, a proposition fully explored in the famous Hudson River steamboat case of *Gibbons v. Ogden* (1821). Seward countered that the states retained regulatory power over the banks of the inland rivers. Again, Seward had adopted a states' rights stance. The federal court dismissed plaintiff's bill. In 1863, on appeal, the US Supreme Court allowed the ruling of the circuit court dismissing the plaintiff's suit to stand. Seward again argued the case for the bridge (as there was no bar to members of the president's cabinet practicing law while in office). His opponent was a US senator from Maryland and leading Union Democrat, Reverdy Johnson. Although the federal Constitution had established separation of the three branches of government and barred multiple office holding, in the High Court it was not unusual to find a member of the executive and a sitting congressman arguing a private suit before members of the third branch.[63]

Seward's argument in Albany River Bridge departed from the strictures of law as laid out, for example, by Webster in his *Gibbons* brief. Instead, Seward made the externalities of commerce and development the centerpiece of his argument. The law may have been in favor of his opponent; after all, the banks of the Hudson shifted over time, and navigable waters lapped over them. But the development of cross-river traffic by railroads, for that is what the Albany bridge was in fact, was necessary if they were going to be efficient carriers of goods. River trade was still important, and the bridge company's plans called for a swing bridge to accommodate larger vessels, but the future meant more bridges. It did not hurt that Chief Justice Taney's opinion in *Charles River Bridge v. Warren Bridge* (1837) had leaned in the direction of economic progress, or that *Pennsylvania v. Wheeling and Belmont Bridge Company* (1852), while upholding the exclusivity of federal interstate commerce (the stance that Troy's counsel took), nevertheless upheld the rights of Ohio River bridge companies against a state challenge.[64]

In these cases, Seward proved himself a shrewd lawyer, capable of mastering arcane legal detail but also elaborating on economic and moral issues. He found ways to introduce relational concepts into his arguments. Near the end of his life, former attorney general (under James Buchanan) and later reporter of the *U.S. Reports*, Jeremiah Black, wrote that Seward "knew less of law and cared less about it than any other man who has held high office in this country," but Black had mischaracterized Seward's obvious abilities. He certainly did not recognize the jurisprudential component of the arguments. On a more personal level, Black's judgment was perhaps inevitable; he wanted to be part of Lincoln's cabinet and may have blamed Seward for being denied a place. Black, as it happened, was also a Democrat and had served Buchanan, Lincoln's predecessor. In any case, Black never had much use for Seward's politics.[65]

Although he did not close his legal practice to serve in his next official capacity as US senator from New York, Seward's skills as a country lawyer faced a sterner test in that forum. He could sway a jury in a local court and the justices of the Supreme Court, but could he sway the other senators? He could conceal the extent and full implication of relational justice in oral argument before the bench, but would he reveal it under the pressure of senatorial politics? What tools could he transplant from his practice, and what new skills had he to master?

CHAPTER 3

"There Is a Higher Law Than the Constitution"

Conscience Whig Senator

By 1849, when he took office as US senator from New York, it would have been impossible for Seward to compartmentalize his legal practice and his political activities. They overlapped in so many ways, not only because he pled cases while he held office in the Senate, but because he thought of politics in legalistic terms and law in political terms. Nothing better had proved this than the intersection of law and politics in his argument for Van Zandt. But a return to public office changed the scope and the nature of the relationship between law and politics in his life. In the Senate, Seward found himself in a different setting than the courts. Although the Senate was a law-making body and many of its members were lawyers, it was politics more than precedent or book law that mattered to its members. Could country practice translate into winning votes in the national legislature?

As he contemplated a return to public office in Washington, DC, Seward looked back on the life and career of John Quincy Adams, recently deceased. The two men had forged a genuine friendship in the later years of Adams's service in the House of Representatives. In the autobiography, Seward's praise of Adams's term as president was fulsome, but Adams's administration lasted only one term, after which Andrew Jackson of Tennessee won the White House. For Seward, looking back, Eden was lost. "The state of the South, under the influence of the institution of slavery, had now become sufficiently strong to induce a combination of all except Kentucky and Louisiana to recover the Southern

Ascendency." Kentucky was the home of Henry Clay, and Louisiana of Zachary Taylor, the Whig Party leaders. From the vantage point of 1871, Seward could see how slavery had divided the nation into sections, the North and the South, with the West as a plum sought by both sides. As yet, "no such maturity of opposition to slavery" had emerged in the North, but it would come. The National Republicans, the party of Adams, would in time become the Whig Party, in opposition to President Andrew Jackson, and although there would be Whigs in the South, a major part of the party would soon share an aversion to the expansion of the "peculiar institution."[1]

In retirement, Seward perhaps admired John Quincy Adams even more than he had when the two men spent time together. He saw in Adams a fellow legalist. The two had corresponded over the Virginia affair. When Adams traveled through New York, in 1843, he stopped at Auburn and stayed with Seward. Seward was honored. When Seward was in Washington, DC, he visited Adams. When Adams died in the Capitol, in 1848, Seward genuinely grieved. Seward even composed a volume in honor of Adams, titled *The Life and Public Services of John Quincy Adams* (1849). Seward admired the public Adams as well as the man. "His purity of life—his elevated and patriotic principles of action—his love of country, and devotion to its interests—his advocacy of human freedom, and the rights of man—brought all to honor and love him."[2]

Adams, as Seward related, was the opposite of the country lawyer, as a young man traveling to Europe on diplomatic missions, and then engaged in a wide variety of state and federal government offices, including secretary of state. Still, Adams had to survive reading law. "Adams completed the usual term of professional study, and then commenced the practice of the law in Boston. It may encourage some who are oppressed by the difficulties attending initiation in the profession, to know, that during the first and only four years of John Quincy Adams's practice, he had occasion for despondency. 'I had long and lingering anxieties, (he afterwards said) in looking forward, doubtful even of my prospects of comfortable subsistence, but acquiring more and more the means of it, till in the last of the four years, the business of my profession yielded me an income more than equal to my expenditures.'" Seward's own eulogy of Adams, appended at the close of the volume, demonstrated his respect, and more, that Adams had been a mentor, albeit a sometimes distant one. He cared not for party, as Seward later professed, but only for the public good. Adams preserved the interest of the new nation among other nations, something that Seward would later strive to do. And Adams, no abolitionist, had strived to end slavery by peaceful means; by law, as his role in the freeing of the ship *Amistad* captives displayed. This was Seward's own quest. He saw himself in Adams.[3]

Adams had never hesitated to tell the House what he was thinking, and never more so during the long and fierce quarrel over the "gag rule" from 1835 until Adams passed away in 1848. Seward took Adams's conduct to heart (even to the point of nearly getting himself censured by the Senate, as Adams had in the House more than once during the gag rule debates). Seward was loquacious in the Senate. Did his words matter? It may be argued that for politicians deeds matter more than words, but in the Senate, Seward's actions were not particularly efficacious. Not to say he did little; he tried to do a lot. But he was not a mover and shaker in the slave' cause. One thus comes back to his words. For a lawyer, words mean a great deal. Words win (or lose) cases. The law is wordy, and published law reports of judges' opinions and litigators' arguments had become a staple of legal education and practice. Whether the word was mightier than the sword is not a question easily answered, but for a lawyer like Seward, words really did matter, and that is how they are treated here.[4]

In the gag rule controversy, Adams had argued that words—the words of antislavery petitioners, the words of their advocates on the House floor, and his own words, should be exempt from censorship. He arranged for his arguments to be published in the newspapers as well as in the House records. Seward also arranged for the publication of his Senate speeches. He took great pains with them before he delivered them, and returned and revised them after he delivered them. Sometimes the arguments in them hardened. Sometimes he added flourishes. Which of the versions mattered more? Here are the published versions, because those are the ones he wanted to reflect his ideas in their final form. He was not the greatest orator of his time. Webster outdid him, and Charles Sumner's long-winded tirades were more imposing. But Seward was an honest speaker, and his speeches were, in some sense, the man.[5]

This chapter focuses on one of these speeches—the first one and in some ways the most controversial of them. It was ostensibly about Henry Clay's proposed compromise bill to bring California into the Union as a free state and make abetting a fugitive slave's escape a national crime. Seward opposed the bill, but the value of the speech is the insight it affords into Seward's developing philosophy of public law. This was his "higher law" speech of March 11, 1850, an answer to Daniel Webster's oration four days earlier.

By this time, the real Seward, the country lawyer who championed relational rights, had the misfortune of being mistaken for a manqué-Seward. Among the advocates of Southern interests Seward had become the archvillain of the abolitionist crew. Among abolitionists Seward was seen as an untrustworthy trimmer. Among those who envied him his office, he seemed the grey eminence behind, well, behind whatever the accuser did not like. Horace Greeley, having decided that Seward was not his man, after the "higher law" speech in the Senate accused him of having "cut himself loose from the restraints which are obligatory upon his brother Senators . . . finds a charter for his senatorial conduct in the casuistry of theologian, the dicta of modern philosophers, and the suggestions of metaphysical theorizers." During his stint in the Lincoln cabinet, rivals like Secretary of the Navy Gideon Welles accused him of being patronizing at best, and treacherous, deceitful, and manipulative at worst. It should be added that Welles was a Democrat.[6]

As Greeley's volte-face and Welles's animus hint, the period from 1828 to 1860 was the great age of political parties in the United States. More than in the years before Andrew Jackson won the presidency, newspapers were partisan venues, voting was tied to political party allegiance, and political participation among those with the franchise, at least in terms of voting, was at its height. Party allegiance among elected officials was also very strong. Advocates for particular interests, for example abolition and unionism, formed their own parties and fought for their own portion of the electorate, but in general the two great parties, Whigs and Democrats, shared the spoils of victory. The campaign of 1850 bore out all of these generalizations.[7]

Although party leaders attempted to bury the slavery question, in 1846, Pennsylvania Whig congressman David Wilmot's Proviso in Congress calling for a ban on slavery in any territory won from Mexico threw the slavery question back on the front pages. The House voted for it, but the Senate blocked it. A first-term congressman from Illinois named Abraham Lincoln supported it, as did Seward from his New York law office. The war with Mexico concluded two years later; large portions of the Southwest, including the future states of Colorado, New Mexico, and Arizona, were accessed by the peace treaty. California had formed a republic of its own, under the prompting of agents provocateurs sent by the Polk administration. The fate of slavery in these lands remained uncertain.[8]

Whig fortunes had improved over the course of President James K. Polk's administration. Seward's decision not to seek the presidential nomination in 1848 was surely influenced by Thurlow Weed's caution over the damage to the Whig Party of a (supposedly) abolitionist candidate (although the Whigs were not likely to name Seward in any case). Seward was clearly the leader of the Conscience Whig (antislavery) faction of the party—in opposition to Cotton Whigs who sought the support of Southern planters. With Seward at the head of the ticket, the South would be lost to the Whigs, perhaps forever. There was also the country lawyer's hesitancy to step on the national stage. Still, Seward toured the Northern states stumping for Zachary Taylor, a Cotton Whig from Louisiana who had no political credentials. Taylor was a slaveholder as well. But he was the victor in the Mexican-American War, and war heroes made strong Whig candidates, as William Henry Harrison's candidacy had proved. In any case, Seward was no shrinking violet when it came to standing in the foyer of the courthouse and addressing large crowds. He made the decision to withdraw but resented having to hide his light under New York vice president Millard Fillmore's bushel.[9]

In the meantime, Seward had emerged as unofficial counsel for the Conscience Whigs. For the next six years, he would argue their cause in and out of the halls of Congress. He would crisscross the Northern tier of the country, giving talks to public gatherings and Whig caucuses on issues and candidates. He fretted, "What am I to do with these importunities to attend Whig meetings. They come by twos and threes, and will come by dozens," then told audiences in New York and Ohio that the right of the emancipated slave to vote must be assured. Laws that discriminated against people of color must be erased. Unlike others whose attachment to the antislavery cause drove them to more and more strident pronouncements, Seward left a side door open to compromise. As he stated his rule, "I assail the motives of no Senator, I am not to be drawn into personal altercation by any interrogatories addressed to me. I acknowledge the patriotism, the wisdom and the purity of every member of this body." This was a clear indication that he viewed his role as counselor, not as partisan, for lawyers in court did not assail the motives or personal morality of opposing counsel. Slavery must not be permitted to expand, but it might exist where it was already.[10]

Sworn into his Senate seat on March 4, 1849, Seward stayed in Washington, DC, to hear President Taylor's inaugural address the next day. It was short and uninspired. Taylor promised, "In the discharge of these duties my guide will be the Constitution, which I this day swear to 'preserve, protect, and defend.' For the interpretation of that instrument I shall look to the decisions of the judicial tribunals established by its authority and to the practice of the Government under the earlier Presidents, who had so large a share in its formation. To the example of those illustrious patriots I shall always defer with reverence, and especially to his example who was by so many titles 'the Father of his Country.'" Seward remained for a month, handling matters of patronage, and then returned to Auburn and his legal practice.[11]

Seward returned for the first session of the new Congress in the late winter of 1849. The last vestiges of Polk's Democratic administration had departed. Taylor's administration was still busy with matters of patronage. Seward entered the old senate chamber (which would become the home of the Supreme Court in 1856) and advanced to the front to take a seat at a desk. Some of the most illustrious members—Webster, Clay, Thomas Hart Benton, and John C. Calhoun were all soon to depart. New faces were present—among them John P. Hale of New Hampshire and Salmon Chase of Ohio—both avowed abolitionists. Congress's activity was largely devoted to matters of patronage. With the new Whig administration in place, Seward renewed his cordial relations with President Taylor, temporarily settled his differences with Vice President Fillmore and found a place for family to stay and friends to visit in the city. But beneath the calm of business as usual, ferment was building over the admission of California. The territory's population had zoomed after the discovery of gold at Sutter's Mill, in 1848, and the territorial government was preparing a constitution to accompany its application for admission to the Union. The next time the Senate met, in December 1849, its demeanor would not be so placid.[12]

On November 11, 1849, the draft California state constitution was ratified by its voters and sent to Washington, DC. The document was long and detailed. It took hours to transcribe the official copy. But it was clearly a free state constitution. It began with a statement of rights, the first of which read, "All men are by nature free and independent, and have certain inalienable rights, among which are those of enjoying and defending life and liberty, acquiring, possessing, and protecting property: and pursuing and obtaining safety and happiness." It incorporated an expanded version of the federal bill of rights, and spoke of persons or inhabitants of the state. Although the sections on political rights limited them to "white male" citizens, the law provided for joint property for wives, a reform based in part on Spanish/Roman law, dueling was illegal, and public education was encouraged. Section 18 of Article I, however, was the most important to southern members of the Senate and the Democratic leadership—"Neither slavery, nor involuntary servitude, unless for the punishment of crimes, shall ever be tolerated in this State." Section 3 of the same article seemed directed to the fugitive slave question: "The right of trial by jury shall be secured to all, and remain inviolate forever."[13]

In the Senate, southern opinion on the admission question grew sour and resentful. Leading southern Democrats condemned the admission as a violation of the Constitution and a danger to the balance of power in the Senate (with the admission of California, the free states would outnumber the slave states). Clay, whose proposals had quieted congressional angst in the Missouri admission quarrel thirty years earlier, had proposed a compromise—admit California and pass a much more stringent Fugitive Slave Act, among other provisions. The five-hour, two-day address had exhausted him, but admirers thronged his seat when he finished. On March 4, South Carolina senator Calhoun, dying from tuberculosis, was carried into the chamber, and James Mason of Virginia read Calhoun's address warning of secession if concessions to slavery were not forthcoming. On March 7, 1850, Seward and his wife Frances listened to Webster surrender any claim to speak for the North or the Whig Party's antislavery wing when he urged passage of the Fugitive Slave Act of 1850 and cautioned abolitionists against violent opposition. On March 11, Seward answered Webster and replaced the aged Whig as de facto spokesman for the antislavery Whigs. Titled "Freedom in the Territories" when Seward had it printed and distributed, it was later known as his "higher law" speech. Its tone and arguments would not have surprised anyone, as during his two terms as Governor of New York, he had made clear his views on slavery. He believed that slavery must die but was not an immediatist in the manner of William Lloyd Garrison and the other members of the American Anti-Slavery Society.[14]

Eyewitness testimony about the March 11 speech is confusing. Northern newspapers reported that the galleries were full when Seward rose. The crowd spilled out into the foyer of the Capitol as well. But Frederick Seward recalled that the Senate was almost empty. Seward was not a natural orator like Webster. His voice lacked the size and tonal variation of the older man. Nevertheless, Seward was, like Webster, thoroughly prepared and brought to the chamber a reputation for his orations. Seward did not believe in the amalgamation or equality of the races, but he was proud that the United States was diverse and inclusive. Its many peoples were soon assimilated to one. They conquered and settled. Alas, "The African race, bond and free, and the aborigines, savage and civilized, being incapable of such assimilation and absorption, remain distinct; and, owing to their peculiar condition, they constitute inferior masses, and may be regarded as accidental if not disturbing political forces." Throughout his career Seward was an optimistic supporter of technology, trade, immigration, and free labor, and slavery was anathema to all of these in his mind. He was thus absolutely opposed to the expansion of slavery to the west.[15]

Did this frank confession of racialist views mean that free people of color could never and should never be assimilated? That they could never be considered full citizens of the communities in which they resided? Were relational rights thus denied to them because of who they were rather than what they had done? Calhoun could not have disagreed, indeed had said much the same about people of color. But over the past three years of campaigning for Whig candidates throughout the North, Seward had said the opposite—that slavery must end and that freed slaves must be allowed all the privileges of other freeborn men. The answer, I think, is that Seward believed free people of color, including freed slaves, were entitled to all the legal rights of other members of the community, civil rights and liberties, but he did not see them as his equals in social, cultural, or intellectual ways. It was a biformity of vision and spirit, a paradoxical contradiction, common among all but a few reformers then, and one among many in US history.[16]

Responding next to Clay and Webster, along with Calhoun, who in his March 4, 1850, Senate speech warned that northern antislavery sentiment would lead to Southern secession, Seward turned to the California question. "The question now arises, Shall this one great people, having a common origin, a common language, a common religion, common sentiments, interests, sympathies, and hopes, remain one political state, one nation, one republic, or shall it be broken into two conflicting and probably hostile nations or republics?" The rhetoric was redolent with reciprocity and unity—"one" over and over, everyone belonging, no one left out. If the nation was to be continental, then California must be admitted. "The world contains no seat of empire so magnificent as this; which, while it embraces all the varying climates of the temperate zone, and is traversed by wide expanding lakes and long branching rivers, offers supplies on the Atlantic shores to the over-crowded nations of Europe, while on the Pacific coast it intercepts the commerce of the Indies."[17]

If the nation were to extend to the Pacific, California was the next natural addition. It begged to be included in the common ground. What then stood in the way? Slavery. But slavery was legal in many of the states, and Seward was a legalist. He hated slavery but did not demand its immediate abolition. Was there a middle course in the law itself? Some way to extend community without empowering the slave interest? Seward knew that Clay's omnibus compromise bill included more than a sop to the South. Clay would have the controversial Fugitive Slave bill as well. "But it is insisted that the admission of California shall be attended by a COMPROMISE of questions which have arisen out of SLAVERY! I AM OPPOSED TO ANY SUCH COMPROMISE, IN ANY AND ALL THE FORMS IN WHICH IT HAS BEEN PROPOSED."[18]

Compromise, Clay proposed. Compromise, Webster urged. Compromise, Calhoun demanded. But Seward applied his own calculus to the politics of compromise: "The equivalent, then, is, for some portion of liberty, some portion of human rights in one region [to be sacrificed] for liberty in another region." This compromise would undermine relational rights, for to admit California as a free state, but fasten the chains of slavery on the nation with a new fugitive slave act, would make denial of reciprocity into national law instead of sectional aberration. Like a good lawyer, he recognized the opposing side's argument. "It is now avowed by the honorable senator from South Carolina, that nothing will satisfy the slave states but a compromise that will convince them that they can remain in the Union consistently with their honor and their safety." But that made no sense in terms of the demographics of community, for "the free states having already, or although they may hereafter have, majorities of population, and majorities in both houses of Congress, shall concede to the slave states, being in a minority in both, the unequal advantage of an equality" in determining the extent and legality of slavery.[19]

Such a concession might comport with history, for "The free states, northern and western, have acquiesced in the long and nearly unbroken ascendancy of the slave states under the Constitution, because the result happened under the Constitution." But the compromise did not satisfy Seward's jurisprudence of relational rights. Picking up where he left off in the defense of Van Zandt, he insisted that the proposed fugitive slave law "deprives the alleged refugee from a legal obligation not assumed by him, but imposed upon him by laws enacted before he was born, of the writ of habeas corpus, and of any certain judicial process of examination of the claim set up by his pursuer, and finally degrades him into a chattel." Nor did it make sense as a matter of the basic division of law into civil and criminal parts: "Relying on the perversion of the Constitution, [the fugitive slave law] makes slaves mere chattels, the slave states have applied to them the principles of the criminal law, and have held that he who aided the escape of his fellow-man from bondage was guilty of a larceny in stealing him." It was a violation of the law of nations and made the United States into an outlaw: "Your constitution and laws convert hospitality to the refugee from the most degrading oppression on earth into a crime, but all mankind except you esteem that hospitality a virtue."[20]

Thus far, Seward had mounted arguments in response to Clay, Webster, and Calhoun. Now it was time to explore his own thinking more openly. Read rightly, he argued, the Constitution could not favor slavery, for "The law of nations disavows such compacts; the law of nature, written on the hearts and consciences of freemen, repudiates them." Slavery was a fact of law, positive law, and yes, "There are constitutions and statutes, codes mercantile and codes civil" that countenanced slavery, but morality and true religion repudiated slavery. "We are not slaveholders. We cannot, in our judgment, be either true Christians or real freemen, if we impose on another a chain that we defy all human power to fasten on ourselves." This was then a constitution that stood behind the written one. It was a constitution based on what men owed to other men in a community. Seward was not a William Lloyd Garrison or a Wendell Phillips. He did not condemn southern senators for defending themselves and their neighbors. He was long averse to "the violence of anger, the pain of suppressed revenge, the malignity of envy, and the miserable craving of avarice." Seward's constitution was a just one, to which all just men would return, in time. To the slaveholder he held out the chance to rejoin the community of liberty. Slaveholders were members of the community too. "You believe and think otherwise, and doubtless with equal sincerity. We judge you not, and He alone who ordained the conscience of man and its laws of action can judge us." G-d would judge the slaveholder. But before that, might come another judgment, and it too would be harsh. "But I must tell you, nevertheless, in candor and in plainness, that the spirit of the people of the free states is set upon a spring that rises with the pressure put upon it." In other words, don't depend on the goodwill of the free North; it had limits.[21]

Seward usually wrote out his speeches, then made notes and spoke from the notes. On this occasion, however, he read the first part of the speech. His voice was not loud, and even with the senate chamber's superb acoustics, he was hard to hear. Twirling his glasses, his dark clothing adding gravity to his words, he almost appeared a college lecturer. He despised inept speakers and constantly worried that his audience might not see the logic of his arguments. In his first year in the state senate, he lamented that three of his colleagues "have made speeches drier than brick-dust upon a question drier than baked sand." He did not notice that the crowd in the galleries and the foyer began to thin as he approached the constitutionality of slavery, a subject not entirely germane to the California admission question, but relevant for the rest of Clay's omnibus compromise plan.[22]

If one could travel back and hear him, perhaps one would sense a hardening in his tone at this point. He was the leading man in his state's Whig Party, and his reputation had spread through the land. But in this session of Congress, he had come to feel that the party did not have his back. He wrote to a colleague, "I am alone all alone in the Senate, in Congress, and almost in the United States—I dare to build on the rights of disfranchised men." His defense of Irish immigrants, Roman Catholicism, and free Blacks had truly estranged him from the Cotton Whigs. At this moment, he did not regard himself as an antislavery radical. He heard himself as the still, urgent voice of the ideal community—the upstate New York that he remembered, and the spokesman for a constitution that conscience dictated. He was not a politician, though he sat in a political body and spoke in a legislative chamber. This was not a political speech. It was a call for a different kind of law than that made in the Senate chamber. The lawyer dominated the politician. Thus, when a political oration could, and perhaps should, have come to the peroration, he instead simply raised another point—the unconstitutionality of slavery.[23]

What then of the Constitution, he asked, and its many implied compromises with slavery? "I deem it established, then, that the Constitution does not recognize property in man, but leaves that question, as between the states, to the law of nature and of nations." Nowhere did the Constitution mention slavery by name. It did provide for the end of the overseas slave trade. It did allow states to bar slavery, including the transit of slaves across their land. (Recall this was before *Dred Scott v. Sandford* (1857) implied that slavery was national.)[24]

Seward thought the illogic of slavery should be evident to everyone, as if the Senate were a courtroom and his argument would win the day. Slavery denied the reciprocity that made society possible. It denied hospitality. He went point by point—even viewing the Constitution as a compact among the states—Calhoun's doctrine of concurrent majorities. If states belonged to the Union as states, what gave any one of them the right to dictate to others what they must do with fugitives? Then he argued the opposite: "The proposition of an established classification of states as slave states and free states, as insisted on by some, and into northern and southern, as maintained by others, seems to me purely imaginary, and of course the supposed equilibrium of those classes a mere conceit. This must be so, because, when the Constitution was adopted, twelve of the thirteen states were slave states, and so there was no equilibrium." The result was a compendium of antislavery constitutional arguments.[25]

He mingled fact with doctrine, slyly accusing the slave states of being harnessed to the slave, in effect, enslaved by slavery. "Slavery, if not the only institution in a slave state, is at least a ruling institution, and that this characteristic is recognized by the Constitution. But slavery is only one of many institutions there. Freedom is equally an institution there. Slavery is only a temporary, accidental, partial, and incongruous one. Freedom, on the contrary, is a perpetual, organic, universal one, in harmony with the Constitution of the United States." Rejoin the larger community of free people, Seward urged the white South. Slavery denied to the slave states the very freedom they denied to the slaves. "You may separate slavery from South Carolina, and the state will still remain; but if you subvert freedom there, the state will cease to exist." For "just in proportion to the extent that [slavery] it prevails and controls in any republican state, just to that extent it subverts the principle of democracy, and converts the state into an aristocracy or a despotism." Neat and brilliantly offered arguments, certain to win the case in court, were it not for the slave state senators' indifference to argument.[26]

If precise arguments based on established law would not win the day, perhaps an appeal to a higher law would? In what would become the most quoted terminology of his career, he continued, "But there is a higher law than the Constitution, which regulates our authority over the domain, and devotes it to the same noble purposes. The territory is a part, no inconsiderable part, of the common heritage of mankind, bestowed upon them by the Creator of the universe. We are his stewards, and must so discharge our trust as to secure in the highest attainable degree their happiness." What was the higher law then? It was not a law above the Constitution, but was a law that the Constitution represented and absorbed. In short, it was the law of relational rights. Seward had explained these to the High Court in *Van Zandt*. Now he explained them to the members of the Senate. These were reciprocal, what everyone owed to everyone else. They were not natural rights, embedded in persons in nature or by God, but communal rights, shared by all people in a community of citizens. In free society, they were rights that conscience dictated. In a society with a government, they were the due process that everyone could claim. But in a slave society the master owed nothing to the slave while the slave lived and labored at the command of the master. This was the very opposite of relational rights. Thus a slave society could not fulfill the reciprocity that the higher law required.[27]

A higher law for the western territories and the states that they would become was similarly not some version of natural law. It was the law of what everyone owed everyone else. It was a law of liberty and dignity, in his mind the kind of law in which all communities should begin anew. To impose the institution of slavery in such places, a legal regime that was anything but reciprocal in its duties, was to traduce the very aims of good law. In such places of novel jurisdiction (old Spanish imperial law had no place in Seward's thinking) the compromises that constituted slavery's place in the Constitution and in the nation were no longer valid. Go back to the beginnings, when higher law was the only law, and men were free to choose their ruling institutions. In this Lockean world, before contract among free men created government, "Shall we, who are founding institutions, social and political, for countless millions; shall we, who know by experience the wise and the just, and are free to choose them, and to reject the erroneous and unjust; shall we establish human bondage, or permit it by our sufferance to be established?" In this world, it was not contract or compact that prevented chaos, but mutual obligation and regard. The nation seemed paralyzed by the crisis, but Seward knew better. "A question, a moral question, transcending the too narrow creeds of parties, has arisen; the public conscience expands with it, and the green wreaths of party associations give way and break, and fall off from it." Thus would the question be resolved.[28]

Seward's logic, stretched to its utmost, seemed to suggest that the North and the West would not mind if the South were to secede and take its slaves with it. That was the view that immediate abolitionists like William Lloyd Garrison and Wendell Phillips of Massachusetts seemed to favor, but that was not Seward's desire. In his jurisprudence, he understood the need for moderation in life as in language. Members of a community had to coexist with one another, not unilaterally impose their view of morality on one another. As he told Lincoln when the president-elect sent Seward a draft of the first inaugural in 1861: "something besides argument or in addition to argument is needful—to meet and remove prejudice and passion in the South, and despondency and fear in the East. Some words of affection—some of calm and cheerful confidence." The result was Lincoln's "mystic chords of memory."[29]

Seward's vision of community included those whose opinions (and laws) he rejected. The Union was a community, and harmony of views was a goal not easily realized. Did a failure to compromise endanger the Union? Seward hoped not, but "I do not overlook the fact that the entire delegation from the slave states, although they differ in regard to the details of the compromise proposed, and perhaps in regard to the exact circumstances of the crisis, seem to concur in this momentous warning. Nor do I doubt at all the patriotic devotion to the Union which is expressed by those from whom this warning proceeds." It was "high excitement," the passion of the moment overflowing into the oratory that made the illusion of disunion seem real. "My confidence in the Union remains unshaken," he affirmed.[30]

But Seward was not given to blithe optimism. He saw in the distance what Clay and Webster believed was at hand—the end of the Union. "I agree with those who say that there can be no peaceful dissolution—no dissolution of the Union by the secession of states; but that disunion, dissolution, happen when it may, will and must be revolution." His confidence rested not on foreknowledge, but on the same sort of legal logic, the same sort of constitutional reasoning, that marked his career to this point. "I have thus endeavored to show that there is not now, and there is not likely to occur any adequate cause for revolution in regard to slavery." The legal grounds for severing the Union lay in the same legal regime that promoted slavery. It was the legal regime the Democratic Party tried to impose on the entire nation and had failed. But advocates for the expansion of slavery would not be silenced. "Slavery has a reliable and accommodating ally in a party in the free states, which, though it claims to be, and doubtless is in many respects, a party of progress, finds its sole security for its political power in the support and aid of slavery in the slave states."[31]

One notes how property, including private property and the national domain, were subordinated in Seward's constitutionalism to the higher purposes of the Constitution. The Constitution did not sanction property in man. The words slave or slavery was never mentioned. But when so much of the South's (and by proxy, the nation's) capital was invested in slave labor, how could Seward's analysis be taken seriously? In other words, Seward had left interest, self-interest, out of his account of communities. The internal slave trade, the value of slave labor, the importance of cotton, sugar, rice, and tobacco to the economy of the nation depended on slave labor. Slavery had to expand to be fully profitable. On this Calhoun was right and Seward conceded the point.[32]

Long regarded as a free trade, pro-capital theorist by scholars, Seward was anything but. He understood, as many students of the antebellum South now believe, that capital was amoral. "So long as slavery shall possess the cotton-fields, the sugar-fields, and the rice-fields of the world, so long will commerce and capital yield it toleration and sympathy." But this was temporary. "Emancipation is a democratic revolution. It is capital that arrests all democratic revolutions." History and current events proved Seward's view, or so he thought. "It was capital, that, so recently in a single year, rolled back the tide of revolution from the base of the Carpathian mountains, across the Danube and the Rhine, into the streets of Paris" referring to the end of the democratic reform movements in Europe. Capital had made an alliance with racism. For "slavery has a guaranty still stronger than these in the prejudices of caste and color, which induce even large majorities in all the free states to regard sympathy with the slave as an act of unmanly humiliation and self-abasement."[33]

In the last analysis, the issue of slavery threatened to dissolve the Union. How could we "as wise and prudent statesmen, enlarge its boundaries and increase its influence." In an almost eerie premonition of Roger Taney's obiter dictum in *Dred Scott* that Congress had no power to exclude slavery from the national domain, Seward insisted that Congress could impose conditions of admission. "The Ordinance excluding slavery is such a condition." For the "right [of Congress] to regulate property, to administer justice in regard to property, is assumed in every territorial charter."[34]

But the ultimate argument lay not in the past but in the eternal. "Where I find a law of God or a law of nature disregarded, or in danger of being disregarded, there I shall vote to re-affirm it, with all the sanction of the civil authority." He could find it everywhere in the founding documents of civil government. "There, is the Declaration of Independence, with its solemn recital of the natural equality of men, and of the inalienability of their essential rights. There is the constitution of the United States, beginning with its sublime summary of the object of the government, and ending with its jealous bill of personal rights."[35]

Seward closed with pointedly political and social remarks. For the first, he meant the Democratic Party. "Slavery has a reliable and accommodating ally in a party in the free states" and "a natural alliance with the aristocracy of the North." His social analysis was even more pointed, and demonstrates that he had one foot in the modern sociology of race. Slavery, as he had implied throughout his defense of Van Zandt, "has a guaranty still stronger than these in the prejudices of caste and color." He attacked white supremacy directly—for "philosophy meekly expresses her distrust of the asserted natural superiority of the white race." Everyone knew, but no one would say that slavery must ultimately rest on racial prejudice.[36]

With the opportunity to pad the speech with references to international law, history, praise of the founders, and other subjects, Seward lengthened the print version to sixty pages. Read word for word that would be 52,000 words, or about nine hours of reading time. Even in the short version, the speech's impact was immediate. President Taylor was not an abolitionist, and neither was Fillmore. Although Seward was not technically an abolitionist, he plainly opposed slavery. This infuriated the South's congressional delegation, particularly as Webster had already conceded the field. Seward had been hard at work writing this speech for months. It was not a spur of the moment outburst. Instead, it was the language closest to his own thinking. It was not politic, nor would it advance his political ambitions. If he could see into the future, it was this speech that would, in time, deny him the chance to seek the nation's highest office. Weed was furious. Seward was his man, and now Seward had blown his chances—all for a brilliant but ill-considered oral argument.[37]

The single phrase "higher law" became the focus of public and party attention. Cautious praise and criticism grew into a roar of "raucous and abusive epithets," on the one hand, and effusive praise, on the other. Senator Thomas Pratt of Maryland, a lawyer himself of strong proslavery opinions, asked the Senate to expel Seward for saying that there was a higher law than the Constitution. To be sure, taken out of context, with it Seward seemed to have taken on the mantle of the nation's foremost abolitionist. It would haunt him in the presidential seasons of 1852, 1856, and 1860.[38]

Had Seward meant that there was a higher law than the Constitution that the Senate must obey, Pratt asked, seeking a retraction, or at least Seward's embarrassment (as it was not likely that the Senate would vote to expel the New Yorker for his rhetoric on the Senate floor). Seward answered that he had been misunderstood. He meant that the Constitution must be interpreted in light of the higher law of humanity. It was the same higher law that he invoked in refusing to render the three men sought by Virginia and in defense of Van Zandt. It was a law that rested on reciprocity, the pieces of which the Seward assembled from various sources, as Seward regularly did in his orations. It did not regard the slave's rights separately from the rights of free persons. Simply put, slaveowners could not foist their peculiar institution on the backs of free settlers, for free settlers could not foist a reciprocal burden on the backs of the masters.

On July 2, 1850, Seward once again took the floor to lambaste the compromise bill. It was failing, as he should have known, though Seward sometimes had a deaf ear when it came to party and sectionalism. (Later in the year, the individual parts of the compromise plan would win in sectional votes.) Still, Seward thought it necessary to bludgeon the dying legislation. This time he did not offer a constitutional exegesis. In his March 11 speech, he had mentioned the federal Constitution thirty-five times. On July 2, he rarely mentioned it. His chief query was the obvious one: why was the admission of California held up? Was it the Texas debt due to Mexico? Was it the boundary of Texas? Or was it the old enemy—slavery? The size of Texas and the eventual admission of New Mexico (presumably as a free state) was a proxy for the slave states' desire to expand their peculiar institution.[39]

Despite Seward's opposition, the Fugitive Slave Act of 1850 passed and provided for federal commissioners to assist in the rendition of alleged fugitives without their having benefit of due process (counsel, jury trial, confrontation, and cross-examination of witnesses). The act gave to the federal judiciary the power to name commissioners and to require marshals to assist the commissioners:

> That when a person held to service or labor in any State or Territory of the United States, has heretofore or shall hereafter escape into another State or Territory of the United States, the person or persons to whom such service or labor may be due, or his, her, or their agent or attorney, duly authorized, by power of attorney, in writing, acknowledged and certified under the seal of some legal officer or court of the State or Territory in which the same may be executed, may pursue and reclaim such fugitive person, either by procuring a warrant from some one of the [federal] courts, judges, or commissioners aforesaid, of the proper circuit, district, or county, for the apprehension of such fugitive from service or labor, or by seizing and arresting such fugitive, where the same can be done *without process*, and by taking, or causing such person to be taken, forthwith before such court, judge, or commissioner, whose duty it shall be to hear and determine the case of such claimant in a *summary manner*.

Without process and in summary manner was shorthand for no due process.[40]

Watching as northern abolitionists and southern slave catchers collided in his own state and in neighboring Massachusetts, Seward passed judgment on the new law. "The Fugitive Slave Law is the worst experiment ever made by government here, to compel confederated states under a general government, differing in domestic, social, and civil economy and discipline to agree." When an abolitionist mob prevented a federal commissioner from delivering a Missouri runaway named William Henry (the connection to Seward would not go unnoticed) to a slave catcher, Seward was the first to put up surety for the leader of the mob, Gerritt Smith. The events took place in Syracuse, near enough to Auburn to be a hometown story. William Henry, a carpenter by trade calling himself "Jerry," had traveled across the Midwest but on his way to Canada and freedom found work in Syracuse. There he was arrested under the 1850 law and held for return to bondage. The Vigilance Committee in the city moved swiftly, summoning lawyers to delay the summary proceeding and then simply breaking Jerry out of jail, removing the physical and the spiritual shackles, and hiding Jerry in a nearby house until he could be transported to Ontario. Under the law, his aides and abettors were liable, and twelve of them were indicted, but the trials were repeatedly postponed, and in the end, only one of the twelve was convicted of a misdemeanor.[41]

Like Freeman's case and the Van Zandt appeal, Jerry's rescue posed problems for Seward's theory of rights. Did relational rights have to devolve into mob rule? Was not that the tactic of the antiabolitionist rioters of the 1830s and 1840s? Certainly, violence was a hallmark of the antebellum era. But surely Seward's notion of rights was legalistic, not violent. His saving point was that the Fugitive Slave Act perverted relationships within communities, pitting law officers against free people who wanted to protect their (Black) neighbors.[42]

The real problem, one that Seward did not address and perhaps did not fully recognize, was that he had idealized community, imagining a place and its people in which prejudice did not outweigh reason, and commitment to the common good was common ground. To be sure, he was not the only one who believed in the possibility of such ideal communities. The Transcendentalists' Brook Farm, Robert Dale Owen's New Harmony, and other Utopian experiments rested on similar ground. That they soon failed did not prevent people of goodwill from imagining that the future held such communities.[43]

For Seward, looking back on Jerry's rescue, the answer to antiabolitionist mobs and antislavery mobs was a faith in the American people resting upon deep and shared community values. He proposed that the US Treasury should be empowered to ransom slaves from masters who consented, paying compensation. "This would work slow and sure." Private property would be protected, and no master need complain, for he had a "veto" in every case. Thus Seward supported not a states' rights-based proposal, but something very much more complex—the notion that the Fugitive Slave Law disturbed, actually ruptured, the relations among citizens within his own and neighboring free states. The law was bad not because states said so but because of its impact on relations among the citizens of the states and within the states. Supposed runaways had rights not because of some absolute inalienable guarantee, but because they were members of the community entitled to be treated just as other members were treated until they were proven different.[44]

The presidential campaign of 1852 was a major disappointment for Seward. He supported an old friend, US Army general Winfield Scott, over Webster, but Scott was trounced by Democratic candidate Franklin Pierce of New

Hampshire. Pierce was a northern Democrat with southern sympathies—a "doughface" (the Whigs called him) because he could be pulled in any direction by the southern wing of his party. There was much about Pierce that Seward should have recognized, if not admired. He'd had a distinguished career, coming from one of his state's elite families, as a successful country lawyer whose practice was confined to his state. He would serve as US attorney for New Hampshire in 1845, a member of the House of Representatives and then a senator, and like Seward, was an officer in the state militia. In Concord, the state capital, Pierce was as much in demand for his skills in front of a jury as Seward was in Albany. Like Seward, he was gregarious and loved company. And like Seward, his wife was a quiet but determined reformer. But here the similarity ended. Pierce had served in the Mexican-American War and favored the expansion of slavery. He would serve only one term in the White House, thought secession was legal (though he did not aid it in any way), and died of alcoholism in 1869.[45]

Pierce's election provoked his rival in the Democratic Party, Illinois senator Stephen Douglas, to one of the rashest acts in Congressional history. The Missouri Compromise of 1820 had drawn a line across the Louisiana Territory at the southern latitude of the new state. In the territories above that line, there was to be no slavery. Douglas, borrowing an idea from Senator Lewis Cass of Michigan, proposed to abandon that compromise and replace it with "popular sovereignty"—settlers in each territory north of the line would decide for themselves whether to organize a free or a slave state. Seward was furious and at the same time saddened at the prospect of making slavery a national institution hidden in Douglas' proposal. The battle over Kansas' statehood became a battle over slavery's extension. Popular sovereignty would give to the settlers of the Kansas territory the authority to write a pro- or antislavery constitution as they chose. As Seward wrote to Frances on his return to the Senate in January 1854: "I am heart-sick of being here. I look around me in the Senate and find all [antislavery men] demoralized. Maine, New Hampshire, Connecticut, Rhode Island, Vermont!!! All, all in the hands of the slave-holders." To Thurlow Weed, he fumed, "So slavery is wrapping us in its black folds, and yet the northern people are wrangling about foreigners and licenses and street preaching." He feared the outcome of a "doubtful struggle to prevent the extension of slavery to the shores of the Great Lakes and Puget Sound." The Douglas bill, as reshaped by Southern senators, opened up all of the northern territories to slavery. Ohio antislavery Whig Benjamin Wade regarded its passage as "the eclipse of the sun." On the floor of the Senate, Seward battled Douglas point by point. Seward even rewrote history, recalling (this time fondly) Webster's March 7, 1850 speech, where "he [never] intended or dreamed that in consequence of [the Compromise of 1850] the Missouri Compromise would or could ever be abrogated."[46]

Seward's address on the proposed Kansas-Nebraska Act in 1854 was even more legalistic in tone and argument than the higher law speech. Even the title under which Seward arranged to publish the address, "Freedom and Public Faith," suggested that freedom rested not just on moral superiority but on law. What kind of law was that to be, what kind of legal relationship among the various migrants to Kansas? He began with an extended brief, reciting the facts that led to the Missouri Compromise, on which precedent the Western portion of the Louisiana Purchase had been settled. Then he applied a version of that law of the case: to wit, when opinion in both houses was divided, here a Senate majority for slavery and a House majority against it, compromise was the rule. "Such concessions are mutual and equal . . . by this mutual exchange of concessions, the transaction takes on the nature and character of a contract, compact, or treaty between the parties represented. By the precepts of public law, such a contract is irrevocable and irrepealable, except by the mutual consent of both or all of the parties concerned. . . . Such was the compromise of 1820." Replacement of the Compromise by the Kansas-Nebraska bill's provision for popular sovereignty was an illegal abrogation of settled law. Once again, as in the California compromise controversy four years earlier, Seward lost. But in the melee the doctrine of relational rights had a new offshoot—the rights of various members of Congress vis-à-vis one another.[47]

As Seward had warned on January 11, 1851, the Fugitive Slave Act did not quiet the issue of runaway slaves. Instead, it continued to inflame passions on both sides of the Mason Dixon line. Rescues, recaptures, threats, law cases, kept slavery at the center of the national news. "I am quite sure that we are at the beginning of a reactionary period in favor of freedom . . . I deplore the return of that poor slave [Anthony Burns, in Boston] to bondage. I would not have the crime of participation in it rest on me for all the power that president or emperor ever held," Seward wrote to Theodore Parker, the Massachusetts abolitionist. The old politics and its party system could no longer contain the contagion. A new party, the Republicans, was forming, and Seward would become one of its number.[48]

So would Charles Sumner, of Massachusetts, chosen by the state to replace Senator Webster in 1851. Sumner was an avid abolitionist and viewed "Bleeding Kansas" (the popular term for the violence between pro- and antislave forces in the territory) with alarm. On May 19 and 20, 1856, Sumner treated the Senate to one of his marathon addresses. Filled with classical allusions, bitter scorn, and personal assaults over the course of two days, its targets included one of the supporters of the Kansas-Nebraska Act, Andrew Pickens

Butler of South Carolina (also a renowned orator). Two days later, after a night of fustian and alcohol with his fellow South Carolina congressman Laurence M. Keitt, Congressman Preston Brooks ambushed Sumner at his desk and caned him into insensibility. Brooks, a Democrat, was Butler's kinsman, and Brooks claimed that southern honor and personal offense required him to punish Sumner. The next day, Henry Wilson, Sumner's fellow Republican from Massachusetts, asked the Senate to take notice of the assault. But he had just been named a senator and deferred to his more senior colleagues. None spoke. No one made a resolution for an inquiry. Seward then rose and made the motion. The violence of bleeding Kansas had arrived at the Senate chamber, a perfect example of the poison which slavery poured into the relations among the members of Congress.[49]

Was this patent evidence of an irrepressible conflict? Was personal animus and political antagonism the source of the nation's travail? Did it mean that all reciprocity was dead, or at least doomed? Not for Seward. Quite the contrary. It was the conflict between two different legal regimes. Free labor embraced relational rights. Slave law rejected relational rights. The conflict could be resolved as all legal conflicts could be resolved. There was yet hope. Seward was not at all negative in his thinking. He was more often than not a booster of bills for homesteaders and for a transcontinental railroad—both of which would spread free communities to the West. The idea was that law could foster the right kind of settlement, a settlement of the West similar to that he saw unfolding in western New York. These initiatives became entangled in political partisanship—should the route of the railroad go through the northern plains or through the Southwest; should homesteading be tied to immigration from Europe and the British Islands, a free population, or the expansion of slavery? Thus progressive legislation could never break free of political divisions. The progressive state has never quite found the solution to that conundrum, and Seward cannot be faulted for failing to see his program to fruition while he belonged to the Whig Party. Perhaps a place in the newly established Republican Party would bring better opportunities?

CHAPTER 4

"An Irrepressible Conflict between Opposing and Enduring Forces"

Republican Party Campaigner

The Kansas-Nebraska Act of 1854, which provided for popular sovereignty on the slavery issue in the Nebraska Territory, brought bloodshed to Kansas (the southeastern part of the territory) and to Washington, DC. It was a bad law with bad consequences, as Seward realized. Although Seward and Weed privately hoped that the controversy would breathe new life into the Whig Party, and that hope was the basis for Seward's successful efforts to retain his Senate seat, they were mistaken. Bleeding Kansas was a fatal blow to the Whig Party. By 1855, shortly after its creation, Seward chose to join the new Republican Party, and thereafter became one of its standard-bearers.

Seward's first Republican Party oration, in the foyer of the Albany State Capital on October 12, 1855, made clear his stance on slavery. "Slavery is not, and never can be, perpetual. It will be overthrown, either peacefully or lawfully, under this Constitution; or it will work the subversion of the Constitution, together with its own overthrow." In other words, the solution was legal not political. Although his private hope for the Republican presidential nomination in 1856 was derailed, he gamely campaigned for the party platform and its candidates in the election of 1856. He continued to inveigh against slavery in the West, and this put him squarely against the US Supreme Court's decision in *Dred Scott v. Sandford* (1857), a case in which a master had taken his slave to a western military outpost (Fort Snelling in Minnesota), allowed him to marry there, and died, leaving him to the not so humane care of mistress and father-in-law, both rabid advocates of slavery.[1]

Seward thought that Chief Justice Roger Tawney's opinion in *Dred Scott* produced even more evil than the Kansas-Nebraska Act. As a member of the Supreme Court bar and a confidant of Justice Samuel Nelson and friend of John McLean, Seward knew more about the court's operations than many other politicians. He was livid at the *Dred Scott* decision, and even more so at Taney's opinion's license, calling it "judicial usurpation" of the functions of the elected branches. Seward even told Congress a year later that he thought there had been an illicit conspiracy between newly elected president James Buchanan and Taney to take Kansas out of politics by way of the Missouri slave case.[2]

Like Nelson and others of his brethren, Taney could have disposed of Dred Scott's plea for his own, his wife, and his two daughters' freedom on narrow grounds. Scott's counsel had argued that his master had taken him to Illinois, and then to the Minnesota territory, and by living there for a time, in effect had freed him. The Missouri Supreme Court had decided otherwise, finding that his former status of slave reattached he returned to his new master in St. Louis. The case came to the High Court on diversity grounds, as the administrator of Scott's master's estate lived in New York, while Scott claimed residence in Missouri. Taney could have disposed of Scott's claim by repeating what the Court had said in earlier cases—domicile determined slave or free status, and state law determined domicile.[3]

Taney, perhaps at the prompting of incoming president Buchanan, decided to take the broader issue of the expansion of slavery in hand and settle it. In addition to upholding the Missouri court's finding, Taney assayed two dicta not necessary to settle the case at hand. The first was that people of African descent could never be citizens of the United States. The second was that Congress did not have the authority under the Constitution to bar slavery in the western territories. The basis for the former was Taney's incorrect reading of the views of the framers. The second was the Fifth Amendment, which in his view would have required compensation for denying slaveholders property rights in the territories. He found that the Missouri Compromise (set aside by the Kansas-Nebraska Act in any case) had been unconstitutional. Republicans decried the dicta not because they were law (only one other justice fully subscribed to them; to be precedent they needed a majority of the justices) but because according to more than one Republican, Taney seemed to be warning that no state could bar the introduction of slavery.[4]

These were years that seemed to disprove Seward's view of legal relationships. Instead of revealing its capacity to render to each what they owed to one another, slave law fostered division and disunion. Throughout these years he insisted with ever more stridency that defenders of slavery could not claim a relational rights defense for their domestic institutions. There was no reciprocity in the slave-master relationship. With Buchanan, another Democratic "doughface," a Supreme Court also in the proslavery corner, and a senate with a Democratic majority, Seward was flummoxed. As a final crisis over slavery grew nearer, his call for relational rights grew less focused and more perfervid.

The Republican Party's organizing efforts, bringing together former Free Soil Democrats, Conscience Whigs, nativists, and other groups had not helped resolve "Bleeding Kansas." Seward, like his mentor John Quincy Adams before him, deeply cared for things that no party truly represented. Yet both men were bound by party ties. They needed party support to remain effective in politics. Though a mainstay of the new Republican Party, Seward stepped back from it in 1857. During the Panic of 1857, he considered leaving politics for his law practice once and for all. Weed cajoled him back, and Seward once more became a visible player in the great game of presidential politics.[5]

Once again on the circuit stumping for party candidates, in 1858, Seward spoke at Rome and Auburn, among other cities in upstate New York. His campaigning might not have been as energetic as in earlier years, but his address at Rochester, New York, on October 25, 1858, was widely reprinted and read. The immediate object of his speech was victory in the gubernatorial race, with the Seward-Weed candidate, Edwin D. Morgan, running behind the Democratic candidate, Amasa Parker. Parker was a well-known upstate lawyer, judge, and former congressman. As a Democrat, he had supported Van Buren, but did not move with Van Buren into the Free Soil Party. Instead, he remained a middle-of-the-road Democrat, supporting the Union when the crisis came, but urging moderation in the treatment of the Confederacy. The Republican vote was fractured by a Know-Nothing candidate, Lorenzo Burrows, and Gerritt Smith, running as an abolitionist. Morgan won with a plurality of the vote, Seward's efforts being a key contribution. The speech was widely reported because Seward warned in it of an "irrepressible conflict" between free labor and slave labor. It added to Seward's reputation as an abolitionist, though that is not what he said. To understand what he said, one has to go back to the presidential campaign of 1848.[6]

In the course of that presidential election year, Seward had campaigned for the Zachary Taylor/Millard Fillmore Whig ticket. He had wanted a different set of candidates (perhaps, if the convention deadlocked, even his own candidacy advanced) but settled for Taylor and traveled through the Midwest by rail, giving more or less the same speech at every city stop. The core of that speech was that the Whig Party, as he saw it, represented free labor in the contest between freedom and slavery. On October 26, 1848, he told an audience in Cleveland that "the first principle" of the party and all right thinking men was "to preserve the Union." Only in it and through it could true harmony come, and despotism be prevented. The second principle was that democracy "is founded in the natural equality of *all* men—not alone all *American* men, nor alone all *white* men, but all MEN of every country, clime, and complexion, are equal—not made equal by human laws, but born equal." What followed naturally and logically was that "slavery must be abolished." Not easily, for "there are two antagonistic elements in American society, freedom and slavery." Freedom was in harmony with the democratic "spirit of our age," and it "elevated" labor. Slavery debased labor with forced toil and blood. The Whig Party was the party of freedom. The Democratic Party was the creature of slavery. Supporters labeled it his "most bold" address on the subject. It certainly gained national attention.[7]

Although the message seemed simple, its application was not. Over the course of his service in the Senate, from 1848 through 1860, he hoped for reconciliation between free and slave states; yet he openly despised slavery. What had changed from 1848 to 1858? The Kansas- Nebraska Act and Dred Scott decision had changed the political landscape. Slavery was winning. That was the message of his 1858 speech. On its face, Seward's Rochester oration was just another Republican campaign speech attacking the Democratic Party. Under the surface, it was a sophisticated exposition of Seward's jurisprudence. Why not reverse the facial and the underlying and explore the jurisprudence openly? After all, Seward was an intellectual as well as a politician. But Seward knew that a frank elucidation of his legalist views would turn off the voters gathered at the rallies. It was not what they were used to hearing. It was not what they wanted to hear. So Seward wrapped the jurisprudential doctrine round with a conventional attack on the opposing party. One owes it to Seward, so often accused of being a mere partisan hack, to unwrap the irresistible conflict to show the message beneath the surface.

The opening passage of the October 28, 1858 address appeared to be mere ballyhoo. "The main subject, then, is whether the Democratic Party deserves to retain the confidence of the American people." But Seward did not descend into invective. He professed to take the high road, offering something close to a lecture on democratic politics. "In attempting to prove it unworthy, I think that I am not actuated by prejudices against that party, or by prepossessions in favor of its adversary; for I have learned, by some experience, that virtue and patriotism, vice and selfishness, are found in all parties, and that they differ less in their motives than in the policies they pursue." Seward rejected party affiliation then slammed the opposing party. For some orators, this would be a familiar Ciceronian device. For Seward, it was the painful fact. Party affiliation was not the answer. It was not even the question. "Our country is a theatre, which exhibits, in full operation, two radically different political systems; the one resting on the basis of servile or slave labor, the other on voluntary labor of freemen."[8]

Some of his audience, certainly those who were well read, knew that Seward was taking this opportunity to respond to two of the most popular contemporary legalist defenses of slavery, George Fitzhugh's *Sociology for the South* (1854) and his *Cannibals All!* (1857). Fitzhugh, a lawyer and Southern propagandist, was also talking about a legal regime; he argued that slavery was not only good for the slave, protecting an inferior race from its worst habits but good for the master. He was proud of the reception of his ideas in the South. Of his first work, he boasted, "That little work has met, everywhere, we believe, at the South, with a favorable reception. No one has denied its theory of Free Society nor disputed the facts on which that theory rests. Very many able colaborers have arisen, and many books and essays are daily appearing, taking higher ground in defence of Slavery; justifying it as a normal and natural institution, instead of excusing or apologizing for it, as an exceptional one. It is now treated as a positive good, not a necessary evil." Fitzhugh called free labor "wage slavery," bad for all except the voracious and immoral factory owners who preyed on the poor laborer.[9]

Fitzhugh also had a political agenda—defense of the Southern Democratic Party against Northern radicalism, abolitionism, and socialism. "The true and honorable distinction of the Democratic party is, that it has but one unbending principle—'The safety of the people is the supreme law.' To this party we think the Nation and the North may confidently look for a happy exodus from our difficulties." The Democratic Party had a monopoly on virtue. "It is pure, honest, active and patriotic now, and will continue so as long as the dark cloud of Abolition and Socialism lowers and threatens at the North . . . It is now able, and it alone is able, to grapple with and strangle the treasons of the North." Lincoln read Fitzhugh, as did the abolitionists, and we may presume so did Seward, or at least he was familiar with Fitzhugh's argument.[10]

Seward confronted the same prospect as Fitzhugh and Lincoln: a house dividing against itself might not be able to stand. Fitzhugh had concluded that "There is no middle ground—not an inch of ground of any sort, between the doctrines which we hold and those which Mr. Garrison holds. If slavery, either white or black, be wrong in principle or practice, then is Mr. Garrison right—then is all human government wrong." Lincoln, at a June 16, 1858 gathering of Republicans in Springfield, Illinois, agreed that "A House Divided against itself cannot stand." Seward knew about Lincoln's speech—it was widely reprinted in Republican papers like Horace Greeley's *New York Tribune*. Seward appeared to agree: "Never did human sagacity utter a more pregnant truth. The two systems are at once perceived to be incongruous. But they are more than incongruous-they are incompatible. They never have permanently existed together in one country, and they never can." But recall that Seward's was a relational jurisprudence, not a mere substitution of his own ideas of right and wrong for Fitzhugh's. The fallacy in Fitzhugh's argument was precisely that—he could not see that masters owed anything to their bondsmen.[11]

Was this incompatibility irreconcilable? If it were, then the slaveholding South and its Democratic allies must be swept away in a Republican tsunami. Why bother with all the discussion of "the irreconcilable contrast between their great principles and characteristics"? Why not focus on the new party's principles? Seward's reply was embedded in his answer to Fitzhugh. It was an answer in a place where Fitzhugh had not gone. It was certainly not in the comparative profitability of two contending labor systems. It was in the weakness of law and community in places where slavery existed. "Slavery, as I have intimated, existed in every state in Europe. Free labor has supplanted it everywhere except in Russia . . . and Turkey. . . . State necessities developed in modern times are now obliging even those two nations to encourage and employ free labor; and already, despotic as they are, we find them engaged in abolishing slavery." As law progressed, slavery receded. That law was liberal, democratic, progressive, and above all relational. The rights of free labor were relational—in the mutual obligations of worker and employer. "In the United States, slavery came into collision with free labor at the close of the last century, and fell before it in New England, New York, New Jersey, and Pennsylvania, but triumphed over it effectually, and excluded it for a period yet undetermined, from Virginia, the Carolinas, and Georgia." What was the difference between these states? The law was the difference.[12]

In what amounted to the inverse of the late John C. Calhoun's thoughts on political economy (making slavery the engine of national progress and profit), Seward offered his own analysis of the South's peculiar institution. It was a combination of economic and social/cultural insights. "The laborers who are enslaved are all negroes, or persons more or less purely of African derivation. But this is only accidental. The principle of the system is that labor in every society, by whomsoever performed, is necessarily unintellectual, groveling and base; and that the laborer, equally for his own good and for the welfare of the State, ought to be enslaved." But undercutting the presumed dialectic of laborer versus master was the matter of race. "The white laboring man, whether native or foreigner, is not enslaved, only because he cannot, as yet, be reduced to bondage." The imposition of slavery thus lay in the overlap of race and history. Slavery was not part of the progress of capitalism. It was a survival of an older, harsher time in a different place.[13]

Seward looked ahead. The future was on the side of free labor. "You need not be told now that the slave system is the older of the two, and that once it was universal. . . . The great melioration of human society which modern times exhibits is mainly due to the incomplete substitution of the system of voluntary labor for the one of servile labor, which has already taken place." By contrast, slavery had come out of Africa, and "This African slave system is one which, in its origin and in its growth, has been altogether foreign from the habits of the races which colonized these States, and established civilization here." Actually, slavery was global, not African, but no matter.[14]

Seward was adept at pointing the finger; every country lawyer knew when the jury needed a villain. But the blame for slavery belonged not to the settlers of the English colonies. "It was introduced on this continent as an engine of conquest, and for the establishment of monarchical power, by the Portuguese and the Spaniards, and was rapidly extended by them all over South America, Central America, Louisiana, and Mexico." The results of slavery in these colonies were plain to see. "Its legitimate fruits are seen in the poverty, imbecility, and anarchy which now pervade all Portuguese and Spanish America." So blame the iniquity on the Iberian Peninsula.[15]

Speaking to an audience of Northern Europeans in Rochester, Seward offered a comparative ethnocentric explanation of the benefits of free labor. While slavery was southern (European and African), "The free-labor system is of German extraction, and it was established in our country by emigrants from Sweden, Holland, Germany, Great Britain, and Ireland." To include the Irish, many of whom were virtually indentured servants by English landowners, was something of a novelty in political rhetoric at the time, but many New York City voters were Irish, and weening them away from their Democratic Party affiliation was one of Seward's major purposes.[16]

Where did the law come into this sharply worded account of labor, ethnicity, and geography? When Seward said labor, did he equate it with physical exertion? With work? Was his point that slave labor was so much more onerous than free labor? No. For him labor was inseparable from a legal regime. In free labor, the worker had a relational right—the right to leave a job, the right to bargain for better conditions, the right to be paid. In slave labor, the slave had no relational rights. He or she might try to bargain for more free time or a garden plot, but no right to any benefits. "One of the chief elements of the value of human life is freedom in the pursuit of happiness." The phrase was instantly recognizable, and the assumption was that national law included the Declaration of Independence. What were those inalienable rights? They were legal rights. Did Southern free white men dare to reject this assumption? Yet their welcome of slavery was proof that they did not accept the Declaration's teachings. They did not realize that slavery was "necessarily improvident and ruinous, because, as a general truth, communities prosper and flourish, or droop and decline, in just the degree that they practise or neglect to practise the primary duties of justice and humanity." The duties were legal ones, but the key word is community. This echoed the higher law theme of Seward's California addresses, in which the expansion of free labor was the extension of communal obligations.[17]

By contrast, "The slave system is one of constant danger, distrust, suspicion, and watchfulness"; in short, a legal system with slavery created a dysfunctional community, for what else could be a community in which half of the laborers could never be members? The slave was not a person in the law. He or she was property. And the more the free North pressed for the lawful end of slavery, the more ungovernable the South grew. The degeneration of law in the South went hand in hand with the degeneration of labor in the South. For slavery "debases those whose toil alone can produce wealth and resources for defense, to the lowest degree of which human nature is capable, to guard against mutiny and insurrection, and thus wastes energies which otherwise might be employed in national development and aggrandizement."[18]

Universal education was another of Seward's legal projects. Its progress marked the difference between free and slave communities. "The free-labor system educates all alike, and by opening all the fields of industrial employment and all the departments of authority, to the unchecked and equal rivalry of all classes of men, at once secures universal contentment, and brings into the highest possible activity all the physical, moral, and social energies of the whole state." Raise up the freedman with education and the entire society rises. Debase the slave laborer by denying literacy by law, and society sinks to the lowest level. What is the mechanism that does the heavy lifting? The law. Insert "law" after free and slave and the message comes clear. "In states where the slave system prevails, the masters, directly or indirectly, secure all political power, and constitute a ruling aristocracy. In states where the free-labor system prevails, universal suffrage necessarily obtains, and the state inevitably becomes, sooner or later, a republic or democracy."[19]

Aware of this, the lawmakers of new states, here Seward was thinking of the Upper Midwest and the Northwest, barred slavery by law and thereby created effective communities whose membership was open to all. "Every new State which is organized within our ever-extending domain makes its first political act a choice of the one and the exclusion of the other, even at the cost of civil war, if necessary." Political divisions followed, not only visible in the law but forced by law. For within their own limits the slave states forbade even the casting of votes for the Republican candidate at the last national election in 1856. Would a truly democratic state do this?[20]

Waiting in the wings was the states' rights argument. Recall that Seward was not a fan of the extreme states' rights views of Calhoun and sided with President Andrew Jackson against nullification. At the same time, in the Virginia affair and in his opposition to the Fugitive Slave Acts of 1793 and 1850, Seward made a strong case for states' rights in the criminal process. States' rights were thus familiar but treacherous waters for Seward to navigate in 1858. "Hitherto . . . two systems have existed in different States, but side by side within the American Union. This has happened because the Union is a confederation of States." Forced to choose between states' rights and national Union, Seward did not hesitate to choose the latter. But he denied that he was choosing. History dictated the choice. "The United States constitute only one nation. Increase of population, which is filling the States out to their very borders, together with a new and extended network of railroads and other avenues, and an internal commerce which daily becomes more intimate, is rapidly bringing the States into a higher and more perfect social unity or consolidation." History celebrated the growing consolidation of the Union. For consolidation read community. But not every state was part of the process. "These antagonistic systems are continually coming into closer contact, and collision results."[21]

Seward looked from the past and the present to the future, from legal and social analysis to politics. "Shall I tell you what this collision means? They who think that it is accidental, unnecessary, the work of interested or fanatical agitators, and therefore ephemeral, mistake the case altogether." The abolitionists were merely harbingers of that future; they did not make it. Instead, "It is an irrepressible conflict between opposing and enduring forces, and it means that the United States must and will, sooner or later, become either entirely a slaveholding nation, or entirely a free-labor nation." The word "irrepressible" and certainly the idea behind it, were not new, but when the speech was printed and circulated, it aroused anger in the slave South. Seward was delighted. He wrote to Massachusetts abolitionist Theodore Parker, "I have great satisfaction in witnessing the contests that the slave-retainers have raised about it."[22]

The problem was that history could not be trusted to constrain the future. The nation's choice between freedom and slavery remained unmade. Seward turned to imagined landscapes: "Either the cotton and rice fields of South Carolina and the sugar plantations of Louisiana will ultimately be tilled by free labor, and Charleston and New Orleans become marts of legitimate merchandise alone, or else the rye-fields and wheat-fields of Massachusetts and New York must again be surrendered by their farmers to slave culture and to the production of slaves." Then would "Boston and New York become once more markets for trade in the bodies and souls of men." All manner of fortune-telling was popular in his day, but Seward did not find palmistry and Tarot card hucksterism attractive. Law must determine whether the nation be free or slave. "It is the failure to apprehend this great truth that induces so many unsuccessful attempts at final compromises between the slave and free States, and it is the existence of this great fact that renders all such pretended compromises, when made, vain and ephemeral."[23]

What had begun as a stirring call to voters had passed through an erudite essay on political economy now became a lesson in history. Historians may question the strict accuracy of Seward's narrative, and there is still much controversy over the pro- or antislave nature of the Constitution of 1787, but Seward's search for historical authority was a standard of antislavery writing, and one reason why he was accounted an abolitionist in both North and South. "Startling as this saying may appear to you, fellow-citizens, it is by no means an original or even a modern one. Our forefathers knew it to be true, and unanimously acted upon it when they framed the constitution of the United States. They regarded the existence of the servile system in so many of the States with sorrow and shame, which they openly confessed, and they looked upon the collision between them, which was then just revealing itself, and which we are now accustomed to deplore, with favor and hope."[24]

Seward engaged in what today is called originalist jurisprudence—claiming to know the intent of the framers behind their published words. "They knew that one or the other system must exclusively prevail. Unlike too many of those who in modern time invoke their authority, they had a choice between the two. They preferred the system of free labor, and they determined to organize the government, and so direct its activity, that that system should surely and certainly prevail." Like Lincoln in his debates with Democratic senator Stephen Douglas earlier in the same year, Seward argued that the Declaration of Independence was incorporated in the Constitution. "For this purpose, and no other, they based the whole structure of the government broadly on the principle that all men are created equal, and therefore free." The framers would have little imagined that "within the short period of one hundred years, their descendants would bear to be told by any orator, however popular, that the utterance of that principle was merely a rhetorical rhapsody; or by any judge, however venerated, that it was attended by mental reservation, which rendered it hypocritical and false."[25]

Seward's recapitulation of the thinking of the framers was a common feature of both abolitionist and proslavery rhetoric. Seward had no doubt that "By the ordinance of 1787 they dedicated all of the national domain not yet polluted by slavery to free labor immediately, thenceforth and forever; while by the new constitution and laws they invited foreign free labor from all lands under the sun, and interdicted the importation of African slave labor, at all times, in all places, and under all circumstances whatsoever." How then to explain the proliferation of slave states and slave ownership? "It is true that they necessarily and wisely modified this policy of freedom by leaving it to the several States, affected as they were by different circumstances, to abolish slavery in their own way and at their own pleasure, instead of confiding that duty to Congress; and that they secured to the slave States, while yet retaining the system of slavery, a three-fifths representation of slaves in the federal government, until they should find themselves able to relinquish it with safety."[26]

Seward had turned the three-fifth clause on its head—no longer was it a concession to slavery; for him it was the promise of the end of slavery. The clause held the Union together until the natural course of emancipation would make its way. His relentless optimism spilled out onto the page: "But the very nature of these modifications fortifies my position, that the fathers knew that the two systems could not endure within the Union, and expected within a short period slavery would disappear forever." Proof of this optimistic assertion he found in the amendment process. "Moreover, in order that these modifications might not altogether defeat their grand design of a republic maintaining universal equality, they provided that two thirds of the States might amend the constitution."[27]

Seward knew that slavery had gone everywhere in the British North American colonies. He permitted himself a hypothetical—the common rhetorical practice of modern law teachers. For this is what the oration had now become—a lesson in US law. "It remains to say on this point only one word, to guard against misapprehension. If these States are to again become universally slaveholding, I do not pretend to say with what violations of the constitution that end shall be accomplished." Only by violating the Constitution and reversing the course of history could slavery become national—as Chief Justice Taney had (allegedly) proposed in *Dred Scott*. "On the other hand, while I do confidently believe and hope that my country will yet become a land of universal freedom, I do not expect that it will be made so otherwise than through the action of the several States cooperating with the federal government, and all acting in strict conformity with their respective constitutions." The answer, then, was more law, better law, in both the states and the federal government.[28]

Back and forth Seward struggled, in ever tightening coils of logic and fact. "The strife and contentions concerning slavery, which gently disposed persons so habitually deprecate, are nothing more than the ripening of the conflict which the fathers themselves not only thus regarded with favor, but which they may be said to have instituted." The framers not only enabled slavery to continue, he conceded that they saw its benefits. "In the field of federal politics, slavery, deriving unlooked-for advantages from commercial changes, and energies unforeseen from the facilities of combination between members of the slaveholding class and between that class and other property classes, early rallied, and has at length made a stand." In short, slavery was profitable. The labor of slaves brought profits; the internal traffic in slaves brought profits; and the breeding of slaves brought profits. The cultivation of rice, sugar, tobacco, and above all cotton by slaves was profitable, and those profits spurred national growth.[29]

Seward believed in the importance of economic growth, and that growth was fueled, at least in part, but the profits of slavery. This was Calhoun's often repeated claim: US wealth was built on southern cotton exports, and cotton required slave labor. Why then attack slavery—the engine of much of the nation's economic progress? Seward was often accused of being a slippery advocate, inconsistent at best and dishonest at worse. But here he faced a true paradox—the most perplexing puzzle of the Western intellectual world. As the historian David Brion Davis demonstrated, societies that made use of slave labor accumulated capital and redistributed the wealth to spur free persons' standard of living. Slavery and progress in the eighteenth and early nineteenth centuries seemed to go hand in hand. Abolitionists rejected this association as mere concomitance and argued that in modern (i.e., postemancipation) times, free white and Black labor was a better model for economic growth. Defenders of slavery responded that progress must rest on a foundation (Senator James Henry Hammond of South Carolina called it "a mudsill") of bondsmen and women. Seward never totally resolved this conundrum, but he saw in it the gravest warning should the free North bow to the slave South.[30]

For Seward envisioned a parade of horrors as a free people succumbed to the slave power. The panic factor was very real in Republicans' minds. The *Dred Scott* decision was not the only omen that worried him. The Democratic dominance of the presidency, the southern dominance of the High Court bench, and plans to expand slavery into the Southwest all bode ill for the project of freedom. "By continued appliances of patronage and threats of disunion, they will keep a majority favorable to these designs in the Senate . . . Through that majority they will defeat, as they best can, the admission of free States and secure the admission of slave States. Under the protection of the judiciary, they will, on the principle of the Dred Scott case, carry slavery into all the territories of the United States now existing and hereafter to be organized. By the action of the President and Senate, using the treaty-making power, they will annex foreign slaveholding States." So the dominos could fall.[31]

The possibility of slavery in the Northern territories lay in Taney's obiter dictum that the Fifth Amendment protected the slaveowner's right to take the slave into free territory or be compensated for the lost property. The last was a reference to the 1854 plan to annex Cuba to which the US minister to the Court of St. James (equivalent today to the ambassador to Britain), James Buchanan, and the Democratic president, Franklin Pierce, both Northerners, acceded. As it happened, the plot, which went nowhere, was one of the sparks that ignited the Republican Party movement. Worse would follow. "In a favorable conjuncture they will induce Congress to repeal the act of 1808 which prohibits the foreign slave trade, and so they will import from Africa, at a cost of only twenty dollars a head, slaves enough to fill up the interior of the continent." Although the framers who owned slaves like Jefferson thought the external slave trade barbarous, and readily sought to ban it, the issue had been reopened in the 1840s by southern politicians and journalists. Again, it failed to gain popular support, in part because it undermined the profitability of the internal slave trade.[32]

The national community would then be perverted by the slaveocracy to protect their peculiar institution. This was for Seward the most feared consequence of continued Democratic electoral supremacy. It meant that the way to reciprocity through ordinary legal practices would be closed. As governor he had used these means to effect reform. As a senator he felt powerless to continue the progress. "Thus relatively increasing the number of slave States, they will allow no amendment to the constitution prejudicial to their interest; and so, having permanently established their power, they expect the federal judiciary to nullify all State laws which shall interfere with internal or foreign commerce in slaves." The slave power would then overawe the free states. "When the free States shall be sufficiently demoralized to tolerate these designs, they reasonably conclude that slavery will be accepted by those States themselves." The conclusion of his logic was almost unbearable. "I shall not stop to show how speedy or how complete would be the ruin which the accomplishment of these slaveholding schemes would bring upon the country. For one, I should not remain in the country to test the sad experiment. Having spent my manhood, though not my whole life, in a free State, no aristocracy of any kind, much less an aristocracy of slaveholders, shall ever make the laws of the land in which I shall be content to live." He called upon that New York experience in his peroration. "Having seen the society around me universally engaged in agriculture, manufactures, and trade, which were innocent and beneficent, I shall never be a denizen of a State where men and women are reared as cattle, and bought and sold as merchandise." Again, the law itself was perverted to subjugate the slave, reducing them to "merchandise." It could not have been done without law, a cruel irony for the country lawyer.[33]

The parade of horrors had begun. "You will tell me that these fears are extravagant and chimerical." They were not. But they could be averted. "But it is only the possibility of defeat that renders them so. They cannot be defeated by inactivity. There is no escape from them compatible with non-resistance." There was no brokering, no negotiation, no way to live alongside slavery and its minions. "The Democratic party must be permanently dislodged from the government. The reason is, that the Democratic party is inextricably committed to the designs of the slaveholders, which I have described."[34]

But there was something in him that hoped for a more moderate resolution. It was there in his California speeches. It was still there. Because he was not a linear thinker but a lateral one. "Let me be well understood. I do not charge that the Democratic candidates for public office now before the people are pledged to-much less that the Democratic masses who support them really adopt-those atrocious and dangerous designs." That was fair. Some Democratic candidates were Free Soilers. Others were bound by party allegiance merely, rather than advocacy of the expansion of slavery. "Candidates may, and generally do, mean to act justly, wisely, and patriotically, when they shall be elected; but they become the ministers and servants, not the dictators, of the power which elects them." The Democrats could not help themselves. They would be swallowed by the Leviathan of the slaveocracy. "It is not more true that 'hell is paved with good intentions,' than it is that earth is covered with wrecks resulting from innocent and amiable motives."[35]

Lest he lean too far in the direction of accommodation, the Democratic Party leaders were not unwitting victims of their own words. "The very constitution of the Democratic party commits it to execute all the designs of the slaveholders, whatever they may be." By 1858, the Democratic Party was split into two. The northern part, led by Stephen Douglas, tried to skirt the question of expanding slavery to the west. Popular sovereignty proved that moderation did not work for the northern Democrats. The strength of the party lay in the South, and there it was dominated by slaveholders and proslavery ideology. Books and newspapers thought to contain abolitionist ideas were burned. No abolitionist speaker was safe. This Democracy "is not a party of the whole Union, of all the free States and of all the slave States; nor yet is it a party of the free States in the North and in the Northwest; but it is a sectional and local party, having practically its seat within the slave States, and counting its constituency chiefly and almost exclusively there."[36]

If that were true (and it was close), then the free and slave parts of the country had already begun the slide apart. Thus far, the South had not seceded because it had no need to secede, not as long as the Democrats controlled the White House and the judiciary. How did the South control the Democratic Party? Seward's explanation drew on a legal analogy to the formation of a commercial venture. "A party is, in one sense, a joint stock association, in which those who contribute most direct the action and management of the concern. The slaveholders contributing in an overwhelming proportion to the capital strength of the Democratic party, they necessarily dictate and prescribe its policy." The slaveholders were the biggest investors in the democracy, and they managed its policies, picked its candidates, and dominated its voting. "The inevitable caucus system enables them to do so with a show of fairness and justice. If it were possible to conceive for a moment that the Democratic party should disobey the behests of the slaveholders, we should then see a withdrawal of the slaveholders, which would leave the party to perish." A final slap at Douglas: "The portion of the party which is found in the free States is a mere appendage."[37]

Seen from a different perspective, the speech had a different aspect. The evil of the Democratic Party was that it divided the nation into two distinct legal regimes creating two distinct and opposite communities. The Democrats in this role were not a party of politicians, they were a body of lawmakers, and the law they made was a perversion of the aims of the founders. Bad law, not bad men or bad politics, was the curse they cast on the nation. The irrepressible conflict was not another term for violent sectionalism; it was a description of the struggle between these legal regimes. Such a struggle, in Seward's mind, could still have a legal resolution. The house dividing against itself need not fall if the wreckers could stop and seek legal repairs. Seward no doubt believed that he could provide a plan for this repair if the nation chose him as its next president.

After the election of 1858, an exhausted Seward traveled to England and then on the European continent. When he returned home at the end of 1859, he faced the campaign for the presidency. This was the occasion for which he, Weed, and his other backers had waited, but they had waited too long. Too much of what Seward had said now came back to haunt his candidacy. Although he tried to assuage fears that he would lead the abolitionists, he was still viewed as one, and although he condemned John Brown's raid on the federal armory at Harper's Ferry, he was suspected of having aided and abetted it. Returning to the Senate on February 29, 1860, he reassured the body that the Republican Party was not the party of violent overthrow of slave state governments and did not plan or support Brown's raid. The "one disturbing subject of slavery" should not lead to disunion. Slavery was wrong, and the High

Court was wrong to imply that slavery could be national, but progress and patriotism would resolve the issue. The North was not hostile to the South, and the Republican Party was not a sectional arm of the abolitionists. It would not force abolition on the South.[38]

In the governor's office, Seward had pledged himself to seek better laws, "to freely submit for your correction any errors and abuses in our laws," which obligation he enthusiastically pursued over the next three years although most of his plans for legal reform did not result in any real changes. From 1843 to 1860, Seward was a "free player," not an executive or a judge bound to enforce the law as it existed, but an advocate, able to argue against existing law for better laws. What would happen to his views, and the liberal vision of community values they embodied, when he was no longer free to obey or not obey given law? (And that is what did happen when he became US secretary of state in 1861).[39]

CHAPTER 5

"I Am to Engage in Conducting a War against a Portion of the American People"

Secretary of State

Seward hungered for the Republican presidential nomination, but a candidate about whom less was known (though his views were close to Seward's) was preferable to the Republicans, and they chose Abraham Lincoln over Seward at the May 1860 convention. Seward was stunned, but only for a moment, and supported the nomination.[1]

Seward had supported Lincoln's campaign, swallowing his disappointment at not becoming his party's choice for the White House and offering praise for the party's choice. In the fall of 1860 Lincoln won in the nation's most divisive sectional contest. In Springfield, Illinois, after he won the election, he played his cards close to his chest, placing conciliatory messages to southern leaders in private hands while refusing to make open concessions beyond the reassurance that he would not touch slavery where it existed nor interfere with the internal slave trade. At the same time, he adopted Seward's 1842 model law guaranteeing suspected runaways a trial by jury. All of which left Seward, still in Washington, DC, as the party's de facto spokesman. In the meantime, South Carolina's legislature called for a secession convention, which duly met and unanimously voted to take the state out of the Union. Still, no other state followed South Carolina's lead—yet. Lincoln hoped that cooler heads and pro-Union sentiment in the South would reverse the course of the secession movement—a vain hope as events revealed. Seward followed that policy.[2]

Well, not exactly followed. As Seward's speeches in the Senate had demonstrated, the idea of relational rights was not limited to handling cases for private parties. Thinking about community membership on a national scale, Seward joined in the effort to find a compromise short of secession. On December 18, 1860, two days before South Carolina seceded, veteran Kentucky senator John J. Crittenden proposed a compromise that would have ensured the perpetuity of slavery. The Missouri Compromise line would have been reinstated, with slavery allowed south of 36 degrees 30 minutes latitude. A committee of thirteen senators was named to consider the proposal. The Republican platform of 1860 barred such a guarantee, and the Republicans in the Senate were left in an awkward position by the proposal. Lincoln, from afar, and Seward, on hand, worked to find a way around the impasse.

Seward described his efforts in a letter to Lincoln on December 26, 1860. Seward had told the compromise committee of thirteen earlier in the week. "First, that the Constitution should never be altered, so as to authorize Congress to abolish, or interfere with slavery in the states. . . . Second, that the Fugitive Slave law should be amended, by granting a jury trial to the fugitive." Third, was the recommendation that states with personal liberty laws should amend them to conform to congressional legislation. The next day Seward added another contribution to the committee debates—that Congress pass a law making it a federal crime for anyone to plan or execute an invasion of any state. Although one could read the addition as a response to John Brown's raid (although the raid was carried out on federal property, and that offense was already covered in the 1790 federal crimes act), it could also apply to secessionists attempting to overthrow legal governments in the border states. The result of the committee of thirteen deliberations was the Crittenden compromise proposal, which went nowhere.[3]

On January 9, 1861, Thurlow Weed announced what everyone in Washington, DC, already knew: Seward was Lincoln's choice to be secretary of state. The secretary of state is not a legal officer in the same sense as the various district's federal attorneys or the attorney general. But the duties of the secretary of state are legal ones, including the receipt and publication of treaties and amendments to the Constitution, and the keeping of the records of the foreign relations of the United States. In addition, the secretary advises the president on negotiations with foreign governments and may carry on these negotiations at the president's behest, helps form foreign policy, reports to Congress on similar matters, and administers the department of state. In Seward's day, the secretary had a very small staff in house, and he wrote directly to and received correspondence from the nation's emissaries to foreign governments and diplomats representing those nations. For all of these reasons, the secretary in the nineteenth century was more often than not a lawyer. Of incumbents from 1789 to 1869, all but two, James Madison and Edward Everett, were members of their respective state bars and practiced law. Thomas Jefferson was the first secretary, followed by Edmund Randolph, Timothy Pickering, and John Marshall. All were lawyers. They were also politicians. Other secretaries whose legal and political careers prepared them for the secretary's duties included James Monroe, John Quincy Adams, Henry Clay, Martin Van Buren, Daniel Webster, John C. Calhoun, and James Buchanan. The secretary of state was the nation's legal voice to the rest of the world. Legal skills that translate include the ability to draft and to read documents, dispute resolution, and respect for adversaries. As career diplomat George Kennan wrote during the Cold War, Americans routinely "transplant legal concepts from the domestic to the international field; to believe that international society could and should operate on the basis of general contractual obligations, and hence to lay stress on verbal obligation rather than on the exact manifestation of political interest." Seward's filled this role from 1861 until he left the secretary's office in 1869.[4]

As the foremost man in the Republican Party and someone Lincoln commended for integrity and loyalty, Seward was a natural choice as a first minister in the cabinet. But I suspect there was something more, something that made the choice a good one for both men, and would, as time passed, bring the two men closer together. They had shared an experience that Lincoln did not share with other members of the cabinet or with leading members of his party in the Congress. Lincoln and Seward both remained country lawyers at heart.[5]

In the meantime, in addresses to Congress, the outgoing president Buchanan denounced secession as illegal, but told Congress that he, as president, could do nothing to prevent secession. With Lincoln still in Springfield, and the prospect of the dissolution of the Union becoming more serious every day, absent a full-dress speech from the president-elect, on January 12, 1861 Seward took it upon himself to state to Congress the Republican Party's stance on secession. He was now placed or had placed himself in an untenable position. More visible than Lincoln, feeling that the crisis—that is, averting the crisis of secession—had fallen on his shoulders, he reverted back to the country lawyer. A firm believer in relational rights in a community, he believed he now had to convince potential secessionists that they must accept a legal solution to the crisis short of secession, although some of the secession state senators had already departed. The galleries were packed.[6]

The problem was this: as the crisis unfolded, Seward believed even more strongly than ever in relational rights—the rights that belong to each member of a community of like-minded people. In a sense, the Union was such a community, the member states sharing duties and enjoying benefits because they were members of the national community. Now the very existence of that community was threatened by secession. How could one use a jurisprudence of reciprocity when some in the community explicitly rejected the very idea of reciprocity? Seward's attempts to resolve this fundamental conundrum—fundamental to his conception of rights at least—would persist throughout the secession crisis and the war that followed.

As printed, "The Union" proposed that political disagreements must be resolved within a legal framework—the essence of Seward's notion of good politics. First came what might have been read as boilerplate rhetoric—appeals to patriotism and a recounting of the shared heroism of northern and southern founders. But in the context of his thinking these appeals were absolutely necessary—for what was the shared heroism of a nation's people but the creation of the political community? All were members, for all had pledged themselves to the Union. This was the community of common believers that secession would destroy. Jefferson Davis, seating himself next to Seward, was deeply moved, and Crittenden was seen to shed tears. Seward warned that "Seditious combinations" threatened the Union and had already thrown the credit and business of the nation into disarray. The Union was "the soul" of the nation, assumed to be "immortal." He named with approval the views of southern members with whom he agreed (their states had not yet seceded) and pleaded for a spirit of compromise without recrimination.[7]

Seward then engaged in a very old rhetorical tactic. He first denied and then pivoted to argue for the very same proposition he had denied. The denial first: "The union cannot be saved by proving the secession is unconstitutional or illegal." Such proof would make little difference to those who had already asserted the legality of their departure. Then came a pivot: But did the departed have the legal right to coerce the Union to "acquiesce" in secession? No. The disunionists could not argue that Lincoln's election was illegitimate because they had left the community. No longer members, they no longer possessed the rights that members shared. Could they, in effect, wage war against the Union? No. There was no constitutional power for the federal government to make war on a state, but the federal government could certainly deal with conspirators within a state who had subverted state government to their own ends.[8]

The closing passages appealed to the good sense of the southern congressional delegations. Why sacrifice safety, happiness, and freedom that came from membership? There was no threat to existing political or social relationships in the legal election just finished. No one need fear the incoming administration. The Republican platform had promised that slavery would not be touched where it already existed. Members of the federal community had to trust the law and the political acts within the legal framework if any community could ever survive. The benefits of prior republican government, that is, membership, were obvious: the federal government alone could prevent war between rival confederacies; the federal government alone could ensure favorable treatment for Americans abroad. With these propositions laid out, the second hour of the speech outlined the proposals that Lincoln had already agreed to, with Seward's additional suggestion that a constitutional convention reconvene to address the slavery issue. In short, more law, better law, acceptance of law by all concerned would save the nation from the horrors of lawlessness.[9]

Back on the Senate floor at the end of the month, Seward was even more reassuring. In a memorial the citizens of New York had sought from him, and through him from the Senate "some plan for adjustment of the troubles which disturb the peace and happiness and endanger the safety of the nation." Rather than actually asking for such reassurance, he offered it. After all, Lincoln planned on being the president of the entire country, not just its northern precincts. Lincoln, another country lawyer, understood how community membership, and relational rights, worked for everyone. The memorial, had he laid it on the Senate floor, had so many signatures that it had to be taken seriously. The message was simple: everyone was devoted to the Union. No one intended or expected it to be riven in two.[10]

In both the January 12 and January 30 orations Seward offered the Senate a version of the relational rights doctrine. For the Union was not just a collection of states, it was the community of all Americans. No American could depart from that community; and all in it owed to one another reciprocal obligations. From its inception, the Union depended for its growth and its strength on these relationships. Division over slavery notwithstanding, Seward and the people of his state rested the case against secession on the relationship of every American to the Union. This was Seward's law. In the days after the January 30 speech, the reestablishment of relations between the Union and the putative Confederacy required more than Seward's moderation. Good relations among members of Congress was surely a start, but it was a pale and shimmering image of actual reciprocity. Forgiveness was only possible if those erring members of the Confederate delegations recanted their departure from the common government.[11]

Although still hoping for reconciliation between the Unionists and the secessionists (even telling domestic and foreign correspondents between December 1860 and the end of February 1861 that such a prospect looked promising), Seward was powerless to reverse the momentum of secession. Though he tried to remain cheerful and hopeful, in private he was despondent. "I hope what I have done will bring some good fruits, and, in any case, clear my own conscience of responsibility, if, indeed, I am to engage in conducting a war against a portion of the American people." On March 2, he indicated his desire to withdraw from the offer that Lincoln had made, although he had not yet been formally appointed. (Lincoln was not president until two days later.) Lincoln urged Seward to reconsider, and Seward did. A month and a half later, the war came, as Lincoln would latter lament in his Second Inaugural Address, though no one wanted it.[12]

Where had Seward the country lawyer gone when Lincoln called on him? Not far away. Seward's roots in Auburn were deeply planted. But his duties as secretary of state, far more than those as a senator, left him little time to travel back. He brought as much of his family as he could to Washington, DC, to help with his extensive socializing. His home was part domicile and part political club. Frances was not comfortable there and did not host the receptions other official wives hosted (remaining in her room when guests appeared), but daughter-in-law Anna, and Fanny (still learning how) played hostess and son Frederick was in almost constant attendance as his secretary. Seward was often so busy that he spent more of his day in his office than in his DC abode. In a sense, this was the same pattern as his law practice in Auburn, with much of his day devoted to clients and legal papers, or to traveling the circuit of upstate courts. It was the nation's business that now claimed him, different business from a country lawyer's, but the routines of work and social life in the one were not entirely distinct from the other. In any case his energy as a country lawyer suited him well as the country's lawyer.[13]

As secretary of state, Seward remained something of the country lawyer. That is to say, he revamped his skill set to perform his new duties. He was still a partisan, in such partisan times how could he be impartial, and now his client was the Union itself. He did not give up his law practice. (The Ethics Reform Acts barring such conduct lay in the future.) His basement in Washington, DC, doubled as his law office. In the midst of the secession crisis a visitor found him there consulting with Edwin Stanton on a patent case. In the *Albany Bridge Case* (1865), argued on appeal before the Supreme Court (Seward had already represented the bridge company in the 1858 Circuit Court case), Seward faced Maryland senator Reverdy Johnson and won. Just as he had made himself an expert on patent law, so Seward would make himself into an expert on international law. Never passive or even silent, he gave counsel to Lincoln, to US emissaries abroad, to foreign dignitaries, and to federal officials. At the same time, he was no longer free to challenge existing law. As counsel for the country he was constrained in his thinking, writing, and speaking as never before.[14]

Sometime in these early days, Seward decided that the State Department must publish its essential correspondence, including his own. Although there was something self-serving in the project, Seward telling everyone how important a part of the war effort his department was, the release of the documents was also essential to the notion of a democratic foreign policy—that is, that the diplomacy of the nation was the people's diplomacy. This became the *Foreign Relations of the United States* (*FRUS*), a series of volumes essential to all students of US foreign policy that continues to this day. Here was the country lawyer opening his file cabinets to the world. The novel aspect of the 1861 volume lay in its comprehensive scope and unified presentation, which enhanced both the utility and the visibility of the documents. "For the first time, documents about a variety of subjects all over the globe were presented under a single cover, rather than being published in an ad hoc manner." Seward censored materials that were sensitive or secret, but the public response to the publication, at least in the North and in Britain, was overwhelmingly positive.[15]

In Lincoln's cabinet, Seward was part of a public law firm. He did not choose his cases nor direct this virtual firm. Instead, Lincoln was the senior partner in the firm, and Seward had to take direction. Lincoln's was a cabinet of lawyers, many of whose credentials rivaled Seward's own. After Lincoln won the presidency over Democratic and Union Party rivals Stephen Douglas, John Bell, and John C. Breckinridge, he turned to lawyers to populate his cabinet: Seward was joined by Secretary of the Treasury Salmon Chase of Ohio, Attorney General Edward Bates of Missouri, and Gideon Welles of Connecticut as secretary of the navy. Welles had never practiced law, though he was a trained lawyer. Postmaster General Montgomery Blair was a lawyer from a family of lawyers. Indiana's Caleb Smith briefly served as secretary of the interior, but after a year of illness in Washington, he returned to his law practice and later a federal judgeship in Indiana. Simon Cameron, the first secretary of war, was not a lawyer, but a year later he was replaced by Edwin Stanton. James Speed, a Kentucky lawyer and close friend of Lincoln, replaced Bates in 1864. Speed was from his early political career in an opponent of slavery, calling it "legalized robbery," not an easy course of action in a slave state like Kentucky. Overall, one could not find a more able or imposing team of lawyers than this, though like many law partnerships, there was rivalry and contention among themselves and with senior partner Lincoln.[16]

Lincoln was comfortable around other lawyers; accustomed to listening to arguments, weighing their relative merits, and then arriving at his own conclusions. Although Seward's loquaciousness might seem out of place in a Lincoln law firm, his manner even pushy or arrogant, Lincoln was especially attentive to Seward's views, as the two of them had traveled parallel paths to power from country lawyer to the highest posts in the nation. The most striking difference was that Seward had traveled abroad; Lincoln had not. This made Seward a perfect fit for the nation's top diplomat. Other members of the cabinet, notably Welles and Chase, openly resented the close relationship between Lincoln and Seward, but the secretary of state post was literally and figuratively next to the presidency. Secretaries of state, from Jefferson, Madison, Monroe, John Quincy Adams, and Martin Van Buren, to Buchanan, had become presidents. Seward had harbored the same dream, but he put it far aside to serve Lincoln loyally. Lincoln reciprocated with trust and affection. What was more, Lincoln ceded diplomatic matters to Seward, although Lincoln had the last word on all dispatches, should he desire.[17]

Both Seward and Lincoln believed that secession posed a legal crisis and that withdrawal from the Union was profoundly illegal. As Lincoln told secessionists in his first inaugural address, "no State upon its own mere motion can lawfully get out of the Union; that resolves and ordinances to that effect are legally void, and that acts of violence within any State or States against the authority of the United States are insurrectionary or revolutionary, according to circumstances." Lincoln believed that the ship of state must be steered by lawyers because the crucial issues were not political or even military (at this time at least), but legal. Lincoln was reported to say to his law partner William Herndon, "Law is nothing else but the best reason of wise men applied for ages to the transactions and business of mankind." The Civil War would test that faith for both Lincoln and Seward.[18]

Lincoln showed his draft first inaugural address to Seward, and Seward marked it up with suggested changes. It was an act of self-abnegation rarely matched in US political history. Here was the address that Seward had longed to write and deliver himself, the honor and the opportunity given to his rival—yet he showed both loyalty and skill in his emendations. These toned down the language, in line with Seward's earlier attempts to mediate the sectional quarrel. Lincoln adopted many of the emendations. Lincoln was a little anxious about the speech, not so much about the content, as much of it he had already delivered to the Cooper Union on February 27, 1860. Then, the target was Chief Justice Roger Taney's obiter dictum in *Dred Scott v. Sandford* (1857) that the Missouri Compromise barring slavery from territories north of 36 degrees 30 minutes latitude was unconstitutional. Now the target was actual secession by seven of the slave states, soon to be eleven.[19]

According to the historian Doris Kearns Goodwin, "Seward's revisions were evident in nearly every paragraph." Most important, perhaps, was Seward's call to stress patriotism, a theme of his recent Senate addresses, softening Lincoln's adversarial tone. One can thus see the final version as a collaboration. Lincoln began the inaugural address with the concession that "Apprehension seems to exist among the people of the Southern States that by the accession of a Republican Administration their property and their peace and personal security are to be endangered. There has never been any reasonable cause for such apprehension." As the leader of the party as well as the nation, he offered that "the most ample evidence to the contrary has all the while existed and been open to their inspection. It is found in nearly all the published speeches of him who now addresses you." In particular, he repeated that "I have no purpose, directly or indirectly, to interfere with the institution of slavery in the States where it exists. I believe I have no lawful right to do so, and I have no inclination to do so." Proof lay in the platform on which he ran and won the presidency: "That the maintenance inviolate of the rights of the States, and especially the right of each State to order and control its own domestic institutions according to its own judgment exclusively, is essential to that balance of power on which the perfection and endurance of our political fabric depend; and we denounce the lawless invasion by armed force of the soil of any State or Territory, no matter what pretext, as among the gravest of crimes." The last was Seward's addition to the Crittenden compromise language.[20]

The most important emendation Seward suggested to Lincoln came in the final passage. Seward changed Lincoln's "With you, and not with me, is the solemn question of shall it be peace, or a sword?" to "I close. We are not we must not be aliens or enemies but fellow countrymen and brethren, Although passion has strained our bonds of affection too hardly they must not, I am sure they will not be broken." Seward urged Lincoln to sound the "mystic chords" that passed "though all the hearts and all the heaths in this broad continent of ours will yet again harmonize in their ancient music." Lincoln adopted this language with little rephrasing. Look again at what Seward wrote—it resonates with the reciprocity due to and from each of the members of the national community. It is a call to remember a relationship that a common history had forged. It is rooted not in absolutes or abstractions, not in threats or bluster, but in what one American owed to other Americans. See how it resembles the duties that all members of the state of New York owed to one another, writ large for the states. It is the distillation of Seward's ideal of relational rights.[21]

In the meantime, Seward settled into the major task of steering the country through troubled diplomatic waters. He had served for years on the Senate foreign relations committee and had traveled throughout Europe, meeting many of its leaders with whom he would have to deal. Thus it was natural for

Lincoln to delegate to Seward those types of day-to-day functions of state, although Seward almost invariably shared drafts with Lincoln or adopted Lincoln's stance on important issues. In important matters Seward showed unswerving loyalty to Lincoln and, in turn, demanded it of his staff. Chief among those officers was William Hunter. Chief clerk Hunter was a Rhode Island appointee of Millard Fillmore, thus a Whig, and on a number of occasions had been the acting secretary of state. If there was anything like a professional bureaucrat, it was Hunter. Seward also brought his son Frederick back from the newspaper business as a personal secretary.[22]

The next task was to replace some of Buchanan's ministers to European governments with reliable Union men. Lincoln and Seward had to collaborate on the task, for it was partly political (rewarding Lincoln supporters with foreign posts) and partly professional (choosing men who knew the language and the customs of the posting and, hopefully, some international law as well). For example, Lincoln wanted William Dayton, a New Jersey senator, for the all-important London position of minister to the Court of St. James, but Seward demurred. He insisted on Charles Francis Adams, as he and Seward had developed a close working relationship.[23]

Seward knew that Adams, a Republican elected to the House of Representatives from Massachusetts in 1858 and the son of John Quincy Adams, was firm on the key issue of secession. On December 27, 1860, Seward, told by Lincoln that he would be named secretary of state, reached out to Adams and the two men talked. Seward explained that he had urged Lincoln to name Adams to the cabinet, probably wishing to seed the cabinet with friends, but Lincoln had not agreed. Seward then convinced Lincoln to choose Adams for the London post. Adams had a temper, but kept it in largely in check during the fevered weeks before the inauguration, joining in what Adams's biographer has called the Seward-Adams "policy of conciliation and moderation."[24]

A test of that policy was the mid-March arrival in Washington of two emissaries from Davis's Confederate government in Montgomery, Alabama. Seven states had seceded and drafted a Confederate constitution. Davis, who knew Seward, sought his aid when Lincoln refused to accept the offer of negotiations. John Forsyth Jr., son of a former secretary of state and currently a Mobile Alabama newspaper editor (and a future Confederate army officer), and Martin Crawford, a Georgia lawyer, legislator, and member of Congress, then applied to the state department for accreditation as representatives of a foreign government. Their commission told Seward that "Seven States of the late Federal Union, having in the exercise of the inherent right of every free people to change or reform their political institutions, and through conventions of their people withdrawn from the United States and reassumed the attributes of sovereign power delegated to it, have formed a government of their own." Seward knew that any formal acceptance of those credentials was tantamount to recognition of the Confederacy. Instead of rejecting them outright, he delayed, sending hints of conciliatory messages through third parties that some accommodation might be reached. Accused later of a range of misfeasance from duplicity to naivete, Seward was simply trying to allow time for a Unionist reaction in the South. The southern emissaries waited in vain for their reception and returned home empty-handed.[25]

Seward, whose career in domestic politics had been devoted to manufacturing public opinion through speeches, newspaper coverage, voluminous personal correspondence, and in-person visiting, understood that the diplomatic struggle was also a struggle for popular support. When he had traveled abroad before the war, he visited and entertained with the idea of making useful connections. This was a form of social capital that would, after 1861, become essential for the campaign to keep European public opinion on the side of the Union. And it worked. For many among Europe's reformers, the war was waged not against domestic rebels but against slavery. And through the efforts of Seward's many agents in Europe, official and unofficial, the "Union won and the South lost this diplomatic duel."[26]

One reason why Seward was effective was that diplomacy was amenable to relational rights thinking. If nations existed in a community governed by international law, Seward could ask what were the rights and obligations of one member of the community of nations to another? In particular, what rights and duties did a nation engulfed in civil strife have to a neutral nation, and what did the neutral have to the former in the midst of a civil insurrection? This was a question that the secretary of state faced on an everyday basis. While handling critical episodes in the federal government's foreign relations was almost a regular part of those duties, there were manuals and guides to those relationships and duties on "the law of nations." Seward had proven himself a quick study on past occasions and happily added treatises on international law to his reading list.[27]

Settling in as secretary of state was only one of Seward's immediate tasks. He was counsel to Lincoln in the making of wartime domestic policy as well, as correspondence over the precarious status of Fort Sumter in Charleston, South Carolina Harbor demonstrated. On March 11, 1861, the commander of the federal forces, General Winfield Scott, passed to Lincoln Major Robert Anderson's report on the status of Fort Sumter. Anderson did not think he could hold the fort without reinforcements. Should the fort be evacuated? Resupplied? Scott was an old friend of Seward's, far closer to him than to Lincoln;

Seward had campaigned for Scott's presidential hopes in 1852. This may have spurred Seward to press a little harder on the still-new relationship with the president.[28]

Seward replied to Lincoln's request for suggestions on the Sumter issue on March 15, 1861. Lincoln had asked for a response in writing, though Seward was sitting in the old state department building a stone's throw away from the White House. He told Frances that "my duties call me to the White House one, two, or three times a day." It was not distance then, but something else that prompted Seward to reply in the manner he chose. When asked about a legal matter (in effect the legality of secession), he reverted to his lawyerly ways. His letter had the structure of a lawyer's response to a client's request. He urged Lincoln not to provoke the South but to go slowly. "If it were possible to peacefully provision Fort Sumter, of course I should answer, that it would be both unwise and inhuman not to attempt it. But the facts of the case are known to be, that the attempt must be made with the employment of military and marine force, which would provoke combat, and probably initiate a civil war. . . . I would not provoke war in any way *now*." After all, the people of the Confederacy had recently been part of the community he and Lincoln led.[29]

Shortly after the March 15 memo, Seward wrote a fuller and somewhat sterner message to Lincoln. Seward adopted the tone that Greeley had condemned in an open letter, some months earlier, as Seward's judge voice, as if scolding a dilatory counselor for not providing paperwork on time for a case on the docket. Nothing had been done to settle the Sumter question in the two weeks since the first letter. It seemed to Seward that Lincoln's caution had become a paralysis similar to Buchanan's. Dated April 1, 1861, it has been called the "April Fool's letter" and denounced as an attempt by Seward to hector the president.

It was Seward's last effort to assert his view of law against the weight of the position he had assumed in the cabinet, and the loyalty he owed the president and the Union. Judging from the opening of the president's response, written the same day, the two men must have conferred face to face before Seward went off to write. It should thus be seen as Seward's summing up of the position he took when the two men spoke. He labeled it "Some thoughts for the President's consideration," and it began with "We are at the end of a month's administration and yet without a policy either domestic or foreign." The delay in formulating a plan was "not culpable" as "the need to meet applications for patronage have prevented attention to other and more grave matters. . . . But further delay to adopt and prosecute our policies for both domestic and foreign affairs would not only bring scandal on the Administration, but danger upon the country."[30]

In the April 1 letter, Seward hinted that one way to avoid further secessionist movements was to incite hostilities against a foreign nation. The idea made little sense, except in one way. Consider: Did the relational rights thesis have any application outside of slavery? Did it perhaps apply in some way to the secession crisis? What were the relations among the free citizens of the nation that could be restored by some act of the administration? Could these, the mystic chords of memory stretching from battlefield to battlefield be revived by a patriotic war against a common enemy? It was not really feasible, and Seward never revisited it, but it suggested that his thinking was never far removed from relational ties. If the Union were not a federation of states, but, as Lincoln and he believed, a single people, then such a war might rekindle what slavery had smothered. When the schism became real, instead of mere words, that is, when it was played out on the battlefield, Seward's relational rights doctrine played differently. Southerners' war on their own country had to be punished, with violence for violence.

Seward served at Lincoln's pleasure, but as the secretary of state post was the foremost in the cabinet, Lincoln had already shown great deference to Seward's opinions and experience as a lawyer, and Seward reciprocated. Again, the reference in the memo to "not sufficiently explained" suggested that Seward had pitched his argument in person earlier that day. "I am aware that my views are singular and perhaps not sufficiently explained. My system is built on this *idea* as a ruling one, namely that we must *Change the question before the Public from one upon Slavery, or about slavery* for a question upon *Union or Disunion.*" Slavery entailed legal questions, but its legality was well established, and Lincoln had already promised that he would not touch it where state law established it. The Republican Party was opposed to the expansion of slavery, but that was a party stance, not a fully developed legal one. Secession was an act whose legality was at issue, and this was Seward's point. "In other words," he told Lincoln, shift the subject from "what would be regarded as a Party question" to one of the crime of insurrection.[31]

In effect, Seward pressed Lincoln to take a legal rather than a political view of the crisis. Sumter had become a focus of partisan debate because of the "last [Democratic] administration." Instead, drop the Sumter issue and return to the question of the defense of federal property. "I would simultaneously defend and reinforce all the Forts in the Gulf, and have the Navy recalled from foreign stations to be prepared for a blockade. Put the Island of Key West under Martial Law. This will raise distinctly the question of *Union* or *Disunion*. I would maintain every fort and possession in the South." Seward concluded with a broad hint that he, as legal counsel, should take the lead in this shift of policy. "But whatever policy we adopt, there must be an energetic prosecution of it.

For this purpose, it must be somebody's business to pursue and direct it incessantly. Either the President must do it himself and be all the while active in it, or Devolve it on some member of his Cabinet. Once adopted, debates on it must end, and all agree and abide." And then, Seward's characteristic, faux modesty, "It is not in my especial province. But I neither seek to evade nor assume responsibility."[32]

The imposition of martial law was within the legal capacity of a president in time of domestic rebellion, so long as the regular courts of law were not or could not operate. It applied as well to "the very ground" over which an enemy had control or contested with the legal government. It could also be imposed by military commanders on the scene, by the commissioners of military courts, or when a government's courts were held in jeopardy. Traditionally, martial law was a last resort in the United States. State courts were very wary of federal martial law in addition. Seward, a former governor, knew that martial law could only be "temporary and local," and its application to localities nominally at peace in the Union was an extreme extension of the presidential wartime power.[33]

Lincoln's response, written the same day (though the original cannot be found in the Seward papers and Lincoln's may have delivered its contents orally, for that would be his custom in later days), after their meeting and the receipt of Seward's memo, was not a rebuke to an inferior. It was Lincoln jotting down his thoughts, just as Seward's memo was the secretary's thinking. Such exchanges within a legal partnership are common. Seward wrote notes to himself all the time. When later historians read such exchanges among coworkers, they can be mistaken (as this exchange was) as evidence of something more than two men batting about ideas, some of which might be laughable if made public. Neither man saw the exchange in that fashion. Lincoln's repeated and then answered each of Seward's points. "Since parting with you" was a reference to their earlier discussion. "My dear Sir: Since parting with you I have been considering your paper dated this day, and entitled 'Some thoughts for the President's consideration. . . . The first proposition in it is, 1st. We are at the end of a month's administration, and yet without a policy, either domestic or foreign." Rather than consider Seward's point as an insult, Lincoln answered as if it were a "count" in common-law pleading. "At the *beginning* of that month, in the inaugural, I said 'The power confided to me will be used to hold, occupy and possess the property and places belonging to the government, and to collect the duties, and imposts.'"[34]

Lincoln could have simply thanked Seward for his concern, or replied briefly that a policy of patience would pay dividends, or not replied at all. Instead,

Lincoln filled out his thinking from what was probably his silence during their earlier meeting. He was stern but not sharp or curt. "This had your distinct approval at the time; and, taken in connection with the order I immediately gave General Scott, directing him to employ every means in his power to strengthen and hold the forts, comprises the exact domestic policy you now urge, with the single exception, that it does not propose to abandon Fort Sumpter [*sic*]." It was the insufficiency of Seward's argument that Lincoln asserted and the inconsistency that he hinted at. Lincoln obviously found the formal tone necessary to curb Seward's tendency, but now well known to Lincoln, to let his words run ahead of his thinking. Lincoln also objected to the relief or remedy that Seward proposed. "Upon your closing propositions, that 'whatever policy we adopt, there must be an energetic prosecution of it . . .' I remark that if this must be done, I must do it." There was no estrangement between the men, however, merely a legal exchange, polite but firm, and wholly in keeping with both men's professional experience. It did not revolve around politics, but around a common understanding of what was permissible when lawyers disagreed. Lincoln continued, "When a general line of policy is adopted, I apprehend there is no danger of its being changed without good reason, or continuing to be a subject of unnecessary debate; still, upon points arising in its progress, I wish, and suppose I am entitled to have the advice of all the cabinet."[35]

As news of Confederate victories filled the newspapers in the first months of conflict, and prospects for Lincoln's policies and the survival of the Union seemed increasingly uncertain, Seward took the lead in arresting and confining suspected traitors, as well as investigating sympathizers to the Confederate cause. Much of the criticism for the denial of the writ of habeas corpus in these cases fell on Lincoln, but Seward was the member of the cabinet who wrote the orders and directed the program. Individuals who sought to raise funds or supply for the insurrection were obvious targets, along with those who recruited troops for the Confederacy. Less justifiable was the suppression of Democratic newspapers and the arrest of Democratic politicians who criticized Lincoln's call for volunteers, the blockade that Lincoln imposed on the Confederacy, and the suspension of habeas corpus itself. Evidence of such acts could be sketchy, for example in the case of former president Franklin Pierce of New Hampshire. Pierce, a Democrat, supported allowing the Confederacy to depart in peace, but he did not violate any laws in doing so. Nevertheless, Seward never had much use for Pierce and credited rumors about his disloyalty. On this occasion, Seward apologized for investigating the matter. In any case, Seward ordered 64 of the 111 prisoners in Fort Lafayette, New York, confined. Seward was still a legalist, and over the period from July 1861 to February 1862, nearly 70 of those confined were released within a short time.[36]

Some of these cases, in the end totaling nearly eight hundred detentions, made their way into the courts. One involved a former Democratic senator from Iowa, George Jones. Jones, whose political career began on the Michigan frontier and who was an advocate for the expansion of slavery to the Northwest, had served in the House of Representatives and then as the first Iowa senator in Congress. His ten years of service there ended in 1859, when President Buchanan appointed him as minister (the equivalent of an ambassador today) to "New Grenada" (Columbia and Panama). He returned to the United States when Buchanan's term ended, and although he did not offer his services to the Confederacy, he did correspond with Confederate president Davis, a longtime friend. Jones's two sons took commissions as Confederate officers. Seward had ordered Jones detained and imprisoned. After thirty-four days Lincoln ordered Jones freed. Jones, who had met Lincoln and Seward to ask for reimbursement for his ambassadorial expenses just prior to his arrest, later claimed to have been blindsided by Seward.[37]

Jones sued in New York State court in a common law action of false imprisonment. The suit sought "to recover damages for an alleged false imprisonment of the former by order of the latter in November, 1861." The complaint alleged that the defendant (Seward), by himself and others acting under his direction; Without legal process or lawful authority of any name or kind, and without cause, had the plaintiff arrested in the city of New York, and confined in Fort Lafayette for the space of four months." Jones lost in the New York court, and sought to remove the case to the federal court for the Southern District of New York, under the act of Congress passed March 3, 1863, titled "An Act Relating to Habeas Corpus, and Regulating Judicial Proceedings in Certain Cases." Seward replied that he acted as secretary of state under authority from the president during the rebellion. Jones's appeal was denied.[38]

The avidity with which Seward pursued suspected "Copperheads," northern supporters of the Confederate cause, seems at first hard to square with the messages of moderation and reconciliation he had expressed in his January addresses to the Senate. Times had changed since then, but the harshness of his pursuit of enemies was still striking to contemporaries. After all, was that really his job to be the nation's policeman? To trample on the rights of men who had not actually raised rebellion? For Seward, rights lay in the relations among members of the community. Rebels and their comforters not only had opted out of the community of citizens that was the Union, but they also aimed to destroy that community. Had Seward adopted a social contract view of rights, he would have believed that the federal government must be bound in its treatment of Confederate sympathizers by the rights and privileges the Bill of Rights afforded everyone. Had he adhered to the natural rights view that everyone's rights derived from nature and followed them whether they were members of the community or had abjured that membership, he would not have been accused first and exonerated later. A relational rights jurisprudence in peacetime could be tolerant and liberal. In wartime it wore a different face.

Seward recognized the challenge of balancing his role as secretary of state with his longtime advocacy of the rule of law. As he wrote to Adams, while the latter was still in Washington, DC, on April 10, 1861, "It is by no means easy to give you instructions. They must be based on a survey of the condition of the country, and include a statement of the policy of the government." These and later missives had a fussy, almost persnickety quality, as if Seward were treating the younger Adams as one of his sons. After all, Seward had been a close friend of Adams's father. "The insurrectionary movement, though rapid in its progress, is slow in revealing its permanent character. Only outlines of a policy can be drawn which must largely depend on uncertain events." Federalism too complicated the task. "We are not only a nation, but we are States also. All public officers, as well as all citizens, owe not only allegiance to the Union but allegiance also to the States in which they reside."[39]

Domestic politics threw its shadow over the affairs of diplomacy, as loyalty to the administration overshadowed Seward's earlier juristic tolerance of opposition. Dissent must not be tolerated. "It may be stated, perhaps without giving just offence, that the most popular motive in these discontents was an apprehension of designs on the part of the incoming federal administration hostile to the institution of domestic slavery in the States where it is tolerated by the local constitutions and laws. That institution and the class which especially cherishes it are not confined to the States which have revolted, but they exist in the eight other so-called slave States; and these, for that reason, sympathize profoundly with the revolutionary movement."[40]

In one sense, the body of the correspondence was Seward's crowing legal accomplishment. It was text, treatise, discourse, and advice. Adams was by his own account often bewildered and sometimes displeased with the barrage of notes. Coming as they did, he was not in a position to see them as a whole. Seward himself may not have fully recognized his achievement, although he was hardly modest in that regard. In another sense, there was nothing of Seward's pre-1861 liberalism in the correspondence.[41]

In these dispatches, the country lawyer had now become an international lawyer. Sitting on the swivel chair at his desk in the old state department building,

Seward fired off instructions to Adams and the other diplomats in the service of the Union. Although current events dictated their content, pulled together they form a free style extended legal brief defending the administration's conduct of the war. The unique circumstances of Seward's place in the cabinet, including Lincoln's dependence on his secretary of state's diplomatic skills, the anomalous character of the conflict (was Lincoln putting down a domestic insurrection or dealing with a genuine belligerent state), and the uncertainties of British and French responses, made the work itself continuously demanding. A man with less energy could not have kept up.

From the first, Seward's dispatches were eloquent but overwrought. It was almost as if he felt that he had to defend the administration at length to its appointees. That defense was a combination of legal and political. As he wrote to Adams on April 10, 1861, before he had departed for England, "Disunion at the very first took on a specious form, and it afterwards made its way by ingenious and seductive devices. It inculcated that the Union is a purely voluntary connexion, founded on the revocable assent of the several States." This was a version of the theory of relational reciprocity. States, like people, belonged in a community. The sovereignty of individual states depended on membership in that community. The Union was the community, and, arguing the other side, "secession, in the case of great popular discontent, would induce consultation and reconciliation, and so that revolution, instead of being war, is peace, and disunion, instead of being dissolution, is union." Secession destroyed the very idea of communal legality. Perhaps this was a speech he would have made to Congress had he, instead of Lincoln, called it into a special session.[42]

Seward continued with his version of the Confederates' argument. "It being assumed that peaceful separation is in harmony with the Constitution, it was urged as a consequence that coercion would, therefore, be unlawful and tyrannical." For how could a dissolved community force its erring members back into the fold? "This principle was even pushed so far as to make the defensive retaining by the federal government of its position within the limits of the seceding States, or where it might seem to overawe or intimidate them, an act of such forbidden coercion." As an addendum (perhaps realizing how long and far the tangent had taken him from his subject and his actual audience), Seward concluded, "I believe that I have thus presented the disunion movement dispassionately and without misrepresenting its proportions or its character."[43]

In a legal brief, one is expected to recount one's opponents' arguments. By doing this, Seward accorded some legitimacy to the rebels' cause. After all, they had lately been his fellow congressmen. It was as well almost reflex for a lawyer arguing a case. Thus perhaps inadvertently Seward had combined the two roles of lawyer and diplomat. He recovered by telling Adams that this was for his benefit and not for the Court of St. James. "You will not be expected to promulgate this history, or to communicate it to the British government, but you are entitled to the President's views, which I have thus set forth in order to enable you to understand the policy which he proposes to pursue, and to conform your own action to it."[44]

Even the specifics, limned as though Seward had sat down opposite Adams, were legalistic. Why send such a detailed message when Seward could have had Adams drop by the old State Department building? The answer was that Seward wanted to create a record on paper of what he said. This is more evidence of Seward's role in launching the *FRUS*. That is what lawyers did, even when they argued a brief in court. Habits of mind among professions like the law did not disappear when lawyers sat in government.[45]

In the second half of the dispatch, the source of the admonitions changed. At first, Seward had spoken like an oracle of law. In the concluding passages, he was Lincoln's lawyer and not his own. Still, Seward framed Lincoln's views in relational terms. "The President has noticed, as the whole American people have, with much emotion, the expressions of good will and friendship toward the United States, and of concern for their present embarrassments, which have been made on apt occasions by her Majesty and her ministers." The Anglophone nations were a special community, and they had a special bond. "You will make due acknowledgment for these manifestations, but at the same time you will not rely on any mere sympathies or national kindness." For each citation of expected friendship (and the possibility of alliance), there was an equal measure of threat. "If, as the President does not at all apprehend, you shall unhappily find her Majesty's government tolerating the application of the so-called seceding States, or wavering about it, you will not leave them to suppose for a moment that they can grant that application and remain the friends of the United States." Make no promises, no quid pro quo. "You will not be allowed, however, even if you were disposed, as the President is sure you will not be, to rest your opposition to the application of the Confederate States on the ground of any favor this administration, or the party which chiefly called it into existence, proposes to show to Great Britain, or claims that Great Britain ought to show to them." At the same time, maintain a firm but fair demeanor, such as one would in court. "You will indulge in no expressions of harshness or disrespect, or even impatience, concerning the seceding States, their agents, or their people."[46]

Finally, Seward returned to his prior stance as a lawyer briefing a case. He added one more admonition against treating the Confederacy as a member of the community of nation states. "We freely admit that a nation may, and even ought, to recognize a new State which has absolutely and beyond question effected its independence, and permanently established its sovereignty," but that was not the case here. "The disunionists will, I am sure, take no such ground. They will appeal, not to the justice, or to the magnanimity, but to the cupidity and caprice of Great Britain." But Adams must exert himself to the utmost to prevent British official recognition of the sovereignty of the Confederacy.[47]

Seward's primary task as secretary of state was to keep Britain and France out of the fray. He ceaselessly wrote to US emissaries in response to rumors from London, Paris, and elsewhere that neutral governments were preparing to recognize, or at least meet informally, with representatives of the Confederacy. With Adams still en route to England in early May, Seward's instructions mixed warning, caution, and his own uncertainty. He showed a draft to Lincoln, and the president suggested some modifications, in particular toning down the bellicose language. The final draft message of May 21, 1861 spelled out Adams's role: "This Government considers that matters have reached such a crisis in which crisis in Europe in which it is necessary for it to take a decided stand . . . At the same time, it neither means to menace Great Britain nor to wound the susceptibilities of this or any other European nation." Seward had to set a course between the Scylla of bluster and threat and the Charybdis of conciliation. What is more, he had to do it through Adams, an ocean away, and Lord Lyons, the new British emissary, in Washington. Thus, "The paper itself is not to be read or shown to the British Secretary of State nor are any of its positions to be prematurely unnecessarily or indiscreetly made known."[48]

The diplomatic circle in which both men moved was itself a community with its own norms. Seward's advice to Adams encapsulated what the older man believed to be the best practices of this community. "You will keep back nothing when the time arrives . . . being said with dignity propriety and effect, and you will all the while be careful to say nothing that will be incongruous or inconsistent with the views which it contains." This was the essential difference between correspondence within the community of diplomats and legal argument in a court of law. Legal argument was public, and all of it was relevant. Diplomatic papers were guides to diplomats, often containing legal materials but never with the force of law. And they were more often private than transparent. Treaties were an exception to this, but treaties were the result of diplomatic negotiation and nothing in that negotiation was part of the treaty, save what was written and ratified. Thus one may see the diplomacy of the war as a kind of shadow legal process, with correspondence as shadow briefs. The country lawyer's skills were taxed to the utmost with all these qualifications and subtleties, as Seward was fast learning.[49]

Externalities to official correspondence from foreign powers, like debates in parliament or Congress, speeches by national political figures, private correspondence from officials and persons who had access to government, might be noted, but they had no official weight. They were not part of the community discourse. "You will base no proceedings on parliamentary debates farther than to seek explanations when necessary and communicate them to this Department. We intend to have a clear and simple accord of whatever issue may arise between us and Great Britain."[50]

This was especially true for any contact between US diplomats and Confederate representatives in Europe. They, too, were not members of the diplomatic corps. "Intercourse of any kind with the so-called [Confederate] Commissioners is liable to be construed as a recognition of the authority which appointed them. Such intercourse would be none the less wrongful to us, for being called unofficial, and it might be even more injurious, because we should have no means of knowing what points might be resolved by it." Confederate emissaries were not members of any legitimate community. They represented a rebel band. "Unofficial intercourse is useless and meaningless, if it is not expected to ripen into official intercourse and direct recognition." If such recognition were forthcoming, however, the outlaws would become part of a community—the community of nations. Then the Confederacy would have relational rights under international law. That must not be allowed to happen. Were such contacts already taking place? Certainly Democrats in Congress and in private life were reaching out to their former political and legal allies in the Confederacy. The contacts formed a backstairs communications network that reached across the Atlantic. Seward had already arrested some journalists and politicians suspected of this. But "It is left doubtful here whether the proposed unofficial intercourse has yet actually begun. Your own present instructions are deemed explicit enough, and it is hoped that you have not misunderstood them. You will in any event desist from all intercourse whatever, unofficial as well as official with the British Government, so long as it shall continue intercourse of either kind with the domestic enemies of this country, confining yourself simply to a delivery of a copy of this paper to the Secretary of State. After doing this you will communicate with this Department and receive farther directions."[51]

The issue likely to cause the greatest diplomatic vexation at the time was the blockade of Southern ports and coastlines. The legality of this under the law of war would have been unquestionable if the South were an enemy belligerent, but not so clear if the Civil War were regarded as a domestic insurrection. British imports to the South might include arms and ammunition, and Southern exports might include cotton and tobacco. This was the trade that the Confederacy hoped would lead to British recognition of the Confederate States of America. That it must not was one of the purposes of the blockade. "As to the blockade, you will say that by the laws of nature and of nations this government has a right to suppress insurrection. An exclusion of commerce from national ports which have been seized by the insurgents, in the equitable form of blockade, is a proper means to that end."[52]

The legality of the blockade was thus a tricky issue. Britain and other European nations—longtime trading partners with the cotton states—had declared their neutrality, which could mean recognizing the Confederacy as a belligerent, if not a sovereign government. That made the federal government a belligerent rather than a nation castigating rebels. Seward rejected this notion, even though it had come in the form of a royal proclamation from Queen Victoria. One belligerent may blockade another if that blockade is effective (not a paper blockade). It might then bar ships of the other warring party from entering or leaving blockaded ports and bar neutral ships within coastal waters from entering or leaving the blockade. Such rules did not apply in civil insurrections, however. The laws of war only applied to blockades when two nations warred. But the Lincoln administration regarded the Confederacy as a collection of rebelling United States citizens. Hence the problem in dealing with neutral sea powers like Britain, a problem so vexing that the usual graceful prose of Seward faltered. "You will admit[,] not insist[,] that our blockade is not to be respected if it be not maintained by a competent force—but you will add that it is now and it will continue to be so maintained, and therefore we expect it to be respected by Great Britain."[53]

The dispatch of May 21, 1861 featured Seward's assessment of the dangers the Union faced abroad. He warned that "This government considers that our relations in Europe have reached a crisis, in which it is necessary for it to take a decided stand, on which not only its immediate measures, but its ultimate and permanent policy can be determined and defined. At the same time it neither means to menace Great Britain nor to wound the susceptibilities of that or any other European nation." The rest of the message concerned the issue of privateers and the imposition of the blockade. On the former, Seward referred to the convention of 1856, to which Britain subscribed, barring privateering. On the latter, Seward pointedly did not mention earlier occasions of British blockades. Instead, he told Adams, "As to the blockade, you will say that by our own laws and the laws of nature, and the laws of nations, this government has a clear right to suppress insurrection. An exclusion of commerce from national ports which have been seized by insurgents, in the equitable form of blockade, is a proper means to that end." Seward thus sidestepped the question of whether the Civil War was entirely domestic (in which a neutral had no business) or a war between nations (in which international law applied). Earlier versions of the missive were more hard-edged. Fortunately, Lincoln, who had seen it before it was sent, altered some of its text, and Seward, instead of ordering Adams to present it to Lord John Russell of His Majesty's Government, told Adams to regard it as his own guidance.[54]

As Confederate victories mounted, Seward's characteristic sangfroid in the dispatches vanished into a logic-chopping testiness. When the British demanded to be treated as a neutral power in the war between the North and South, Seward snapped to Adams, "We propose, as a nation at peace, to give to Great Britain as a friend what she as a neutral demands of us, a nation at war. We rejoice that it happens so. We are anxious to avoid all causes of misunderstanding with Great Britain; to draw closer, instead of breaking, the existing bonds of amity and friendship." Seward did not want Britain to insist on treatment as a neutral, because that would imply that the Civil War was an international war. When Britain, with respect to a blockade imposed by New Granada on ports in the hands of its insurgents, demanded that the ports be opened, Seward took further umbrage. "The opinion of her Majesty's government, after taking legal advice, is, that it is perfectly competent for the government of a country in a state of tranquility to say which ports shall be open to trade and which shall be closed; but in the event of insurrection or civil war in that country, it is not competent for its government to close the ports that are *de facto* in the hands of the insurgents, as that would be an invasion of international law with regard to blockade." This was unacceptable applied to the US Navy blockade of Southern ports. "The Congress of the United States has by law asserted the right of this government to close the ports in this country which have been seized by the insurgents." Sometimes Seward could barely contain his anger. "The inefficiency of the British laws to prevent violations of our rights is deeply to be regretted. We shall necessarily be obliged to exercise vigilance in detecting the unlawful character and objects of British vessels approaching our coasts." Irony alternated with pedantry, a mode of discourse that would continue through three more years of dispatches, as Seward continued to insist that US participation in the Paris Convention of 1856 on the rights of neutrals required an amendment to protect the personal goods of neutral persons everywhere, and the British refused to accede. The same tenor marked the controversy over the building of Confederate raiders in Britain by private companies.[55]

Seward continued his efforts to prevent southern sympathizers from reaching Britain. "On the 5th instant [of August 1861] I was advised by a telegram from Cincinnati that Robert Mure, of Charleston, was on his way to New York to embark at that port for England, and that he was a bearer of dispatches from the usurping insurrectionary authorities of Richmond to Earl Russell . . . Upon this information I directed the police at New York to detain Mr. Mure and any papers which might be found in his possession until I should give further directions. He was so detained, and he is now in custody at Fort Lafayette, awaiting full disclosures." Mure was a private English citizen and connected to the British diplomatic service by family ties. The letters, after minute examination, did not contain criminal matters, save an attempt to promote the Southern cause. In fact, they had begun with an initiative from Lord Russell to open negotiations with the Confederacy. Lyons had acted quickly to quash the plan, but it had already spun out of control.[56]

Mure's circuitous route to New York City raised Seward's suspicions. The bag he carried raised even more suspicions. It was a dispatch bag from the Charleston British consul to the British foreign office. The latter official, Robert Bunch, was a spymaster, and Mure was his agent. In international law the contents, if correctly marked, were untouchable. Still, "The marks and outward appearance of the bag indicate that its contents are exclusively legitimate communications from the British consul at Charleston to H. B. M.'s government. Nevertheless, I have what seem to be good reasons for supposing that they may be treasonable papers, designed and gotten up to aid parties engaged in arms for the overthrow of this government and the dissolution of the Union." Seward sent the dispatch bag to Adams, with instructions to give it to Lord Russell, and Mure, who had long been in the sights of Seward's agents, was indeed part of an espionage plot. When Lord Lyons objected to the detention of British subjects like Mure (and others), Seward's response alternated between forced civility and high dudgeon. That, too, would continue throughout the correspondence among the British and US diplomats. Mure was released on October 17, 1861, on parole, after promising not to visit any of the Confederate states.[57]

On November 16, 1861, Seward learned that former US senators James Mason and John Slidell, sent by Confederate secretary of state Robert M. T. Hunter to convince Britain and France to aid the Confederate cause, had been captured at sea by US Navy captain Charles Wilkes and were on board the US Navy vessel *San Jacinto*. Seward knew both men from their common service in the Senate, was aware of the two men's mission, and expected that they would travel on a confederate warship or blockade runner. As it happened, they were aboard the British mail vessel *Trent*. The British had anticipated something of this, but they learned of the event, as did Adams and Seward, without warning. For three weeks after the information of the interception at sea, without instructions from Seward, Adams remained "a passive and impotent spectator." Pressed by Lord Russell, Adams could only profess ignorance of the matter, though his silence suggested that the seizure was not at the instruction of Seward, Welles, or anyone in Washington.[58]

Hearing the same reports, Republican newspapers burst with delight. The *New York Times* expected every good citizen to start quoting from international law authorities like Hugo Grotius, Samuel von Pufendorf, Emmerich Vattel, and Henry Wheaton to prove the legitimacy of the catch. A British observer wryly noted that everyone in Boston seemed to be walking about with a copy of Henry Wheaton's *Elements of International Law*. Seward's son Frederick wrote from his father's side to his mother, back in Auburn, that "the whole community and the press have done little else but discuss diplomacy and the precedent of internal law."[59]

Wheaton, the third reporter for the US Supreme Court, was a familiar figure in Washington, DC, during his tenure at the court, and served as US ambassador to Denmark and then to Prussia after his service to the court ended in 1827. He passed away in 1848, the Reports and his *Elements of International Law* (1836) a lasting monument to his influence. Six editions of the latter work were published before 1861, the last two with corrections and additions made by Wheaton. As the first compendium of international law written in English, its influence was widespread in the Anglophone world.[60]

Wheaton defined sovereignty at the outset, for international law was the law of nations, not the law of internal affairs. Internal sovereignty rested on the power of rulers and laws; external sovereignty was independence from foreign powers. Beyond these general precepts lay a myriad of particulars. The bottom line of sovereignty was not just recognition by other states, but the ability of a state to remain independent of other states. If, however, a state, having declared its independence, wished to enter into the community of nations, those nations had to recognize its existence. In line with this was his general assumption that international law lacked the finality of positive law (as nations had little power to compel obedience on other nations, save by conquest), but instead represented reasonable rules to ensure fair play among nations, even those at war. It was a descriptive treatise, not a prescriptive one (unlike some of its predecessors), but included concepts like reciprocity that, although based on pragmatic considerations (like violate reciprocity and expect consequence) that came close to moralizing.[61]

Civil wars did not extinguish the sovereignty of a state, although belligerents might seek aid from outside forces. The war and its impediments might interrupt the normal relations between a sovereign state and other states. The other states would be expected to continue to observe the rules of international law, or they could take a side in the Civil War, and thus become the enemy of one side or the other. The rights of neutrals and the rights of enemies in these cases diverged. If a foreign state professed neutrality, it would be bound, along with the sovereign state experiencing civil insurrection, to obey the laws regarding neutrality. During a civil war, sovereign states had the absolute right of self-preservation, and this not only applied to their internal affairs, but to their conduct with respect to foreign powers. Absolute rules on these matters, unfortunately, were impossible to lay down, no more than to impose.[62]

For Seward, the federal diplomatic corps, and by implication, the Confederacy, the key issues revolved about the rights of neutrals. Were Britain, France, and the other European powers really neutral, or did they covertly aid the rebellion? For Davis and his diplomats, the goal was recognition from Britain and France and, failing that, material assistance in the war effort from Britain and France. The first question in the case of the Confederate emissaries taken from the *Trent* was whether they had immunity from prosecution as traitors or some other offense under federal law. If they were accorded diplomatic status by Britain and France, they had immunity wherever they might be apprehended. But prior emissaries from the Confederacy were not given diplomatic status by Britain and France, so this issue was moot at best.[63]

In past years, particularly during the French Revolutionary and Napoleonic Wars, Great Britain had disregarded the neutrality of the US in regard to its ships on the high seas and its shipping in ports that Britain was blockading. In theory, no state should exercise its rights to the detriment of other state's rights, a version of John Stuart Mill's utilitarianism that Wheaton did not cite, but again, "non-interference" was a general rule to which there were always going to be exceptions. The great exception was a "necessity" whose conditions nations were free to define as they saw fit.[64]

The distinction between coastal waters and international waters was another of the subjects that the blockade raised for neutrals. A nation could claim sovereignty over waters within a certain distance from its shores. The old definition was a cannon shot from shore, along with the waters about all ports, bays, and promontories. The technical ability to measure the precise distance at sea did not yet exist. In this sense, a blockade was legal. But blockades raised special questions, and Wheaton gave them special attention.[65]

The basic principle was that neutrals could not trade with a foreign power across a legal blockade. They could not do it as a public act, and they could not do it in a private capacity. But this last species of trade was one of those borderline issues that the British had crisscrossed over and over, depending on whether they were neutral or were themselves at war. Making this complication even more complicated, the interdiction of neutral trade or private aid to a belligerent depended on an actual state of war between two powers, and the Lincoln administration never declared war on the Confederacy. To make such a declaration would be to treat the Confederacy as a sovereign power rather than a temporary alliance of civil insurrectionists. Instead, the blockade rested on the right of a country to defend itself against internal enemies. Residence in a neutral country would not protect a merchant or other business against reprisal from his own country. Property coming from an enemy's plantation, exported by its owner, living abroad, was subject to capture, even if carried on a neutral ship. Property taken or retaken in this way had to be condemned as contraband by a "competent authority." But each nation had its own rules and precedents for this, and was "exclusive of the judicial authority" of any other nation. This "foreclosed the question of the validity of the capture."[66]

The rights of neutrals in these situations were established by conventions, by treaties, and by international reciprocity. A belligerent could not wage war in the territory or the waters belonging to a neutral power, for example capturing a vessel of an enemy, but the rights of neutrals in the territory and waters of a belligerent were complex. Wheaton had more trouble finding binding principles in this section of the book than any other. For example, what was to be done with the pursuit of a hostile vessel into neutral waters? The rule he proposed was that voluntary entrance into neutral waters in pursuit of a hostile ship was forbidden, but counterexamples were abundant. The neutral state was, correspondingly, required to return to the original owners any property taken in such cases.[67]

Seward had Wheaton's work by his side the entire time that he dealt with the *Trent* affair. In light of what he assumed would be Britain's willingness to meet with Confederate representatives, would Britain also allow the construction of Confederate raiders? Its neutrality merely meant that Britain would not give military aid to the Confederacy, although private shipbuilders and merchants were not barred from continuing to trade with the South. Thus the diplomatic relationship that November was touch and go. Although the Confederacy had no direct line of communication with the British government (ironically, that was to be Mason and Slidell's task), English newspapers regarded the affair as a "gift" to the seceding states. After all, was Captain Wilkes's stopping and boarding the *Trent* to seize the two men and search for their documents not an act of war against a neutral power?[68]

The taking of the Confederate diplomats from the *Trent* while the ship was in international waters, and the incarceration of the two men in Boston harbor fortress, was clearly a violation of international law. But what had the Constitution to do with international law? Was the US government bound by the precepts of the law of war? In subsequent years, the United States was the only major maritime nation to refuse to sign the Hague Convention and the Paris Declaration on neutral shipping rights, protesting that the conventions did not protect neutrals traveling on enemy ships. The practical question was how to assuage British feelings, but the British had no wish to go to war so soon after the debacle of the Crimean War, and after much personal effort among US and British ministers on both sides of the Atlantic, further formal animosity was averted, although preparations for war on the British side continued into the next year.[69]

Lincoln wanted to keep the two emissaries and prepared a draft response to the British that would have involved arbitration. He did not know that delay in response would lead, according to Lyons's instructions from the Palmerston government, to the departure of the British legation from Washington and, perhaps, a war at sea. Members of his cabinet agreed with Lincoln, although Bates and Welles favored some sort of return of the two captives. Public opinion, roused by the Republican press, was hawkish. The British were reported to be equally roused, and Palmerston's government was doing little to quell it. Although the Queen wanted peace, peace hovered over the abyss. Seward knew better and took Lincoln's draft, politely, apart. The key on the US side was Seward's note to ambassador Lyons, a less than masterful piece of international lawyering according to Charles Francis Adams, Hamilton Fish, and other contemporaries. The foremost modern biographer of Seward, who happens to be an international lawyer, disagreed. He thought Seward had acted and written brilliantly, and here he had changed the course of history.[70]

Seward called on all his resources, intellectual and political, to compose a suitable reply to Lyons. His labors showed how far the country lawyer had come along a steep learning curve. He "closed his door" (which was usually open to all manner of visitors) and worked through the day and night of December 20, 1861. He worried, "If I decide this case in favor of my own Government (i.e. by keeping the two men in custody) I must disavow its most cherish principles (of neutral rights on the open seas). If I maintain those principle . . . I must surrender the case itself (i.e. allow the two Confederate emissaries to depart)." He chose the latter course. He mollified Lincoln, quieted dissent in the cabinet, and did due diligence with Wilkes, the newspaper reports, the messages from England, and various international law authorities. He muted the passions of the day, satisfied the British, and still maintained US honor and maritime law.[71]

Seward's response to Lyons, composed as it was away from the looming shadow of Lincoln, was an echo of this former relational legalism. It sought a middle course, an enlightened course, a peaceful course, as though England and the United States were members of the same Anglophone community. The essence of his December 26, 1861, message was that Wilkes had acted alone, without instructions, and without the foreknowledge of Seward, Lincoln, or Welles. The men and the officers of the *San Jacinto* had behaved civilly, without undue force. Wilkes had proceeded in "a simple legal" fashion against a "neutral vessel carrying contraband of war" for the use of a belligerent. The problem was that the Confederacy was not really a belligerent, it was a collective of insurrectionists, but that matter would be settled later. Wilkes had made one mistake, which was crucial to the diplomatic solution Seward proposed. Seward had adapted the skills of the country lawyer as mediator to give a legalist cast to the case, and so save both the nation's honor and Britain's.[72]

According to international law at the time, Wilkes was supposed to carry the *Trent* to a neutral port and have its cargo and credentials investigated. Instead, he had done the merciful act of allowing the ship, its papers, and its cargo to proceed. Thus the evidence of a violation of British neutrality was never produced. As a result, the United States had to do what it always had (as a neutral power itself) insisted "all nations ought to do to us." The last bit, resting the entire matter on US practice, was suggested to Seward by Ambassador Adams in a December 3 missive. Adams pointed to Secretary of State James Madison's 1804 instructions to ambassador James Monroe—demand protection of US shipping's neutral rights. Seward credited the suggestion: "I was really defending and maintaining not an exclusively British interest, but an old, honored, and cherished American cause, not upon British authorities but upon principles that constitute a large portion of the distinctive" US policy. The fact that it was the British whose ships of war violated US neutral rights in the years prior to the War of 1812, was a nice point that Lord Russell would have immediately noted.[73]

Seward arranged for the swift and secret departure of the two Confederate diplomats. They proceeded to England and France, where their presence made little difference. They were not officially received. Seward celebrated the peaceful resolution of the *Trent* Affair in a dispatch to Adams. "The American people could not have been united in a war which, being waged to maintain Captain Wilkes's act of force, would have practically been a voluntary war against Great Britain. At the same time it would have been a war in 1861 against Great Britain for a cause directly the opposite of the cause for which we waged war against the same power in 1812." Nevertheless, British support for the Confederate war effort, clandestine but accurately reported to Seward, went on apace. The Palmerston government insisted that it had no control over the private firms producing the Confederate raiders, even though the crews of the raiders were largely recruited from the British Isles. The movement of troops to Canada continued, and the Canadian government was not able or willing to prevent Confederate irregulars from raiding settlements in New York and Vermont. Thus relations with Britain continued to roil US diplomacy, and Seward's output of instructions to Charles Francis Adams regarding these matters expanded to fill volumes.[74]

Seward was never quite sure of Britain's support, but his relations with Lyons were cordial, and when common ground revealed itself, the two men could move in lockstep. In England, Lord Russell and Charles Francis Adams had established, if not a warm relationship, a working one. The Atlantic slave trade was already prohibited by a variety of treaties among the Atlantic world nations, and the Royal Navy was actively policing the treaty by the end of the 1830s. Here British and Lincoln administration interests coincided, and an agreement to suppress the overseas slave trade further isolated the slave South from European aid. Thus it was relatively easy for Lyons, Seward, and their respective governments to conclude, and on April 25, 1862, ratify when has come to be called the Lyons-Seward Treaty. Lincoln was pleased, and the Senate, remarkably (given some of its number opposed to any form of abolition) unanimously ratified the treaty. The treaty had three courts whose benches included British and US judges to hear and determine cases of slavers seized and searched at sea. The courts sat in New York City, Sierra Leone, and the Cape of Good Hope (the latter two sites were then under the control of the British Empire). There was no appeal from the judgment of the courts. Although the US naval squadron assigned to the treaty enforcement had little success, the Royal Navy ships almost entirely shut down the illicit slave trade between Cuba and the Confederacy.[75]

Still, the shadow game of British private citizens' covert support for the Confederacy continued. In the late spring of 1863, the British government seized the Confederate-commissioned brig *Alexandra*. Built of reinforced oak to withstand conventional cannon fire, the ship was procured surreptitiously by agents of the Confederacy from the same shipyard that built the *Alabama* and *Florida* raiders. The British government brought a trial case against the ship and, in effect, prevented it from sailing until near the war's end. Adams, who had labored mightily to gain this end, was pleased, and Seward was delighted. When the papers surrounding this case were presented to Congress, at the end of 1863, both men celebrated.[76]

In the meantime, Republican members of Congress surged ahead of the Lincoln administration, and Seward, in planning for the end of slavery. It was long on Seward's to-do list. Yet here, with the opportunity to take the lead in the antislavery crusade, he hesitated. He was the country's ablest counsel in this time of crisis. The country lawyer had become the lawyer for the country. But not for all his countrymen.

CHAPTER 6

"To the Arbitrament of Courts of Law and to the Councils of Legislation"

Hesitant Emancipator

Wrapped up as he was with keeping the European powers from aiding the Confederacy, Seward did not pay as much attention to the domestic slavery question as did Lincoln. This was something of a reversal of the two men's interests during the 1850s. The evils of slavery were the central focus of Seward's assault on the Democratic Party and his relational rights arguments through the 1840s and 1850s. Lincoln was not nearly as concerned with slavery until the mid-1850s. But what to do about slavery would become one of the central concerns of the northern war effort. How would Seward's jurisprudence relational rights measure up to the challenge of ending that "peculiar institution"?[1]

Perhaps the answer is simple: Lincoln now led, and Seward followed. Lincoln knew that the border states, all slaveholding regions, loyalty was vital to the suppression of the insurrection. Both men knew that the loyalty of the border states, slave states of Delaware, New Jersey, Kentucky, Maryland, Missouri, Tennessee, and Virginia, along with the southerner-populated portions of Indiana, Ohio, and Illinois, was essential if the Union was to survive. Directly attacking slavery risked alienating those states, some of which were already teetering on joining the Confederacy. Thus any move against slavery must be tied to the war effort. That would include striking at slavery in the Confederacy and giving sanctuary to slaves who fled from Confederate states. But it would not include, at least at first, any declaration that slavery was to end. For Seward, this would mean that emancipationist impulses must bow to wartime realities. Lincoln's need to restore the Union limited what Seward could do or say to fulfill the implicit promise of relational rights with respect to slaves.[2]

What then of this clear and present test of Seward's relational rights jurisprudence? Jurisprudence is the study of the laws. Seward often wrote and spoke about good law and bad law in the context of slavery. But he was not a consistent or a deep thinker on the abstract nature of law. Modern critics have held this against him. As William Gienapp concluded, "In spite of his obvious influence, Seward never comprehended fully the power of his words. Basically a conciliator, he overestimated his ability to mitigate in private the intensity of his public remarks, and he failed to foresee the impact that some of his speeches would have on his public image." Had Seward merely blustered about the illegitimacy of slavery to aid and abet the cause of his political future? Had he not been prepared to follow his own jurisprudential logic?[3]

Surely this hard judgment seemed to apply to his treatment of the Democrats' defense of slavery. In 1860, Seward had accused slavery and the Democrats of demoralizing the nation and causing talk of disunion. But Seward had never demanded emancipation of the slaves. Relational rights forbade secession but did not require forced abolition. Here Seward disagreed with the Gerritt Smith school of abolitionism. Because slavery was part—albeit a despised part—of long-standing relationships of free persons within the nation, the remedy lay within the discretion of the slave owner.

In that furious campaign year of 1860 Seward had fumed, "I care not what reckless men say in the heat of debate, or under the influence of interest, passion or prejudice, that it is a matter of indifference whether slavery shall pervade the whole land . . . that freedom and slavery may take their chances." For Seward it was plain that "every man demands freedom for himself . . . I know this national idea is just and right." Could not the noble sentiment of freedom prevail over the base motive of greed? Reread the Senate speeches; the campaign speeches, the invited orations, and slavery appears in almost all of them as an evil that must and will be terminated—in time. That was before secession; before the war came; surely the fires of war would consume slavery.[4]

Seward's ideal of law, a law that better men could employ to better the world based on the relations among men in a community, had been easy to apply to the distant project of universal emancipation when addressing a friendly audience on the eve of the 1860 election. Seward did not find it so easy to propose the same solution to slavery's evils when the war came. On April 1, 1861, in the exchange of memos with Lincoln, recall that Seward suggested, "I am aware that my views are singular and perhaps not sufficiently explained. My system is built on this *idea* as a ruling one, namely that we must *Change the question before the Public from one upon Slavery, or about slavery* for a question upon *Union or Disunion.*" In a message to William L. Dayton, the new ambassador to France, dated April 22, 1861, Seward's new caution, or was it reticence, on slavery was obvious. "I refrain from any observation whatever regarding the morality or immorality the economy or waste, the social or unsocial aspects of slavery." Secession was an attempted "revolution" (the word he had suggested to Lincoln to replace treason in the draft inaugural address) but when it was suppressed, Seward expected that slavery would remain where it already existed. Seward reminded Dayton that both men acted "at the instructions of the president." After all, but a month and a half earlier, Lincoln had promised that his administration would not touch slavery where it already existed. That policy was still alive when Seward wrote to Charles Francis Adams on February 22, 1862. A Union victory would leave a party opposed to slavery in control of the federal government, but "slavery in the slaveholding states would be left in the care of the people in those states," those people being white and free—and some of them former slave owners.[5]

As late as the end of 1862, Seward still did not grasp the full ramifications of the Emancipation Proclamation. It was a wartime step, dictated by wartime needs, but it fundamentally changed legal relationships surrounding slavery. Whether he opposed the Proclamation's promulgation or simply wanted to delay it remains a contested issue among scholars, but to Adams on November 30, 1862, Seward incorrectly summarized it. "The President's message grasps the subject of slavery earnestly and confidently. It would be unbecoming, even if it were possible, to predict the reception which his bold suggestion of gradual and compensated emancipation will meet." In it, the president had not proposed gradual and compensated emancipation. Freeing of the slaves in portions of the Confederacy still in rebellion as of January 1, 1863 was absolute and permanent. According to the Proclamation, slaves of rebels would not be returned to their bondage at the end of the war, nor would slaveholders in those regions be compensated. If Lincoln had, in past years, supported gradual and compensated emancipation, that time had passed. Seward, always something of a compromiser on this point, never quite accusing his Southern senatorial counterparts in language like Charles Sumner's or Thaddeus Stevens's (Seward attacked the Democratic Party, not its southern members by name) had nevertheless been far ahead of Lincoln on the manumission question. But both the president and his secretary of state regarded the slavery and emancipation questions in the context of winning the war and preserving the Union, rather than on the grounds that the abolitionists pressed.

Perhaps in 1862 Seward simply assumed that a victory over the Confederacy would doom slavery without the need for federal emancipation?[6]

In the meantime, momentum in Congress for an amendment to the Constitution barring slavery was building. At first, Seward kept out of the way. The congressional debate over the fate of slavery when the war ended commenced in earnest in February 1864 and continued for another year. Republicans agreed that the Constitution must be amended to accomplish this goal. In March, Illinois senator Lyman Trumbull reported out of the judiciary committee the language that would be the basis for the next year's debate: that "neither slavery nor involuntary servitude, except as a punishment for a crime whereof the party shall have been duly convicted, shall exist within the United States, or any place subject to their jurisdiction." The one echo of the "old Constitution" doctrine of strong states' rights was the plural possessive, "their" rather than the collective, national "its"—for the United States. A second section did what the Republicans had hesitated to do when the session of Congress began: "Congress shall have the power to enforce this article by appropriate legislation."[7]

Waged in the presidential election year of 1864, with the outcome of the war no longer in doubt but its end still not in sight, perhaps the need to keep Lincoln in office and a Republican majority in Congress seemed more important to Seward than close legal argument about slavery? Intraparty rivalries, personal factions, and cross-aisle differences all seemed to come to a head in the year-long debate over the amendment. Seward, waiting at Lincoln's side, did not yet employ his office or his experience to aid in what, given his earlier views of slavery, should have been a natural step. He watched as Congress debated the end of the peculiar institution.[8]

At the same time, Lincoln did not have a formal role in the proposal for ending slavery once and for all, but his thinking was evolving in parallel with the movement for the end of slavery. He no longer considered colonization as a corollary of emancipation, for example. Nevertheless, he had not yet thought through the legal requirements of equality for the freedmen. Seward might have helped Lincoln think through the problems associated with emancipation, but he too was focused on the support of the border (slave) states in the conflict, and beyond that, the prospect of millions of armed white Southerners rejoining the Union. Neither Lincoln nor Seward were ready to tackle those questions. Thus, while Lincoln referred to a nation "conceived in Liberty, and dedicated to the proposition that all men are created equal," and closed with "a new birth of freedom" in his November 19, 1863 "Gettysburg Address," he did not mention an end to slavery with victory over the Confederacy. Despite the later widespread myth that Lincoln dashed off the address during the train ride down from Washington, DC, he prepared major speeches in advance, and this was no exception.[9]

The night before Lincoln's address, after Seward and Lincoln had traveled to Gettysburg on November 18, a crowd gathered at the boarding house where Lincoln was staying. They wanted a speech. He declined. They moved next to the house where Seward was staying, and he obliged them, much as he had when they came to his door in Auburn. He arranged for his remarks to be published in newspapers, so he had to have prepared them previously. "I said forty years ago that slavery was opening before this people a grave-yard that was to be filled with brothers." Slavery would destroy community, and with it all the relationships of a free people. Now that had come to pass. "I knew that the cause that was hurrying this Union into this dreadful strife was slavery," but no one listened. As often as he raised his voice in warning, it was ignored or shouted down. But now it was heard. "I thank God for the hope that when that cause is removed, simply by the operation of abolishing it, we shall be one country." How would slavery be ended? "I believe this strife is going to end in the removal of that evil which should have been removed by deliberate councils and peaceful means." He repeated that "we shall therefore be united, only one country, having one hope, one ambition, and one destiny." Note how he linked the end of slavery (without mentioning it) to the goal of restoring a national community. Only when that unity returned could relational rights govern racial relations.[10]

But Seward had not said how slavery would end, much less that freedmen would have all the rights and privileges of their white neighbors. In the Senate Seward had never hesitated to speak on issues involving the expansion of slavery or the impact of the slave power on national policy. He had always favored persuasion and gradualism. Patently, that had not worked. With Seward silent on the means by which slavery was to end, it was James F. Wilson of Iowa who opened the debate on the abolition of slavery. Born in Ohio, and a defender of civil rights before there was a civil rights movement, Wilson entered the House of Representatives in 1861 and remained there until 1869, serving as the chair of the House Judiciary Committee during Reconstruction. He returned to Congress in 1883, as a senator from Iowa and served for two terms.[11]

On March 19, 1864, Wilson offered his thoughts on a thirteenth amendment to the Constitution on the floor of the lower house. The reader is struck by how similar the claims in it are to Seward's "irrepressible conflict" speeches. Wilson proposed that slavery be forever prohibited in the United States, except as punishment for a crime, and that Congress have the authority to pass legislation to enforce the amendment. He conceded "that a proposition in the Congress of the United States to so amend the Constitution of the Republic as to weaken or destroy slavery is a novel thing. . . . It was long the custom in this body whenever slavery became excited and angry, to try to appease its wrath by offering it some new hold on the life of the nation." Wilson was no doubt referring to the gag rule barring the acceptance of antislavery petitions in the House of Representatives from 1835 to 1844 and in the Senate from 1836 to 1850. The result, he thought, was that slavery enslaved the nation "and a most cruel task-master it proved. Its political career was an incessant, unrelenting, aggressive warfare upon the principles of the Government, the objects for which the Constitution was ordained." Slavery "defiled everything." Seward had already said as much.[12]

But Wilson faced the same conundrum that Seward had—the framers had allowed slavery to flourish. "This issue is no reflection on the wise and good men who laid the firm foundations and fashioned the sublime architecture of our Constitution." Like Seward in past days, Wilson theorized that the framers simply had no idea of the corrupting influence of slavery on the republic. The proof of this invincible ignorance was secession itself. "It is impossible to believe that the master workmen who gave to us this best of human Governments, in the least degree suspected that they were transmitting with it the seeds of dissolution." The framers had built into the Constitution the means for the protection of republican liberty. The Amending Clause "is the safety-valve of the Constitution, so constructed and guarded as to prevent hasty and inconsiderate action, and utterly destructive of every pretense for forcible revolution." This was a backhanded comment on the Confederacy's refusal to wait for an amendment protecting slavery in their rush to secession, although in the secession winter of 1861 Wilson would hardly have supported such an amendment himself. Like Seward, Wilson found the key to unlocking the puzzle in the Preamble to the Constitution, each of whose parts Wilson applied to emancipation. "The last, the grandest, the most sublime of the objects declared by the people in the ordination of the Constitution is, 'to secure the blessings of liberty to ourselves and our posterity.'"[13]

In the Senate, where Republicans had a far larger majority of seats than the Democrats (none of the twenty-two seats of the Confederate states were filled), the idea of an amendment was gaining strength during 1864. Republican Lyman Trumbull of Illinois had taken part in Lincoln's deliberations on emancipation, and he was the first to raise the question again. But Trumbull, "highly skilled" in the courtroom and facile with the law and "cold and calculating" in his role as chair of the judiciary committee, was a moderate, and he too seemed to regard the amendment as a way to ensure that the "slave power" would never regain its former strength in the Congress. (The amendment would change the basis for representation, ending the two-thirds rule. What was more, if given the right to vote, former slaves were not likely to elect their former masters.) Henry Wilson of Massachusetts made a similar speech, talking for so long that the galleries emptied.[14]

The next impetus for the amendment came from an unexpected source—Senator Reverdy Johnson of Maryland. Seward and Johnson had been co-counsel for clients. They had also opposed one another in court. Johnson was one of the foremost lawyers in the nation, much sought after for complex cases. He had represented John Sandford in *Dred Scott* and had won for his client. He supported the war effort, and in the Senate was a leader of the Union Democrats. On April 5, 1864, he gave a long and detailed speech in favor of an amendment. For a lawyer/politician from a slave state to reject the states' rights position on slavery was something of a body blow to his party. The newspapers reported that his speech was booed by fellow Democrats. Republicans flocked across the aisle to shake his hand.[15]

Johnson was not an ideologue of any stripe. A former Whig, like Seward, his was as distinguished a legal pedigree as the nation offered—his father, the attorney general of Maryland, and his legal colleagues William Pinkney, Luther Martin, and the young Roger Taney. Johnson would briefly serve as US attorney general. His approach to political issues was akin to his approach to legal cases. He was a conservative thinker. In *Dred Scott*, according to opposing counsel (George Ticknor Curtis, Justice Benjamin Curtis's brother), Johnson offered "a forcible presentation of the southern view of our Constitution . . . I believe that he held those opinions with entire sincerity." "Our constitution" meant the "old Constitution" that Lincoln and Alexander Stephens lauded in the year before secession, the Constitution of limited federal powers and strong states' rights. Johnson was not apologetic in his advocacy of the amendment, and saw it as a necessary next step after the war. His advocacy did not ignore the concerns that defenders of slavery had raised about relations between the two races, but he concluded that the war had changed the legal status of slavery. "To manumit at once nearly four millions of slaves, who have been such by hereditary descent during their lives, and who because they were such, it being one consequence of their condition, have been kept in a state of almost absolute ignorance, is an event of which the world's history furnishes no parallel. Whether it will be attended by weal or by woe, the future must decide. That it will not be followed by unmixed good or by unmixed evil, is perhaps certain." In light of how divisive slavery had been, and race relations would remain after victory, general emancipation was simply a matter of right, whatever its consequences. One notes that Johnson did what Lincoln did in his Cooper Union

Address of 1860, Seward had done in 1858, and Wilson did a few months earlier: use history to claim that the framers expected slavery to end. There was nothing of reciprocity in his remarks—no idea that former slaves' membership in the community required more than ending their bondage.[16]

Johnson was convinced that slavery had an expiration date, and the war had hastened that date. He recalled that in 1847 he had listened as John C. Calhoun told the Senate "that republican freedom could not exist without African slavery, and proclaimed his attachment to the Union and to the Constitution upon the ground," an opinion he opposed then and now. He disagreed with those who claimed that Congress could end slavery by legislation, as Ashby had proposed, or that the president could end it by fiat (Johnson still opposed the Emancipation Proclamation), or that (as in the dissents in *Dred Scott*) the courts could end it—but that was the precise reason that he wanted Congress to pass the amendment. Fending off questions about the status of slaves if the war had ended before the amendment was in place with as fine an oral argument as was ever presented before the Court, a precisely legal argument, he managed to support the amendment without recanting any of his earlier views. The clincher was a powerful counterargument: "But even if [permanent emancipation] could be done by either [Congress or the president] as far as the slaves in the rebellious States are concerned, it would fall far short of the object which in common with a large majority of the Senate, and, as I believe, of the country, I have at heart; for can either the executive or Congress under the war power emancipate the slaves in the loyal States?"[17]

A careful reading of Wilson, Trumbull, and Johnson fails to reveal anything quite like Seward's relational rights. If slaves were to be freed, were they thus full members of the postwar community? Did they have, or could they expect, all the rights and immunities, along with all the duties and obligations, of all other members of the community? Were they full citizens, or only citizens by courtesy of their former masters' treason? For if one were to base emancipation on relational rights, the answers to all these questions might be quite different from the narrow, contractual justification that the three senators provided for freedom. Amending the Constitution to bar slavery did not address any of the questions of the reciprocity due to newly admitted members of the national community—the key question for Reconstruction.

Johnson did not have this dilemma. His was the old attachment to states' rights. For the federal government to interfere with the sovereignty of states still in the Union by pressing the amendment on the states would violate the basic tenets of federalism. In a remarkable volte-face, Johnson brushed away this strong version of states' rights doctrine and the old Constitution. "To a limited extent the States are sovereign . . . but if [these opponents mean] to contend that the United States are not also in the same sense and to another extent equally sovereign, [they are] mistaken." To say "the only true sovereignty was that which belongs to the States . . . in my judgement, there never was a greater political heresy." The Constitution rested on "we the people," not we the states (in fact on Gouverneur Morris's rewriting of the Preamble's original draft in the Committee on Style and Arrangement, but no matter). Calhoun's version of states' rights was put on death watch, ironically, by his South Carolina successors when they seceded.[18]

Note that like Seward, Johnson admonished the Confederacy, but unlike Seward did not excoriate the slaveholder or, except for a few passing remarks, argue that slavery itself was an abomination. To do so would have accused, by implication at least, some of his fellow congressmen who presently owned slaves. To complete the Constitution's promise of inclusion they needed to understand and accept why slavery must be abolished. Then they and their former bondsmen and women would share the benefits of citizenship.[19]

Were it characterized in this fashion, Seward should have been in the front rank of those calling for the amendment, but Johnson did not follow Seward's prewar line of argument. Instead, he fell back on the far less radical Lincoln-Seward wartime position that the end of slavery would appropriately punish secession. "The conspirators who are now almost exclusively governing the South, or to speak more accurately, tyrannizing over the South, have for more than thirty years been plotting and anxiously looking to the accomplishment of the treason, the destruction of the Union." And his target was the ideology that underwrote slavery. "The moral and religious mind of the country has become nauseated by the teaching that scripture authorizes and approves slavery, and sanctions its perpetual existence, and that it authorizes such slavery as exists in the Southern States, and does it because its victims are not of the same color of their masters!" Slaves wanted freedom. "How do they prove that in that particular we differ from the black man? Do we not see that he is willing to incur every personal danger, which promises, if successfully met, to throw down his shackles and to make him stand upon God's earth, upon that earth created for all, as a man and not as a slave." Johnson's speech was prescient. On April 6, a day after the news reports of Johnson's speech sped out from Washington on the telegraph lines, news came to the Senate that Maryland voted to end slavery in a revised state constitution.[20]

With the amendment movement gaining traction, the next step should have been consideration of the extent and nature of the civil rights of future freedmen and women. Here the idea of reciprocal relationships could have played a central role—for once slaves were citizens, they should ideally have all the rights and privileges, along with all the duties and obligations, of all other citizens. Enforcement of those rights and privileges would have fallen to Congress. The Thirteenth Amendment was the first of the amendments to include a formal enforcement clause: "Congress shall have power to enforce this article by appropriate legislation." Did that clause mean that the amendment added civil rights legislation to the enumerated powers of Congress? Even if the second clause of the amendment provided for congressional legislation on civil rights, what were those rights? Were they absolute? In whose hands would the elaboration of those rights lie—the federal government (and Congress) or the state governments? Would the putative end of slavery by amendment rather than ordinary Congressional legislation imply that Congress did not think it had the constitutional authority to impose on the states equal treatment of freedmen and women? If the status in law of the men and women freed by ratification of the amendment were left in the hands of the states, would various states have different regimes, just as they had different views on slavery and freedom before the war? Strong abolitionists assumed that equality under the laws would follow freedom, indeed was a natural concomitant of freedom. Twice they voted down Kentucky senator Garrett Davis's motion to bar all Blacks from voting and holding office. On April 8, the Senate passed the draft of the amendment reported out by the judiciary committee. According to newspapers, the galleries of the chamber were packed with spectators, including many women. The final draft was largely the work of Trumbull. Charles Sumner had tried to add language as a preamble that "all persons are equal before the law," but the committee did not choose to follow his proposal. Instead, the proposed amendment read, "Section 1. Neither slavery nor involuntary servitude, except as a punishment for crime whereof the party shall have been duly convicted, shall exist within the United States, or any place subject to their jurisdiction. Section 2. Congress shall have power to enforce this article by appropriate legislation."[21]

In the meantime, Seward was assailed by the radical wing of the Republican Party for being too conciliatory toward the rebels and for not pressing for complete emancipation. On the other side of the political spectrum, Unionist Democrats demanded that he be booted out of the cabinet for fomenting bad relations with foreign powers and meddling in military affairs. In the cabinet, Chase and Welles intrigued against him. In the Senate, Sumner (whose cause Seward had championed in 1856 after the Brooks affair) lobbied Lincoln to drop Seward. Seward offered Lincoln his resignation, but the president declined. Seward was indispensable.[22]

Seward repaid Lincoln's loyalty on the hustings. As he told voters on September 3, 1864, "The Union men in all the slave States that we have delivered are even more anxious than we are to abolish slavery. Witness Western Virginia, Maryland, Missouri, Louisiana, Tennessee, and Arkansas." Indeed, all of these states had or would soon end slavery on their own, and slaves had liberated themselves in these states, and with the exception of Maryland, state legislatures had not ended slavery. It was only the Emancipation Proclamation, limited to areas in rebellion, that freed slaves from their Confederate masters.

> Although altogether unauthorized to speak for the President upon hypothetical questions, I think I can give an answer upon the subject of slavery at the present day—an answer which will be explicit, and I hope not altogether unsatisfactory. While the Rebels continue to wage war against the Government of the United States, the military measures affecting slavery, which have been adopted from the necessity to bring the war to a speedy and successful end, will be continued, except so far as practical experience shall show that they can be modified advantageously, with a view to the same end. When the insurgents shall have disbanded their armies, and laid down their arms, the war will instantly cease, and all the war measures then existing, including those which affect slavery, will cease also; and all the moral, economic, and political questions, as well questions affecting slavery as others, which shall then be existing between individuals and States and the Federal Government, whether they arose before the civil war began or whether they grew out of it, will, by force of the Constitution, pass over to the arbitrament of courts of law and to the councils of legislation.[23]

By invoking "courts of law and councils of legislation," Seward was not abandoning the freedmen to the animus of their former masters in the former confederate states. Instead, he was trying to recover something of the relational rights argument from the ruins of the devastated South. For he realized that the fate of the former slaves would, whatever program of reconstruction followed victory, be left to their former masters. Law—from courts and in statutes—must build the bonds of reciprocal duties among free men. Imposing equality from without would not work unless whites wanted it to work. Good law would incorporate the freedmen and women into full membership in the reconstructed states. Bad law would impose a new regime of discriminatory regulations. What Seward did not realize or credit was the thoroughgoing racialist animus of the defeated foe. It was not slavery that drove them; that is, they were not motivated by the attempt to reinstitute slavery, so much as they were motivated by deep-seated racial prejudices. The former Confederates were simply not able or willing to regard Blacks in their midst as members of their communities. Seward should have surmised all this, for he had traveled in the South and knew the minds of its white leaders. Seward did not mention to the voters what they undoubtedly already knew: An amendment to the Constitution outlawing chattel slavery had already been introduced in Congress. Lincoln favored it, but did not campaign for it, again because slave states remained in the Union, and victory in the 1864 presidential campaign was still uncertain. Seward and Lincoln both worried that Congress could not end slavery; the Proclamation was merely a wartime order by a commander in chief regarding confiscated property. Hence a bill proposing reconstruction based on the end of slavery simply could not be signed. Lincoln pocket vetoed it in July 1864.[24]

In early September 1864, with news of the taking of Atlanta, Georgia, and the fall of Mobile Bay, Seward, always optimistic, was triumphal. "You receive the Executive Government in a condition very different and highly improved." He told New York State's voters. "We found it practically expelled from the whole country south of the Delaware, the Ohio, and the Missouri, with the most of the army and navy betrayed or fallen into the Hands of insurgents, and a new and treasonable Confederacy. . . . We cheerfully give the Government back to you, with large and conquering armies and a triumphant navy, with the hateful Confederacy falling into pieces, and the rebellious States, one after another, returning to their allegiance."[25]

There followed the miniature legal brief which had become the essence of his writing and speeches. Lawyering was so deeply engrained that it bled through everything he did. It was in some ways simplistic, as if he were presenting the summary of a case to the jury. Here they were, the voters of upstate New York. The centerpiece was relational rights talk, but not the rights of the future freedmen. The question was what to do with the rebels. "They rejected Lincoln and set up a usurper. The Executive power of the United States is now, therefore, by force, practically suspended, between the usurper Jefferson Davis and that constitutional President, Abraham Lincoln. The war is waged by the usurper to expel that constitutional President from the Capital, which, in some sort, is constantly held in siege, and to conquer the States which loyally adhere to him. The war is maintained on our side to suppress the usurper, and to bring the insurgent States back under the authority of the constitutional President."[26]

Seward then offered proof—evidence—of the treasonable designs of the Democratic Party in the North, not just to offer the presidency to their own candidate, but to negotiate away the war gains and allow the Union to fall into ruin. Actually, the evidence for the motives of the opposing party was surmise and suspicion, but the manner of presentation was again legalist. Let me prove, Seward offered. "They are not content with plotting sedition in secret places, but they go up and down the public streets uttering treason, vainly seeking to provoke arrests in order that they may complain of a denial of the liberty of speech. The impunity they everywhere enjoy under the protection of constitutional debate shows at one and the same time that their complaints are groundless and that the Union in the element of moral stability is stronger than they know." The supporters of the Confederacy had cast themselves out of the community by violating all of its fundamental rules. They must not be allowed to win the election.[27]

When Seward referred to courts and legislative solution to the fate of the former slaves in the South, and the fate of former rebels and their abettors in the North, he implied that those courts and legislatures would act like New York's, a foolish and naive assumption as events proved. One also notes that Seward did not stress the antislavery stance of the administration nor press for a relational-rights doctrine of emancipation. There were extenuating circumstances, however. First and foremost, New York was a hotbed of Democratic support. Not all were Copperheads (antiwar), but the governor, Horatio Seymour, commanded strong support among voters. He was a Union Democrat and supported the war effort, but repeatedly criticized Lincoln's (and Seward's) policies of suppression of dissent and for the Emancipation Proclamation. The legislature was Republican, and both US senators were Republicans, but New York City, traditionally Democratic, was a potential source of Democratic votes for General George B. McClellan, Lincoln's opponent.[28]

With the outcome of the hotly contested presidential campaign still in doubt, on September 4, 1864, the Senate Republicans passed what was to become the Fourteenth Amendment. Once party and president began to move the rock up the mountain, Seward not only joined in the effort, he became something of its cheerleader. He worked behind the scenes, organizing among former Whigs, corporate backers, and New York friends into what historians La Wanda and John Cox called the Seward "lobby." Opponents decried Seward's methods as underhanded and even corrupt, But all through December he worked to ensure that New York's congressional delegation voted for the Amendment.[29]

Why had Seward moved from hesitancy to full speed ahead? He was not driven by attachment to his arguments; he was not an ideologue. The one man with whom Seward was in step was Lincoln. Although Lincoln's December 6, 1864 annual message to Congress did not lead with the proposed amendment; his view of it was clear. At the end of his address, in a single longish paragraph, he treated the amendment as if its passage was a foregone conclusion. He was factual but did not rehearse the facts in an argumentative way. Perhaps he knew that Congress was as tired as he was and had spent a year debating the amendment. "At the last session of Congress a proposed amendment of the Constitution abolishing slavery throughout the United States passed the Senate, but failed for lack of the requisite two-thirds vote in the House of Representatives. Although the present is the same Congress and nearly the same members, and without questioning the wisdom or patriotism of those who stood in opposition, I venture to recommend the reconsideration and passage of the measure at the present session."[30]

Lincoln's Fourth Annual Message to Congress was written with the assistance of Seward. In it, the two men showed how far they had come. It began with recognition of Seward's contribution to Lincoln's presidency. "The condition of our foreign affairs is reasonably satisfactory." The entire first third of the message documented the nation's foreign relations. The next third recounted expenditures and income. Lincoln then passed to a project that touched on Seward's other interest—the recreation of the ties that bound the people of the two regions into one. "Important movements have also occurred during the year to the effect of molding society for durability in the Union. Although short of complete success, it is much in the fight direction that 12,000 citizens in each of the States of Arkansas and Louisiana have organized loyal State governments, with free constitutions, and are earnestly struggling to maintain and administer them. The movements in the same direction, more extensive though less definite, in Missouri, Kentucky, and Tennessee should not be overlooked."[31]

Finally, Lincoln offered something on the proposed constitutional amendment. "At the last session of Congress a proposed amendment of the Constitution abolishing slavery throughout the United States passed the Senate, but failed for lack of the requisite two-thirds vote in the House of Representatives. Although the present is the same Congress and nearly the same members, and without questioning the wisdom or patriotism of those who stood in opposition, I venture to recommend the reconsideration and passage of the measure at the present session." Lincoln (here, Seward's voice is almost discernable) suggested that such a great change must rest on a relational basis—it could not be imposed from above. "In a great national crisis like ours unanimity of action among those seeking a common end is very desirable—almost indispensable. And yet no approach to such unanimity is attainable unless some deference shall be paid to the will of the majority simply because it is the will of the majority. In this case the common end is the maintenance of the Union, and among the means to secure that end such will, through the election, is most dearly declared in favor of such constitutional amendment."[32]

The message ended with Lincoln's offer of pardon and clemency. For acts that were clearly treasonous under federal law, all who commanded the war against Union troops could have been tried and convicted for a capital offense. Instead, Lincoln reported,

> A year ago general pardon and amnesty, upon specified terms, were offered to all except certain designated classes, and it was at the same time made known that the excepted classes were still within contemplation of special clemency. During the year many availed themselves of the general provision, and many more would, only that the signs of bad faith in some led to such precautionary measures as rendered the practical process less easy and certain. During the same time also special pardons have been granted to individuals of the excepted classes, and no voluntary application has been denied. Thus practically the door has been for a full year open to all except such as were not in condition to make free choice; that is, such as were in custody or under constraint. It is still so open to all.

That was a wartime measure to reduce the support the Confederacy had among its own. But something of the generosity owed to Seward, whose views of the importance of reestablishing membership in the national community were now so close to Lincoln's that the two were inseparable. On the same day, Lincoln submitted the name of Salmon P. Chase to the Senate for the now vacant post of chief justice of the Supreme Court. The Senate confirmed the nomination at once, unanimously. Chase was the most persistent of the antislavery voices in the cabinet, and the nomination was a valedictory of sorts for the abolitionist movement.[33]

Lincoln had the last word on this project of final freedom in his second inaugural address on March 4, 1865. What he did not say was as important as what he did say. At the start of the war, "One-eighth of the whole population were colored slaves, not distributed generally over the Union, but localized in the southern part of it. These slaves constituted a peculiar and powerful interest. All knew that this interest was somehow the cause of the war. To strengthen, perpetuate, and extend this interest was the object for which the insurgents would rend the Union even by war, while the Government claimed no right to do more than to restrict the territorial enlargement of it." An able summary of the difference of political opinion in 1860, this was also a statement that confirmed the legality of slavery where it already existed. The war changed everything. "Neither party expected for the war the magnitude or the duration which it has already attained. Neither anticipated that the cause of the conflict might cease with or even before the conflict itself should cease." Slavery was an offense against G-d and man. "If we shall suppose that American slavery is one of those offenses which, in the providence of God, must needs come, but which, having continued through His appointed time, He now wills to remove, and that He gives to both North and South this terrible war as the woe due to those by whom the offense came, shall we discern therein any departure from those divine attributes which the believers in a living God always ascribe to Him?" But if G-d judged, Lincoln would not. "It may seem strange that any men should dare to ask a just God's assistance in wringing their bread from the sweat of other men's faces, but let us judge not, that we be not judged." Lincoln was plainly looking ahead to some kind of reconstruction based on the reconciliation of whites in the North and whites in the South—"A just and lasting peace among ourselves."[34]

The old Congress met again in December 1864. Its successor, with a strong Republican majority in the lower house after the election of 1864, would assemble briefly in March 1865 and then not again until the end of 1865. Thus the two-thirds needed for passage of the Thirteenth Amendment in the House was still not certain. The next month's debates in the House were not without drama, but added little substance to the legal arguments. Democrats opposed to the amendment cited it as evidence of a plan to destroy the sovereignty of the states and prevent genuine reunion. A few members played the racist card—the amendment would lead to the eventuality of Black equality, plunging the nation into the depths of miscegenation. Even without this claim, a legalized racism was a central theme of the Democratic opposition to the amendment. Legalized racism rejected any claim that free or freed people of color had to have equality before the law. Republicans replied by lauding the heroism of the Black Union soldiers, but except for a few genuine radicals like Charles Sumner, stopped short of promising civil rights for the freedmen. Democrats still insisted that the amendment would be an unconstitutional enlargement of the powers of government. Republicans replied that state legislatures would have the final say, conforming to the original intent of the framers. Seward worked overtime to keep radicals, moderates, and conservatives in the party pulling together. Even more important was his effort to placate or suborn the aid of New York Democrats. Lincoln interceded personally, a moment captured in Steven Spielberg's prize-winning movie *Lincoln* (2012). The time had come to end the national nightmare of chattel slavery. The House passed the amendment on January 31, 1865, by a vote of 119 to 56, followed by cheering from the gallery and in the streets of the Capital.[35]

Seward should have been cheering with them. After all, the Thirteenth Amendment exemplified his liberal jurisprudence—progressive change toward greater equality through law. As to its object, well, Seward had lambasted the slaveholders as an un-American aristocracy. They had upset the founders' project of emancipation over and over again by their avarice and immorality. Slavery "was never established rightfully anywhere." It had subverted the meaning of the Constitution. To slay this monster the Republican Party had arisen. It had guided the nation through its greatest trial. And then the war came, and the reknitting of the Union suddenly became more important than the end of slavery—or at least the end of slavery had to be fashioned to promote the wartime aims of the government. But now that war was over. Peace had come. Was all that fustian no more than party politics? Or was Seward's loyalty to Lincoln, and to the partition of duties—Lincoln the domestic and political, Seward the diplomatic—so compelling that Seward simply bowed to Lincoln's primacy. And Lincoln was not entirely forthright in his support for the end of slavery, much less for the rights of the freedman after emancipation, until he won reelection.[36]

On February 22, 1866, at the Cooper Institute in New York, Seward made his last full public statement on the treatment of the freedmen and women. In response to the invitation, he pled his own exhaustion for reasons discussed in the next chapter, but could not refuse to give the Washington birthday address where Lincoln had spoken six years earlier. He was sanguine. "The union—that is to say the nation—has been rescued from its perils." The greater portion of the job was done. What remained was not nearly as important as what he and Lincoln's administration had achieved. The rest was "merely a difference of opinion" about the restoration of full relations between the former confederates and their countrymen. Questions like these were always "worthy of deliberate examination and consideration." He did not subscribe to the radical Republican agenda. Race relations must be worked out within communities of people who lived and worked together, not imposed by Congress. Slavery was gone, without compensation; secession was gone, without recrimination. He did not add that none of the leaders of the rebellion suffered the pains of traitors, although Jefferson Davis had not yet been restored to his freedom. "I apprehend no serious difficulty or calamity" from the controversy between the president [Andrew Johnson] and the majority of Congress. Loyal men from the now loyal states stood and waited while Congress passed law after law, and imposed "burden after burden" on them. When they were admitted to Congress, the job of restoration would be "complete." The issue then outstanding, over the Freedmen's Bureau, renewed by Congress, vetoed by Lincoln's successor, Johnson, was "unimportant."[37]

What then of the relation between free men's law and the law of slavery? Seward had not abandoned his attachment to relational rights, but his focus had shifted. In a choice between enforcing the rights of the newly freed on their former masters and reintegrating the former Confederates into the Union family, he chose the latter. The freedmen were not left in the cold, however. Instead, as he had argued in his September 1864 address, they could rely on the same institutions that protected the relational rights among the already free—the courts and the legislatures. How could he not have seen how newly reincorporated state legislatures had imposed "black codes" on former slaves, forcing them into convict labor? How could he have missed the malign results of presidential Reconstruction under President Johnson? He did not, and privately favored the Civil Rights Act, but forced in his own mind to choose, he chose to support the rights of white men rather than Black men.

He was not quite done with slavery. One of Seward's tasks as secretary of state was to send the Thirteenth Amendment to the states for ratification. Three-fourths of them had to ratify, and one of the conditions of readmission to full participation in the political life of the Union for the seceding states was the ratification of the new amendment. When Georgia ratified the amendment on December 6, 1865, the federal constitution officially barred slavery and involuntary servitude (except for punishment of crimes). Again, as secretary of state, Seward received the ratifications from state legislatures and announced that the amendment was part of the Constitution. He would do the same for the Fourteenth.

CHAPTER 7

"The Union Has Been Rescued from All Its Perils"

Elder Statesman

On February 3, 1865, Seward and Lincoln attended a peace conference with Confederate emissaries on the steamer *River Queen* off Hampton Roads, Virginia. It ended inconclusively except for an accord on prisoner of war exchanges. Seward's role in it, as in the talks with southern emissaries nearly four years earlier, was unclear. Had he hinted that the Confederate states could reenter the Union without ratifying the Thirteenth Amendment? Exactly what had he promised? Still, further victories over Robert E. Lee's troops made Lincoln's Inauguration on March 4 a success. Then came misfortunes, not in single spies but in battalions. On April 5, Seward fell from his carriage and suffered serious injuries to his arm and shoulder. Nine days later, Lincoln was shot by John Wilkes Booth and died the next day. On the same night of April 14, part of the plot against Lincoln and his cabinet, former Confederate soldier Lewis Powell attacked the bed-ridden Seward with a knife and nearly killed him. Seward and the nation never quite recovered from these events.[1]

Seward's face and neck bore the scars of Powell's Bowie knife, though a neck brace worn as a result of the carriage accident saved the secretary's life. His sons Frederick and Augustus, a soldier nurse, and a state department messenger were also injured, Frederick so seriously that his death was feared for a time. William recovered slowly. Another blow was struck on June 21, when his wife Frances died after a long struggle with many ailments, possibly from a stroke. A year and a half later his beloved daughter Fanny died, at age twenty-one. His long convalescence and her own tuberculosis had done for her what general ill health and travel had done for her mother. The mounting sorrows changed his personality and dampened his abilities for a time. He lost the dynamism that had been his hallmark, though he did return to work full time at the end of July.[2]

A lesser man would have retired, and Seward had even thought about it on the eve of Lincoln's second inauguration, but Seward had become so close to Lincoln, meeting in formal and informal settings, telling stories, framing policy, correcting and emending one another's texts, that a symbiotic relationship had developed. When Lincoln was assassinated and Seward nearly killed, that relationship gained a new and even stronger almost spiritual bond. A part of Lincoln adhered to Seward so deeply and profoundly that Seward saw himself as carrying on Lincoln's program even though Lincoln's successor, Vice President Andrew Johnson of Tennessee, bore little resemblance to his predecessor. It was also true that Seward had urged Johnson on Lincoln when Vice President Hannibal Hamlin's radical abolitionism became unpalatable to the new Union party Seward helped build for Lincoln's reelection.[3]

Through his recuperation during the spring and summer of 1865, Seward's saw his wounds as the country's wounds, and his slow recovery he likened to the slow but inevitable reknitting of the nation. If Washington D.C. observers noted how the "wear and tear" of public service was visible on his features, he rejoined "Time alone is necessary to heal our wounds." He told one visitor to his bedside, "These southern people will come back in peace, and in obedience." Some did, but more did not, a future that Seward could have foretold but could not have prevented. For Seward had more than a little to do with Lincoln's Amnesty message of 1863–1864. Its relative leniency to the rank and file Confederates was even closer to Seward's thinking than Lincoln's. The peace and pardon plan was Seward's idea—the requirement that returning Confederates surrender their slave property and the end of slavery once and for all was Lincoln's idea. Seward's decision to remain in the cabinet, and his increasingly strained efforts to conciliate all parties as the breach widened between Republicans and Democrats during the first years of Reconstruction made him a controversial figure. As in the early days of the war, calls for his firing came from all sides. Johnson refused to let him go. Thus Seward's role in Johnson's Reconstruction plans was not an aberration at all, though it brought down the wrath of the radical republicans on both men.[4]

Like Lincoln, Johnson left foreign affairs to Seward. The most immediate diplomatic issue after Johnson took office was the continuing French adventure in Mexico. In 1862, France, along with Great Britain and Spain, had occupied Mexican Gulf ports to demand repayment of loans made to the Juarez government in Mexico. Britain and Spain were repaid with customs duties, but France claimed a much larger debt, and when Mexico could not pay, sent troops to occupy the interior. In 1863, Napoleon III arranged for Prince Maximilian of Austria to rule as Emperor in Mexico City, and France's intervention became a full-scale war. After France withdrew its troops in 1866, US neutrality turned to covert and then open support of Mexico's Republican government. But comparing the volume and tenor of Seward's Civil War correspondence with the US emissary in France, John Bigelow, with the correspondence in 1866 and 1867 on the French-Mexican War one hardly sees the same Seward. True, Seward had "kept himself informed," but had not urged US intervention beyond invoking the Monroe Doctrine (secretary of state John Quincy Adams's warning Europe that the Western Hemisphere was a US sphere of influence). Seward pressured the French to withdraw, but his "drumming his fingers" waiting for them to leave and his "pin-pricks" when they delayed, did not affect their plans.[5]

In 1867, the French completed their troop withdrawal, leaving Maximilian with only his Austrian and Belgian forces. They were defeated, and he was captured and executed by Juarez in early 1867. The republic was restored. It was a quirky episode in French imperialism, but it absorbed Seward at a time when he needed to be needed. Unlike his involvement with other foreign ventures before and during the war, however, his part in the French-Mexican affair was comparatively slight.

Seward's major achievement and most famous legacy in the realm of foreign affairs during the Johnson administration was the purchase of Alaska from Russia. One should see this achievement in context—Seward did not believe in conquering territories, building empire by the sword. He preferred negotiation and then integration of the new territories into a larger and more diverse community. Students of Seward's diplomacy may not always agree on his motives, but his methods were clearly demonstrative of relational rights: the community of commerce and improvement would be tied together by mutual treaties framed through negotiation, every party understanding and accepting what the other parties wanted.[6]

Russia had supported the Union war effort at the same time as Russian officials worried that settlers, fishermen, and miners from Washington would overwhelm Russian outposts in what would later be called the Alaska Territory. Seward's expansionist plans for the area were well known to the Russians, for Seward had proposed something like the purchase as early as 1850, on the Senate floor. At the same time, expansion then was the source of potential evils. For if "we all know the advantage of expansion," he told an audience of Republicans in 1860, "they are augmented wealth and population." But there were dangers. "What then is the danger that attends expansion?" Expansion "increases the strains upon the bonds of Union." In 1860 this was the possibility that new territories would add to the representation of the slave states. Had not Chief Justice Roger Taney's opinion in *Dred Scott* hinted that slave owners could take their chattel property anywhere in the territories? But that was no longer a problem in 1867. The strain was of a different sort—the sort that the framers of the federal Constitution faced in the 1788 ratification debates. Where did ultimate legal authority rest for expansion? Could a federal republic spread over a vast territory survive sectional and political factions? During the ratification debates the Federalists promoted the idea of dual sovereignty—that the new federal government and the existing states each retained their sovereign governmental powers, save for those functions necessarily ceded to the federal government. That constitutional solution was tested and survived secession and Civil War. Seward was confident it would survive further expansion.[7]

In the winter of 1866–1867, the plan for the purchase of Alaska firmed, as Seward reached out to the tsar of Russia with an offer. After a short period of secret negotiations, primarily on the price (7 million dollars), a draft treaty was presented to the cabinet. Johnson's initial hesitancy had vanished, a draft was polished on the night of March 29 at Seward's house, and only then was Charles Sumner, head of the Senate's foreign affairs committee, shown the document. The price edged up to 7.2 million, and Seward and Russian ambassador Baron Stoeckl signed the treaty the next day. The Senate, called into special session on April 1, after some criticism of Seward by the Republican radicals, ratified the document on April 9, 1867. The exchange of ratifications took place on June 20, 1867. A transfer of title followed on October 18, 1867.

Russia still had not been paid when the lower house decided to impeach Johnson on February 24, 1868. When Seward stood by the president, even arranging to find funding for his legal defense in the Senate, the House decided to embarrass Seward. Funding for the treaty was not passed until July 14, 1868, with Massachusetts' Nathaniel Banks, Seward's old ally, leading the charge. Seward's lobbying efforts were ineffectual, though he enlisted Weed and others in the project, until Banks intervened. If past dealings were precedent, there should have been volumes of correspondence, meetings, gatherings, lobbying, and intrigues but again there was comparatively little. Public support for the purchase was generally favorable, although Seward's former ally, now bitter opponent Horace Greeley called the purchase "folly" in his *New York Tribune*. There were the usual conspiracy theories about payments to certain government officials. Apparently Stoeckl had pocketed a significant portion of the payment for his "expenses."[8]

The acquisition of Alaska was something of a last hurrah for Seward. He lacked the energy (though not the ambition) to negotiate the acquisition of additional foreign territories. He compiled a list of the claims against Britain arising from Confederate sea raiders' destruction of Union merchants' property, but they went unpaid until three years after he left office. The gregarious and garrulous talker was still there, but the subjects were more disjointed, and the purpose behind them harder to read. As Charles Francis Adams wrote to his father on June 29, 1867, Seward "speaks and thinks slowly, repeats himself, gets wound up and doesn't seem to have a clear idea what he is after." The unplanned addresses to visiting admirers were shorter; the planned addresses and speeches were less frequent; and with Frances gone, the letters to friends and children were shorter.[9]

Where once Seward would go on for hours, now he replied to delegations at his door with simple thanks. For example, when he was back in Auburn briefly visiting at the end of July 1864, news came of General William Sherman's entry into Atlanta. Typically, a crowd gathered at Seward's house and asked him to speak. "He then spoke at some length" on the military and political significance of Sherman's victory. By contrast, asked to comment at Cooper Institute late in February 1866, on the conflict between President Johnson and the Republicans in Congress, he offered short, banal remarks on the good intentions of both sides, a reminder that "the Union has been rescued from all its perils" and closed with a vignette of folksy but unclear application worthy of Lincoln. When he accompanied President Johnson on the "swing around the circle," a whistle-stop campaign trip between August 27 and September 15, 1866, Seward only spoke "briefly." A year later, when the two men visited Chapel Hill, North Carolina, Seward again spoke for a short time. Compare this to his lengthy campaign speeches in the 1840s, 50s, and as late as 1864. Then, he was always "aware" of his audience. In later speeches, he wandered, sometimes losing touch with his auditory.[10]

Seward disagreed with important parts of Johnson's domestic program, including his resistance to the Freedman's Bureau and the Civil Rights Act, but he did not abandon the president when the president was impeached. He even raised money for Johnson's legal counsel. When he returned to Auburn in October 1868 to cast his vote in the presidential election, Seward gave a short talk before friends. They naturally expected the Republican to explain why he had stood by a Democratic incumbent through thick and thin. "It is not my purpose to vindicate, or even to explain, the part I myself have had in these transactions and debates. I simply say that, as I stood firmly by the wise and magnanimous policy of President Lincoln in his life, so I have adhered to the same policy since his mortal remains were committed to an untimely grave, and I have adhered with equal fidelity to his constitutional successor." He still served when Ulysses S. Grant was elected president in 1868 but retired with the rest of Johnson's cabinet shortly thereafter.[11]

A superficial optimism was still part of his public demeanor, but now it seemed a reflex. There was also a profound sadness, a recognition that, as the country opened its second century, "we shall be passing away." Some of this weltschmerz must be attributed to his declining physical powers, though he told well-wishers that he was exercising regularly. He was still restless, and still traveled, to Cuba, Mexico, and Alaska, but instead of passages of wonder, the travel was a flight from reality and, more so, from the shadow of death that surrounded him. There was no law practice to return to, and unwilling to stay in Auburn for long, in the same house with his son William and daughter-in-law (as he had long ago with his father-in-law), he resumed his travels, first across the country, then around the world. He traveled on the railroads that he had helped fund, and made use of the inventions whose patent rights he helped protect. Along the way he assembled a coterie of young people to replace the ones he had lost, even adopting one as his child, but nothing really replaced Frances and Fanny.[12]

Perhaps Seward had lived too long? Suffering from a variety of debilitating ailments; barely able to take care of his basic needs; losing the train of his thought so often that he forgot that train's destination were the rewards of surviving beyond the three score and ten years vouchsafed to the righteous. Seward had lived in comfortable surroundings, but he had been sick with a variety of ailments and mishaps. He certainly understood loss, though it was not uncommon for men of his generation to bury their children. Lincoln, too, had suffered the early death of loved ones, including his children Edward and William. Tuberculosis had taken Seward's beloved Fanny. It was still the "white plague." Cholera, dysentery, diphtheria, typhoid fever, and pertussis were still killers of children. While black plague and smallpox were no longer endemic, they had not disappeared. Cornelia had died at one year from smallpox. Those of us who have lived long enough may remember the polio summers of the early 1950s, a time when every parent feared for every child's life in in the United States, and in 2020–2022 the COVID-19 pandemic.

If retirement was a physical necessity, Seward nevertheless remained aware of national politics. On the eve of the 1868 election, he spent days closeted writing and revising a campaign speech. He came out for Grant and the Republican Party. He could not trust the Democrats to follow Lincoln's lead in Reconstruction. The long apologia was published, but his spoken remarks, as was now his custom, were brief. Again in 1872, he took an active interest in the national election and wrote a brief letter, for publication, supporting Grant. Seward did not live to see the election results, an occasion which, in years past, had absorbed so much of his attention.[13]

In the last half-year of his life, he undertook two literary projects. The first would have fulfilled the promise he had made to Frances at the end of his gubernatorial incumbency of a treatise on American politics and law. As he left the governor's office in Albany in the winter of 1842–1843, gathering up and arranging his papers, Seward wrote to Frances about a plan, "To supply myself with occupation of a higher order than the practice of the law, for such spare time as I may find, I think I can employ myself in writing a commentary upon American government, politics, and law, which would be a work not unworthy of the considerate [of the topic] I have acquired." He had then begun gathering bits and pieces of this commentary on law—and politics—delivered over the past thirty years.[14]

Thus it is not surprising, though disappointing, that given a chance to bring the bits and pieces of his pre-war thinking together, the autobiography of 1871 offered not a critique of democracy's failings or a prescription for better laws but an uncritical account of American progress. "The colonies easily passed from the state of constitutional resistance to that of self-assertion and independence." There was war, and it could not be ignored, but "throughout the Revolutionary War the struggle of the new nation was conducted and managed by a party more bold and liberal than its conservative opponents." The revolutionaries had anticipated Seward's own goals of unity and reform, and their victory "brought the people to a unanimous acceptance of the principles of independence, liberty and equality." Who could write something like this when slavery and the oppression of Native peoples not only survived the war, but in some places were strengthened by it? Or when loyalists lost everything for simply honoring sacred oaths to crown and law? Seward had earlier in the work recognized the evils of slavery and Indian removal. Had he forgotten his earlier words?[15]

In 1871, when he returned from his world travels, Seward saw courts and legislatures in the former Confederacy performing as he had hoped they would at the end of the war. The "black codes" by which all-white legislatures reenslaved black workers under presidential reconstruction were gone. Replacing them were white and black legislatures working under new constitutions that appeared to guarantee a lot more than mere freedom—education, jobs, and political participation. Civil rights acts passed in Congress gave aggrieved former slaves access to federal courts. Perhaps, Seward must have thought, he had been right all along. Enable federal protection of the rights of former slaves and, over time, they would take their place in the community alongside whites. These achievements depended on the strength of the Republican Party in the South and the promise of prosperity—both of which would fail after Seward died.[16]

Echoes of the relational rights doctrine reappeared in his account of the framers' efforts; "that constitutional ordination would best preserve, perpetuate, and transmit to posterity the great boon which had been secured." In other words, republican law and constitutions would protect the legacy of the Revolution. But what to say about the persistence of the stigma, if not the chains, of slavery? Again, Seward offered a palliative: Many wanted the states to retain the full measure of their newly won sovereignty, and the personal liberty that they had from the "burdens of government." The better answer the founders discovered was a federal union. "Earnest, enlightened, and energetic men, however, early uncovered that a stronger, firmer, and more controlling national constitution would be necessary to preserve internal peace and harmony." Thus began the struggle over states' rights versus the federal government. Both sides were armed with legal skills. The advocates of the former were none the less revolutionaries, and during the turbulent 1790s regained popular sympathy that the Federalists had wasted with the Alien and Sedition Acts. Who was the more progressive element? The War of 1812 resolved the question in favor of the Republicans, the party that Seward joined as a young man. But over time, the Jeffersonian Republicans became the traditionalists, and in 1824, Seward "spoke for the new movement," whose leader was John Quincy Adams.[17]

Had Seward finished this portion of the autobiography, it might have explained how the law worked, or did not work, or might have worked, in a democratic republic. It might have provided a fuller version of a relational rights jurisprudence that Seward in earlier years had pieced together in speeches and letters, or at least placed that ideal of law in context. But Seward did not finish the autobiography. He might have tried to expand on earlier formulations of relational rights when he discussed Native Peoples in Alaska. Post–Civil War expansion of land and resources law to Plains Indians had been a fig leaf to cover appropriation of Indian lands and subsoil resources; but Seward was not responsible for that. He was responsible for the fate of Native people in Alaska as they were incorporated into the larger American community. In a speech he gave at Sitka, on August 12, 1869, he commended the native peoples of all lands, "I have seen all around me persons enjoying robust and exuberant health. Manhood of every race and condition everywhere exhibits activity and energy." The land above and the earth below begged for exploitation;

riches that would improve life for everyone. This was the booster Seward of upstate New York in the 1820s and 1830s. Of the Native Peoples, he worried that "savage communities" required space and time to develop into more productive societies, again applying the rubric of his native New York. He did not, as some modern critics (who want to erase his contributions and remove his statues) call the Native Peoples savage. He merely engaged in the sort of underdeveloped social anthropology of the day. Thus he did not condemn Russians for the massacre of Native Peoples, but he blamed Native Peoples for warring on one another. Relational rights were nowhere in sight.[18]

Instead of finishing the autobiography, he turned to a travel account, including occasional thoughts on various subjects. This was his "table talk," an example, like his autobiography, of another nineteenth-century literary genre. The first English specimen of this genre was Richard Milward's 1689 collection of his mentor John Selden's occasional comments. Selden was a member of the bar, a legal and theological scholar, and something of a skeptic. He believed strongly in the separation of church and state, that the clergy must be subordinate to the civil magistrates, and that tolerance was a good thing—views that made him suspect to the established clergy in England. His wit was as famous as his learning. Of the law he wrote, "ignorance of the law excuses no man, not that all men know the law, but because it is an excuse every man will plead and no man can tell how to confute him." The most famous American sample of this type of table talk in Seward's time was Oliver Wendell Holmes's *The Autocrat of the Breakfast Table*, a collection of occasional pieces that the Boston doctor and raconteur published in the *Atlantic Monthly* in 1857 and 1858, and later in a single volume. The setting was a Yankee boarding house and around the table were various residents, treated to Holmes's opinions on just about everything, delivered with sometimes biting wit. For Seward, one was particularly apt: "you can hire logic, in the shape of a lawyer, to prove anything you want to prove." Seward may have read Holmes; there's a copy of the 1858 edition of the book at the Seward House Museum, with the inscription "William H. Seward Jr." (Seward's son).[19]

Every day from February to July 1872, Seward dictated (for his use of his arms and hands was now severely limited) a short paragraph for the manuscript table talk. Although his travels were the focus of the aphorisms, the work as a whole displayed a new, enlarged, and more diverse sense of community. February 12: "Ours is the best latitude for dinners. Go either north of 45° or south of 35° and you will find that meats, fish, game and vegetable seem inferior. At the north, the climate checks the growth of product; at the South, it enervates the producer, and takes away the appetite of the consumer." So much for southern cooking. Seward was wise as well as wisecracking. February 21: "When we speak of 'civilization,' we generally mean the amount and kind of civilization that we have reached ourselves. We deny the title of 'civilized people' to many nations versed in profound learning and experience of which we are ignorant." And prescient. February 28: "Chinese, English, and American, all deplore the vice of opium-eating, as fraught with great danger to the future of the Chinese people. Yet there probably is not half as much harm done there by eating opium, as there is done here, by drinking rum, nor half the amount of crime resulting from it." He did not quite finish the table talk, although it was later published. Its comfortable reciprocity in judgment hints that Seward had returned to his earlier optimism. The world was a community. He had traveled through it and sampled with pleasure its variety. Globalism was the final piece of relational rights.[20]

Relational rights, reciprocal relations within a community, could have been a very conservative jurisprudence—for the community could have been narrowly construed as everyone like us. But from the very first, Seward's idea of community was liberal—it included blacks and Indians, newcomers and old-timers, Jews, Catholics, Irish, and even, as the last entry in the table talk demonstrated, East Asians. Seward's jurisprudence was democratic. That is, it rested on a polity in which all citizens were included. It was capacious—it could expand to include newcomers like the Irish along with those whom earlier law had excluded from community, like African Americans and Chinese immigrants (victims of discriminatory California law). The antebellum years saw the flowering of that democratic vision of community. The Reconstruction years saw another flowering. So, when Chinese laborers were induced to come to America and work on the railroads and in the mines were denied basic rights by state law, Seward helped frame the Burlingame-Seward Treaty of 1868, establishing formal relations with China and guaranteeing to the Chinese workers the "same privileges, immunities or exemptions in respect to travel or residence as may there be enjoyed by the citizens or subjects of the most favored nation."[21]

Seward, long ahead of his time, welcomed diversity, and his jurisprudence—sometimes—empowered it.

Conclusion
Seward's Law

By calling relational rights a jurisprudence, I have defined it as a category of legal thinking, although it also appeared in Seward's political speeches. I find that it suffused and gave them coherence. But Seward's intellectual contribution to the law has never heretofore been accorded its proper place or value in our legal history.

Antebellum America was a formative time in the development of American jurisprudence. The fulcrum and fount of that jurisprudence was the Constitution, but antislavery and proslavery advocates gathered around strikingly different versions of that Constitution. In aid of these, they offered an array of theories. There were believers in the old Constitution, a Constitution of limited federal government and expansive state sovereignty, a Constitution that promised national security and Union, but little in the way of social or dignity rights. There were those who proposed a radical view of the Constitution, that it offered the basis for a full array of human rights and protected the dignity of all who lived in the republic. That was a far seeing but minority view of US law. I concluded that Seward belonged to neither of these camps, though historians have variously placed him in one or the other. He was not a fervent nationalist. He was not a fierce states' righter. He was cautious, but not a conservative, and antislavery, but not a radical.[1]

Evolving from his practice as a country lawyer, Seward believed that fundamental legal rights grew from a communal obligation that all who lived in civilized society owed to each other. And because the master owed nothing to the slave, and the slave owed unceasing toil, and his or her body itself (for the internal slave trade) to the master, slavery was the antithesis; indeed, it poisoned this ideal of law. His vision of law was blurred in the maelstrom of the Civil War and did not recover anything like its earlier vibrancy in the postwar period. In one sense, then, it was a victim of the secession he had once so blindly dismissed, and then of the fierce struggle to save the Union from its enemies. What was more, relational rights did not comprehend the corrosive effect of racism on all relationships. For racism corrodes social duty and reciprocal obligation in a far more subtle, if just as pervasive, a manner as slavery. Reintroduced into law as Jim Crow, it certainly would have fit Seward's jurisprudential attack on slavery, but Jim Crow did not emerge until Seward had passed away.[2]

Seward applied his relational jurisprudence to other topics than slavery. He was in favor of reform of penal law and prisons, of the extension of public education, of cheaper and more accessible means of transportation, and a myriad of other progressive projects. All of these improved relations among members of the community. His diplomacy was relational, resting upon a network of agreements among nations and treaty relations negotiated on the basis of mutual advantage. Slaves, because bad law left them out of the community, could not benefit from relational improvements. Thus, Seward's jurisprudence always circled back to the issue of slavery because the antiphony of democracy and slavery was the central tension, and the great irony, of politics and law in Seward's day.

Seward saw the Constitution not as a fixed set of rules, but as an instrument to empower humane progress. It was "the spirit of the laws" that mattered, not just the text. To elucidate this spirit, he freed himself from time and space. He looked backward to the framers and forward to a world without slavery. He ranged in space across the country and across the Atlantic. He was comfortable as a seer. "If we act as we did hereafter [the Revolution] as we have hitherto, we shall be continually changing old things, old laws, old customs, and even old constitutions for new ones." This urge to improve must not go unregulated. "Political progress, if not regulated with moderation, may move too fast." Lawfulness was the moderating influence. "We may change everything, first complying, however, with constitutional conditions." He did not explore the theoretical obstacles to this conception. He simply went at it, over time, his approach evolving as his view of the fundamental law evolved. "This progress is very unequal, but it is nevertheless certain and irresistible." His invocation of the "irresistible" progress of the law preceded his warning of the "irrepressible" conflict between freedom and slavery by fourteen years.

Read together, the latter becomes a surmountable obstacle, not an end in itself. This was the essence of Seward's idea of good law. Perhaps what he saw in the law was what he valued in himself, the virtues of moderation and toleration, and the inevitability of the progress of liberty. He assumed the law would foster progress, and progress meant the end of slavery, the welcome of immigrants, the establishment of public education, and the reform of prisons and other public institutions. There was no overarching theory or ideology behind these impulses. Instead, the relationship was deeper, sunk in history, but like history, often misread.[3]

Couched in conciliatory tones and flexible in application, Seward's law was unyielding in one sense. The answer to political strife was more and better lawmaking. But to work, law had to rest on the realities of politics. A law so far out of touch with popular feelings would not be obeyed. So the task of the lawgivers was to find ways for law to accommodate dissent while still working toward certain goals. For Seward, any law would not do. The law must look forward to the greater good for the greater number. It must elevate and inspire. It must encode the ideals for which, he believed, the republic was founded. Democracy without law was a riot of self-interested majorities, democracy rooted in law was true liberty.[4]

Seward envisioned rights existing in an ideal community, and such a community, where race and riches did not matter so much as mutual obligations, never existed. But would it never exist? Seward's idea of democracy went hand in hand with the end of aristocratic limits on many facets of political participation. Departing from efforts to tame the "excesses of democracy" in the first years of the new nation, lawgivers in the next generation were citing their democratic credentials with pride. A republic was becoming a democracy. A leading edge of that transformation was the movement to codify the laws, making them transparent to the ordinary citizen and taking the mystery out of them. As Robert Rantoul Jr. told a Fourth of July 1836 gathering in Scituate, Massachusetts, the older mysteries of the common law must give way to democratic reform, for a law that could not be understood by the common man was one that stood in the way of "the fundamental principles of a free government." Governor Seward tried to reform the law in New York along these lines.[5]

At first glance, nothing could be more different from the rise of democratic law reform than the expansion of a system of chattel slavery. The first implies, if not embodies, the equality of persons. The second debases one group of people as property and elevates another group as property owners. Such biformities in US life, to borrow terminology from Michael Kammen, are not uncommon. In his classic study of slavery in colonial Virginia, Edmund Morgan argued that Virginia elites convinced poor whites that their rights depended on their cooperation in adoption of Black slavery. Despite resistance by a handful of delegates to the constitutional convention, slavery (though not by name) found its way into the Three-Fifths Clause, the Rendition Clause, and the slave trade provisions of the federal Constitution.[6]

If the federal Constitution was hardly a democratic document, the open spaces in its text nevertheless allowed states to innovate with the franchise, office holding, and other reforms. Thus, as Michael Klarman has written, "because of various fortuities in its drafts, the Constitution could be adapted—without formal amendment—to the powerful democratic trends of the Jacksonian Era." In 1831, Seward, then a newly elected member of the New York State Senate, in advocating the popular election of mayors, made the point plainly: "the tendency of all our principles of government is to democracy."[7]

The New York State constitutional convention of 1821 had advanced these democratic trends—making it easier for debtors to pay over time, or at least to avoid debtors prisons, opening the franchise to landless men, beginning reform of asylums and prisons, and other steps toward democratic equality. In 1827, it ended slavery. But those steps did not include reforming the franchise for free people of color. Instead, it removed property qualifications for whites and left them in place for free Black male voters.[8]

The earlier gains of free Blacks in many of the Northern states were undergoing the same contraction as in New York. State constitutional revisions contributed to the proslavery constitutionalism of the day. One after another, amendments protected the rights of white men while diminishing those of Black men. For example, in 1851, Indiana forbade Blacks to settle; Iowa passed similar legislation the same year. They followed the steps of the Illinois (white) voters three years earlier, and six years later, in 1857, Oregon excluded Black migrants. The California State Constitution, largely the work of lawyer Stephen J. Field, barred Blacks from enjoying state citizenship. Slave masters were free to bring their slaves with them when visiting the state, and only the threat of abolitionist mobs protecting runaways deterred masters from domiciling in the Northwest Territory. Thus the same institutions of law, legislatures, and courts that enabled the rise of democratic politics empowered the slaveholder to buy, sell, rent, breed, and abuse other men and women.[9]

Seward confronted this paradox over and over in his public life. As he mused on it in a message to an 1844 Albany conference on the Irish troubles, "The rights asserted by our forefathers were not peculiar to themselves. They were the common rights of mankind. The basis of the Constitution was far broader by far than the superstructure which the conflicting interests and prejudices of the day suffered to be erected." Mankind was a community, and the members of that community owed to one another the principles "promulgated in the Declaration of Independence." It was the aim of "all liberal statesmen" to "promote" those principles, and "the end of that progress will be complete political equality among ourselves, and the extension and perfection of institutions similar to our own throughout the world."[10]

Seward's contribution to legal ideas, his relational jurisprudence, the theory of rights and obligations that supposedly grew out of the mutual duties of members of a community, could have provided a major reinterpretation of this ailment in US law, but again, it and he were never seen as a major contribution to jurisprudence. Perhaps this was the fate of the country lawyer? Because of the nature of his practice, the country lawyer makes relatively few momentous contributions to the law per se. The intellectual monuments of US jurisprudence, the works of an elite circle of judges, legal academics, and practitioners, become constitutional "doctrines" bearing what law teacher Karl Llewellyn caricatured as the "singing reason" of the law, however. Seward did not leave his behind.[11]

Then again, perhaps Seward's younger contemporary Charles Francis Adams offered a more accurate appraisal? Adams offered that Seward was "never a learned man" in the classical sense of the word for "the chief characteristic of his mind was his breadth of view. In this sense he was a philosopher studying politics . . . forming for himself a general idea of government." He was knowledgeable in many subjects, but not a genuine expert in any of them but politics and law. His addresses, whether a report on the state of the state of New York in 1840 or an address to Alaskans in Sitka, in 1869, always contained a pastiche of science, technology, sociological and ethnographic ideas, boosterism, and law, as well as political observations. In other words, Seward was something of what the cultural anthropologist Claude Lévi-Strauss called a "bricoleur." He is one who takes a variety of existing materials, ideas, and customs, and weaves them together. For Lévi-Strauss, the bricoleur was essential to the development of cultures. The bricoleur builds intellectual structure by fitting together events as well as ideas. Relational rights is an example of bricolage. This is precisely what Seward did—drawing from his ever-widening experience, but never really leaving the country lawyer behind, and in the end, returning to Auburn as if he had never left. Thus relational rights became part of a larger web of ideas. He compiled, rearranged, and reset his notions—the very process that his critics decried as inconsistent and unreliable. His conversation, so voluminous and so broad, mixed story and analysis, becoming a running commentary on the process of government. He was not an observer of his own method. The bricoleur does not need to be introspective, but Seward was self-aware to this extent—he knew where politics and law should go.[12]

Were Seward to have followed his periodically announced intention to drop out of politics, perhaps he could have devoted more time to relational rights, and the coherence and importance of his legal thinking would have been more evident? But burying his own contribution under layers of political rhetoric, he denied to later biographers a clear vision of his thinking. In missing the importance of his long career as a country lawyer, they then miss what country lawyering contributed to his way of thinking.[13]

Ideas like Seward's do not float in some intellectual ether. They arise in the context of human activity. The country lawyer was at his best in bringing together parties whose legal differences had led them to court. To this extent he was tolerant of differences and understood reciprocity in the law. The country lawyer was a fierce advocate, but at the end of the day knew that his opponents that day might well be his co-counsel on the morrow. Seward's relational theory of rights could appear to be a species of trimming. In politics, the ability to reach across the courtroom to the other party's side might be seen as equivocation. Certainly Seward was taxed with this partisan sin by other politicians. But in lawyering, the ability to work with one's opponents is an invaluable skill, for the ideal of lawyering is to reach a win-win solution to a dispute. Insofar as much of Seward's practice, for example in patent law, required mastery of equitable remedies, he spent days negotiating fair remedies. In equity practice this kind of lawyering was not just optimal; it was essential. For in equity, all rights are relational. The goal is always to find justice for all those who stand before the bench.[14]

Such moderation was not particularly useful in Seward's day, a time of immoderation culminating in a bloody civil insurrection. Although there is no doubt that he adapted his skills as a country lawyer to his political career, brokering alliances within his own political party and across the aisle to the opposing party for his own ends, more often than not his aim was a larger purpose. He really did believe in the essential role of law in preserving and advancing a regime of relational rights. The skills he developed on the hustings and in Congress provided a venue to present this doctrine, but garbed in conventional political language, it did not shine through clearly.

Then, as Seward became an able and trusted counsel to Lincoln in both foreign and domestic affairs, his foremost goal became the preservation of the Union. Advocacy of relational rights remained a cornerstone of this approach to law, but it was applied first and foremost to his treatment of the secessionists and diplomacy. There was no room for liberality in the prosecution of a civil war and no tolerance for the Union's enemies. His views of neutrality were similarly strained by the need to protect the interests of the Union. Nevertheless, he tried, on at least two occasions, in the "April Fool's Day" memo and his response to the *Trent* Affair, to bring relational jurisprudence back into his official duties as secretary of state.

Even in the darkest days of the Civil War, Seward did not cease to believe that good politics must be was the handmaiden of law, not its unprincipled manipulator. Law should come first; political interests and parties and candidates second. Bad politics—the politics of self-interest—made bad law. There is more than a little of the revolutionary era ideal of disinterested civic virtue in this vision of law. Although historians have moved away from the notion that selfless disinterestedness motivated the revolutionary generation, Seward, who grew up in the penumbras of their achievement (for the Auburn region of New York was a cockpit of revolutionary sacrifice), gloried in it. No conservative, his career was nevertheless a throwback to the ideal of public service.[15]

True, that ideal of republican self-sacrifice, so shining in the time of the War for Independence, had long been dulled by the public and private corruption the Revolutionaries had so feared. The years prior to the Civil War were filled with graft and self-dealing in federal and state government. In the bloodbath of the Civil War the sacrifice on the field of battle and in the disease-ridden camps did not deter corruption in the federal or the Confederate governments. Where was everyday law and order, constitutional law, higher law, law in courtrooms, and law and legislative halls in the bloodbath of the war? In Reconstruction, many in both North and South hoped that the lessons of war included a rededication of public service, but others merely found new venues for illicit ventures.[16]

The weakness of the country lawyer as jurisprudent was the limitation of his vision. He went from case to case. He did not see, or seek to see, the biggest picture because that vision does not help a client in court. The few times that Seward tried to go beyond established law, for example in his 1847 *Van Zandt* brief and his 1850 higher law speech, he failed to convince his auditory. That would not disturb a lawyer like Charles Sumner, who did not have a country practice and routinely vaulted beyond settled law in his public addresses, but the country lawyer in Seward did not recognize his limitations. The result was that Seward's law, like its author, did not evolve when slavery was gone. He and it were not able to envision a day when equality under law would become a national project. His vision of legal equality stopped at real equality, or at least at government programs to ensure equality.[17]

Seward did not blame this limitation on his own lack of vision because he did not see the limitation. Instead, he pointed his finger at the limitations that party affiliation imposed on everyone. As he revealed to one correspondent in 1848, "you know that every concession to or for slavery by the Whig party for ten years past has been a triumph over me. But there are two things neither of which I can ever do. The one is to share the responsibility of any concession. The other is to oppose a candidate of the Whig national party." As much as Seward personally abhorred slavery, his response to it was limited by political ties. "All the Whigs of New York, to whom I owe so much" would not permit him to go beyond these limits. These were the same limits that practicing law imposed. One must remain within the rules laid down by the courts. These were the same limits that being a governor imposed. Sitting in the Senate, the limits of what he could say were expanded. As a Republican, rather than a Whig, those limits again expanded. But not very far. As secretary of state, he could not jeopardize the war effort or the Union, and that meant compromise with the loyal Democrats.[18]

The country lawyer was limited by institutional affiliations. In a letter to New York abolitionists William Jay and Gerritt Smith, Seward explained how he thought change might occur absent constitutional amendment. Slavery was illegal in New York State for twelve years when he wrote, but slaveowners were still bringing their chattels into the port of New York. "I regard the judiciary as the proper tribunal to expound all constitutional questions," and to it he would yield all personal and public support. But what if the judiciary upheld the slave laws? Then Seward could argue against them, but he had to obey, just as Story, McLean, and others who opposed slavery had to obey.[19]

The country lawyer's notion of relational rights doctrine would have protected men like Van Zandt from the impositions of slave law and western settlers from the imposition of slavery, but they did not confer on slaves a natural right to be free. Because it was rooted in existing community values, rather than natural rights or the social contract, relational rights was restricted by existing community prejudices. Seward's world was one in which Black people were subordinate, and he saw them as their patron and benefactor, not as equals. All the books and travels, all the letters, could not change his worldview. As he wrote to William Jay and Smith in 1838, "I believe all men may become competent to the responsibilities of self-government. I think also that nations and races may become debased by ignorance so as to be destitute of the intelligence and virtue requisite for the discharge of those responsibilities." Compare this with the autobiography and the table talk of 1871–1872. Little had changed in his thinking.[20]

The limitations of the country lawyer are not tragic, and Seward's life was anything but a tragedy. But his contributions to the law itself, for example the guarantee of trial by jury for alleged runaway slaves, reading programs in the penitentiaries, and parochial school support, were limited in scope and did not merge into a larger regime of legal reform. As soon as he was gone, they too faded—repealed or underfunded by Democratic successors in the governor's office. But if their time had not come in Seward's incumbency, they would become state policy in the fulness of time. One can say with some justice that Seward was ahead of his time.

Finally, one can understand why the project of relational rights took second place to the restoration of the Union. Reconstruction was a time when the implications of Seward's relational ideal of law could have flourished. Instead, its limitations became all too obvious. He faced Hobson's choice—to ensure the equality of the races in communities where racism was deeply ingrained, or to work for the inclusion of former rebels into the Union. Though he argued for the legal and moral equality of everyone under the law, in practice, and that is where the country lawyer lived, racism among whites—in the North as well as the South, among the Republicans as well as the Democrats—was already creating two communities across a militant color line. Instead of pressing Lincoln and then Johnson to ensure and protect the freedoms of the former slaves, he wished the government to restore the white citizens of the South to their former station in the community.[21]

Did Seward's thinking about relational rights really matter, then? They mattered to him, although the country lawyer was never much of a theorist. Did they matter to others around him? Seward was an important figure in his time. Was his thinking about law also important? Seward's contemporary Ralph Waldo Emerson's famous essay on "Self-Reliance" opened, "To believe our own thought, to believe that what is true for you in your private heart is true for all men,—that is genius. Speak your latent conviction, and it shall be the universal sense; for the inmost in due time becomes the outmost,—and our first thought, is rendered back to us by the trumpets of the Last Judgment." Seward undoubtedly believed that his view of rights was important, and moreover, that it could and should be adopted by courts and legislatures.[22]

But, and this is an important but, as others' voices were growing more strident, his did not. As others' ideas were growing more radical, and hence confrontational, his remained rooted in the ideal of relationships. Thus in answer to the charge that he was politically fickle, that he was driven by the hope of political advantage, comes the defense that he was the very opposite of inconstant. From the late 1830s through the onset of the crisis, and then at its end, his attachment to relational rights remained stalwart. He did not change, and perhaps therein lay the other charge against him—that when the end of slavery did not bring the integration of the freedman into the polity, he could not see how limited relational rights were.

If, as seems the case, relational rights did not attain pride of place in antebellum US jurisprudence, and historians have not recovered its place in Seward's thinking, does it follow that the notion has no place in our own thinking about law? A relational rights jurisprudence untethered from Seward's own is not limited to race relations. A more expansive and inclusive view of community than Seward's could have employed relational rights in a more expansive and inclusive fashion. If everyone is part of the community, that is, if everyone who works, lives, and desires to be part of the community, then their rights and obligations under the law are go beyond obedience. Law abidingness, the barest form of relational morality, does not capture this kind of reciprocity. Relational rights implies that we owe to others according to their needs, not according to their ability to pay, or their political clout, or their connections to those in power. Much of the law that appeared after Seward's generation had passed away, including the safety net of Medicare, Medicaid, affordable care, social security, and noncontributory welfare provisions for health and non-fee-paying public services can most easily be justified by relational rights jurisprudence. Seward understood something of this when he championed public education and the rights of immigrants. Perhaps he should get some credit for the expanded version of relational rights that now undergird our welfare state?[23]

Acknowledgments

I am grateful to Thomas Slaughter of the University of Rochester history department and the editor of Seward's family papers, who read and commented on two early versions of the book, and then read it again for the press; to Jeffrey Ludwig and Zachary Finn, at the Seward House Museum, particularly Dr. Ludwig, who corrected and emended the manuscript with care and kindness; to James D. Folts, head of researcher services at the New York State Archives, for generous assistance on Seward's presence at the New York Court of Appeals; and to Andrew Burstein and Nancy Isenberg, of the Louisiana State University, Sarah Barringer Gordon, of the University of Pennsylvania Carey Law School, Mark W. Summers, of the University of Kentucky, Mark Tushnet, of Harvard Law School, N. E. H. Hull, distinguished professor emerita at Rutgers Law School, and Williamjames Hull Hoffer, of the Seton Hall University department of history, for agreeing to read and comment on various versions of the manuscript. The American Founding Group at the University of Georgia, including Nathan Chapman, Keith Dougherty, Rob Ferguson, Harrison Frye, Ted Rossier, and Michael Taylor, offered valuable assistance on the closing chapter. Derek Chang and another member of the faculty board read the manuscript for Cornell University Press, and their comments were kind and very helpful. Michael McGandy, my editor at Cornell was patient and, more important, saw merit in the project from inception to publication. Clare Jones was my assistant editor and Kathleen Murphy my production editor, and they surmounted all obstacles my clunky handling of the manuscript posed. Bill Nelson did the cartography, a super job. Kristen Bettcher arranged for the copyediting, which Irina Burns accomplished. All mistakes that remain of course are mine.

Notes

Introduction

1. William Henry Seward, Speech on the Admission of California, March 11, 1850, in US Senate, in George E. Baker, ed., *The Works of William H. Seward* (Boston: Houghton, Mifflin, 1888) [hereinafter Baker, ed., *Works*], 1:83.

2. William O. Douglas, "The Lawyer and the Public Service," *American Bar Association Journal* 26 (1941), 633; Louis D. Brandeis, "The Living Law" Address to the Chicago Bar Association, January 3, 1916, in *Brandeis on Democracy*, ed. Philippa Strum (Lawrence: University Press of Kansas, 1995), 65.

3. Robert H. Jackson, "The County-Seat Lawyer," *ABA Journal* 36 (1950), 497; Douglas, *The Autobiography of William O. Douglas, The Court Years, 1939–1975* (New York: Random House, 1980), 42.

4. Norman A. Graebner, "Commentary on 'Abe Lincoln Laughing,'" in *The Historian's Lincoln*, ed. Gabor S. Boritt and Norman O. Forness (Urbana: University of Illinois Press, 1988), 20; Doris Kearns Goodwin, *Team of Rivals: The Political Genius of Abraham Lincoln* (New York: Scribners, 2005), 193.

5. On Webster and Pinkney, Peter Charles Hoffer, *Daniel Webster and the Unfinished Constitution* (Lawrence: University Press of Kansas, 2021), 53–54. Ironically the idea of the country lawyer came into prominence as the real country lawyers were fading into obsolescence. William Domnarski, "The Country Lawyer Remembered," *American Scholar* 58 (1989), 283.

Seward met Aaron Burr in Albany when the older man petitioned to be readmitted to the New York bar to oppose Seward's client. Seward recalled that Burr was courteous and friendly but not a good lawyer and ultimately lost the suit. The date of their meeting was recalled by Seward in 1871 as 1823, see Frederick W. Seward, ed., *Autobiography of William H. Seward, from 1801 to 1834, with a Memoir of His Life and Selections from His Letters from 1831 to 1846* (New York: Appleton, 1877) [hereinafter *Autobiography*], 97–98, but the actual date may have been later, in 1831. Walter Stahr, *Seward, Lincoln's Indispensable Man* (New York: Simon and Schuster, 2012), 33, when the case actually came to be heard at the chancellor's court in Albany.

6. Stacy Pratt McDermott, *The Jury in Lincoln's America* (Athens: Ohio University Press, 2012), 125–126; Seward, note on Henry Wyatt's trial, June 15, 1846, *Autobiography*, 812.

7. Brian Dirck, *Lincoln the Lawyer* (Urbana: University of Illinois Press, 2007), 71.

8. Laura Edwards, "Response to Rebecca Scott's 'Discerning a Dignitary Offense,'" *Law and History Review* 38 (2020), 572–573.

9. Seward family library digital archive mainly included *American Annals* and other works of documents, encyclopedias, law books, histories, government publications, travel guides, and Seward's published speeches; https://sewardproject.org/seward-book-list/public/holdings/64646. Most of these came from his father in law's library. Information from Jeffrey Ludwig, educational director, Seward House Museum. Oddly missing were Joseph Story's *Commentaries on the Constitution* (3 vols.), but he had a copy of Harriett Beecher Stowe's *Dred*, possibly for or from Frances. On law practice, see David Hoffman, *A Course of Legal Study*, 2nd ed. (Baltimore: Neal, 1836), 2:758; M. H. Hoeflich, *Legal Publishing in Antebellum America* (New York: Cambridge University Press, 2010), 35–36; John G. Baker, "Indiana Judges: A Portrait of Judicial Evolution," in *A History of Indiana Law*, ed. David J. Bodenhamer and Hon. Randall Shepard (Athens: Ohio University Press, 2006), 306; Seward to Frances Seward, April 27, 1847, in Frederick W. Seward, ed., *Seward at Washington, Senator and Secretary of State, with a Memoir, and Selections from His Letters, 1846–1861* (New York: Derby and Miller, 1891) [hereinafter *Seward at Washington*], 1:45–46; Mark E. Steiner, *An Honest Calling: The Law Practice of Abraham Lincoln* (DeKalb: Northern Illinois University Press, 2006), 55; Derek Roebuck, Francis Boorman, and Rhiannon Markless, *English Arbitration and Mediation in the Long Eighteenth Century* (Oxford, UK: Arbitration Press, 2019), 278 (country lawyers as mediator). For a description of Seward, see Glyndon G. Van Deusen, "Life and Career of William Henry Seward, 1801–1872," *University of Rochester Library Bulletin* 31 (1978), 1.

10. See, e.g., Daniel Walker Howe, *The Political Culture of the American Whigs* (Chicago: University of Chicago Press, 1979), 22–23 and after. Here and after, Seward proved himself a bricoleur, on which see the conclusion of this book.

11. Whitney R. Cross, *The Burned-Over District: The Social and Intellectual History of Enthusiastic Religion in Western New York, 1800–1850* (New York: Harper and Row, 1950), 247; Stahr, *Seward*, 21, 45, 49–50; on the Higher Law speech, see chapter 3 in this book.

12. Seward, "The Destiny of America," September 14, 1853, in Baker, ed., *Works*, 4:128. The law firm is Greenfield Labby, and the comment appears in Robin Finn, "Casey Greenfield versus the World," *New York Times*, February 17, 2012, https://www.nytimes.com/2012/02/19/nyregion/in-casey-greenfields-personal-custody-fight-the-makings-of-a-public-expert.html. Relational rights in this and other modern usages means that members of a group—family, community, nation—owe reciprocal rights and duties to one another. These can be statutory, but they do not rest entirely on statute or positive law. They are a jurisprudence, a way of thinking about law in both private and public places. See, e.g., Jennifer Nedelsky, *Law's Relations: A Relational Theory of Self, Autonomy, and Law* (New York: Oxford University Press, 2012), 7, 76, 256; Martha Minow and Mary Lyndon Shanley, "Relational Rights and Responsibilities: Revisioning the Family in Liberal Political Theory and Law," *Hypatia* 11 (1996), 4–29. Borrowing the term to describe Seward's jurisprudence is my idea.

Note that this was not the same as a Lockean "contract" made by individuals that creates the state. In social contract theory, the laws that follow from this contract, laws that come from courts, guarantee to individuals certain rights. Peter Laslett, "Introduction," in *John Locke, Two Treatises of Government* (Cambridge, UK: Cambridge University Press, 1967), 111. Seward's relational rights did not come from the state, nor did they rest on an original contract, although Seward mentioned Locke four times in his public addresses, none of the mentions seriously engaged Lockean social contract theory. Baker, ed., *Works*, 4:126, 132, 190, 191.

Nor could Seward's law be reduced to a simple moralism of rights and wrongs, as Seward did not base his view of law on his morals, nor did he discourse on morality in his letters or his public addresses, save to impeach the morality of states corrupted in the contest for railroads (Baker, ed., *Works*, 1:306); the advantage to the morality of internal improvements (Baker, ed., *Works*, 2:203); the reform of state prisons and the criminal law (Baker, ed., *Works*, 2:327, 427, 481, 661, 662); the morality of Irish naturalization and access to the schools (Baker, ed., *Works*, 3:237, 489), all of which were boilerplate. He understood that law and morality were two different realms.

Nor was Seward's idea of rights some form of custom. Custom as a source of law looks backward to distant times and assumes fixed relationships. On only one occasion did Seward hint that the ethos of a particular group of people was a part of relational rights, and that was when he claimed that freedom was the ideal of northern Europeans. See, e.g., Seward, "Irrepressible Conflict," Address at Rochester, New York, on October 25, 1858, *Albany Argus*, 1. In general, Seward saw society and social relationships as evolving over time, a progress toward greater freedom.

1. "There Is No Law of This State Which Recognizes Slavery"

1. Seward to Thurlow Weed, September 24, 1843, *Autobiography*, 682; John M. Taylor, *William Henry Seward; Lincoln's Right Hand* (Washington, D.C. Brasseys, 1991), 59; Merrill D. Peterson, *The Great Triumvirate, Webster, Clay, and Calhoun* (New York: Oxford University Press, 1987), 394.

2. Lord Palmerston, quoted in Walter Stahr, *Seward, Lincoln's Indispensable Man*, 178; Baltimore *American and Commercial*, November 12, 1858; *Albany Evening Journal*, November 3, 1860; Gideon Welles, *Lincoln and Seward: Remarks upon the memorial address of Chas. Francis Adams, on the late William H. Seward, with incidents and comments illustrative of the measures and policy of the administration of Abraham Lincoln. And views as to the relative positions of the late President and secretary of state* (New York: Sheldon & company, 1874), v, 8; George McClellan to Mary Ellen McClellan, October 31, 1861, quoted in Stahr, *Seward*, 304; Seward to Thurlow Weed, December 31, 1842, quoted in Stahr, *Seward*, 84.

3. Glyndon Garlock Van Deusen, *William Henry Seward, Lincoln's Secretary of State and the Negotiator of the Alaska Purchase* (New York: Oxford University Press, 1967), 565. Van Deusen described Seward as "a little, red-haired, beak-nosed lawyer with a ready tongue and much charm," in *Horace Greeley: Nineteenth-Century Crusader* (New York: Hill and Wang, 1953), 38. On Seward variously as a puppet of Weed and a "dexterous" and cunning pol, see, e.g., Sean Wilentz, *The Rise of American Democracy: Jefferson to Lincoln* (New York: Norton, 2005), 277–278, 640–641; David Potter, *The Impending Crisis, 1848–1861* (New York: Harper and Row, 1976), 86–87; and Kenneth Stampp, *And the War Came: The North and the Secession Crisis, 1860–1861* (Baton Rouge: Louisiana State University Press, 1950), 19.

4. Discussions with Thomas Slaughter, the editor of the family papers and a biographer, have persuaded me that hints I have found of certain dysfunctional personality traits, for example regarding Seward's decision not to enter the presidential lists until

1860, are not essential to the argument or any contribution of the present essay. Readers of formal biographies of Seward will find ample speculation on such matters.

5. Full biographical details are available in Van Deusen, *Seward,*; Taylor, *Seward,* and Stahr, *Seward.*

6. *Autobiography,* 2–23. These are my impressions from reading the autobiography, but they are based on Seward's words. The collator and editor of the volumes, including the autobiography and the letters, was Seward's son and frequent aide de camp Frederick Seward. The selections are accurate in one sense (nothing like Jared Sparks's emendations of Washington's papers, for example) and biased in another. He loved and respected his father. The portrait that emerges is thus a favorable one. Not every historian agrees.

7. *Autobiography,* 27–28; Alan Taylor, *The Civil War of 1812* (New York: Knopf, 2010), 205–206, 224–225.

8. Travel and travel accounts were a major part of the booming book culture in the period after 1815. See, e.g., John D. Cox, *Traveling South: Travel Narrative and the Construction of American Identity* (Athens: University of Georgia Press, 2005), 36–37, 143 (for northern travelers slavery was the worm in the bud); for more on Americans on the move, see Amy S. Greenberg, *Manifest Manhood and the Antebellum American Empire* (New York: Cambridge University Press, 2005), 140; George D. Oberli III, "Post Office," in *The World of Antebellum America, A Daily Life Encyclopedia,* ed. Alexandra Kindell (Santa Barbara, CA: Greenwood, 2018), 2:468; Wayne Duerkes, "Housing and Community," in Kindell, ed. *The World of Antebellum America,* 417.

9. George Dangerfield, *The Era of Good Feelings* (New York: Harcourt, Brace, 1952), in which a time of "nationalist exuberance" (xi) gave way to panic and then sectional discord (201–202); *Autobiography,* 53. Seward did not spend much time in the autobiography on what would, in fact, absorb much of his time during his adult years—the practice of law. The volume of correspondence on family matters was huge, on the law practice very small by comparison, and almost invariably mundane.

10. Van Deusen, *Seward,* 6–7; "Death of Hon. Ogden Hoffman," *New York Times,* May 2, 1856; Anthon and Duer biographical information from Appleton's *Cyclopedia of American Biography* (New York: Appleton, 1900).

11. Stahr, *Seward,* 18, 19; Frederick W. Seward, *Reminiscences of a War-Time Statesman and Diplomat, 1830–1915* (New York: Putnam, 1916), 10; Trudy Krisher, *Fanny Seward, A Life* (Syracuse, NY: Syracuse University Press, 2015), 21–22. There are hints that the marriage was often in need of patching up. See, e.g., Frances Seward to William Henry Seward, April 20, 1838, Seward Family Papers, Seward Family Digital Archive, University of Rochester Collections: "And did you really think dear Henry that it was a good and sufficient apology for not writing to me that you had been engaged in public business and could not find time. I had waited impatiently ten long days, you letter came at last and caused some bitter tears, but I foresaw it all when you consented again to become a candidate for popular favour and ought to have been better prepared, these are hard lessons." See also Patricia Johnson, "I Have Supped Full of Horrors," *American Heritage* 10 (1959): 60–101. The marriages of others of his cohort, for example Lincoln's, were often fraught with domestic drama. See Stephen Berry, *House of Abraham: Lincoln and the Todds* (New York: Houghton Mifflin, 2007), 10ff. The instability of the antebellum family even became a political motif in the secession crisis,

see, e.g., Elizabeth Varon, *We Mean to Be Counted: White Women and Politics in Antebellum Virginia* (Chapel Hill: University of North Carolina Press, 1998), 156.

12. *Autobiography*, 613. Legal practice at this time is described in the introduction to Alfred S. Konefsky and Andrew J. King, eds., "Legal Education in Early Nineteenth Century New England," in *Webster, Legal Papers, The New Hampshire Practice* (Hanover, NH: University Press of New England, 1982), 1–18.

13. Tony A. Freyer, "Legal Innovation and Market Capitalism, 1790–1920," in *The Cambridge History of Law in America, II: The Long Nineteenth Century, 1790–1920*, ed. Christopher Tomlins and Michael Grossberg (New York: Cambridge University Press, 2008), 458–468; Morton Horwitz, *The Transformation of American Law, 1780–1860* (Cambridge: Harvard University Press, 1977); *Louisville Daily Journal*, March 3, 1860.

14. Robert T. Swaine, *The Cravath Firm and Its Predecessors, 1819–1946* (New York: Ad Press, 1946),1: 62–66; Alfred D. Chandler, *Scale and Scope: The Dynamics of Industrial Capitalism* (Cambridge, MA: Harvard University Press, 1990), 53; Van Deusen, *Seward*, 53; Daniel W. Stowell, introduction to *The Papers of Abraham Lincoln: Legal Documents and Cases* (Charlottesville: University of Virginia Press, 2008), 1:xxxv; David Donald, *Lincoln's Herndon* (New York: Knopf, 1948), 38–39; *Herndon's Life of Lincoln*, ed. Paul M. Angle (New York: Fawcett, 1961), 169–171; John J. Duff, *A. Lincoln, Prairie Lawyer* (New York: Holt, Rinehart, and Winston, 1960), 35–50 (John Todd Stuart); 78–117 (Stephen T. Logan and Herndon); Timothy H. Huebner, *Liberty and Union: The Civil War Era and American Constitutionalism* (Lawrence: University Press of Kansas, 2016), 101–102 (Lincoln's politics), 212–213 (Seward and Chase).

15. Compare, e.g., Legg v. Robinson, 7 Wend (NY) 194 (1831) with Culver v. Avery, 7 Wend 380 (1831). Seward's practice did not take him to the Supreme Court often. Box 86, folders 4–10, Seward Papers, University of Rochester Library Collections, show that Seward continued to practice law when he sat in the Senate.

16. Williams v. Bank of Michigan, 7 Wend (NY), 539 (Court for Correction) (1831); Livingston v. Peru Iron Co., 9 Wend (NY) 511 (1832) (Court for Correction); Garr v. Gomez, 9 Wend 649 (1832) (Court for Correction); Jackson v. Fitz Simmons, 10 Wend (NY) 2 (1833) (Court for Correction); Davis v. Packard, 10 Wend (NY) 50 (1833) (Court for Correction); Jackson v. Roberts' Executors, 11 Wend. (NY) 422 (1833) (Court for Correction); Fleet v. Youngs 11 Wend (NY) 522 (1833) (Court for Correction); Parks v. Jackson, 11 Wend (NY) 442, 459 (Court for Correction) (Seward, senator).

17. 11 Wend (NY) at 463.

18. Fulton Deoch, ed., *New York to Niagara, 1836: The Journal of Thomas S. Woodcock* (New York: NYPL, 1938); Frank Walker Stevens, *The Beginnings of the New York Central Railroad: A History* (New York: G. P. Putnam, 1926).

19. Stowell, introduction, *Legal Documents*, 1:xxx; Alfred S. Konefsky, "The Legal Profession," in *The Cambridge History of Law in America*, Michael Grossberg and Christopher Tomlins (New York: Cambridge University Press, 2008), 2: 73; Duff, *Prairie Lawyer*, 43, 79.

20. St. George Tucker quoted in E. Lee Shepard, "Breaking into the Profession: Establishing a Law Practice in Antebellum Virginia," *Journal of Southern History* 48 (1982), 393; Paul D. Carrington, "Teaching Law in the Antebellum Northwest," *University of Toledo Law Review* 23 (1991), 4; Harold Holzer, "Reassessing Lincoln's Legal Career," in *Abraham Lincoln Esq.: The Legal Career of America's Greatest President*, ed. Roger Billings and Frank Williams (Lexington: University Press of Kentucky, 2010), 15; Story quoted

in Norman W. Spaulding, "The Myth of Civic Republicanism: Interrogating the Ideology of Antebellum Legal Ethics," *Fordham Law Review* 71 (2003), 1424.

21. Material derived from Peter Charles Hoffer, *Uncivil Warriors: The Lawyers' Civil War* (New York: Oxford University Press, 2018). See, e.g., Christopher Neff, "Those Cunning Spiders, The Lawyers: In Search of An Antebellum Legal Ethos," *Journal of the Legal Profession* 33 (2009), 326; Timothy S. Huebner, *The Southern Judicial Tradition: State Judges and Sectional Distinctiveness, 1790–1890* (Athens: University of Georgia Press, 1989), 133–134; Lieutenant General Jubal Anderson Early, *Autobiographical Sketch and Narrative of the War between the States* (Lynchburg, VA: n.p., 1912), 12; Thomas E. Schott, *Alexander H. Stephens of Georgia, A Biography* (Baton Rouge: Louisiana State University Press, 1988), 29.

22. Henry Adams, *The Education of Henry Adams* (Boston: Massachusetts Historical Society, 1918), 104; Seward, "The Physical, Intellectual, and Moral Development of the American People," speech delivered at Yale College, July 26, 1854, in Baker, ed., *Works*, 4:176. Seward was almost always photographed in profile. The best is the restoration of a photograph by Adam Cuerden, in the Library of Congress collection, Prints and Photographs division, ca. 1861.

23. *Autobiography*, 54; Peter Charles Hoffer, *John Quincy Adams and the Gag Rule* (Baltimore: Johns Hopkins University Press, 2017), 30, 34. On the way in which the ideological first party system became the far less idea-centered second party system, see Lee Benson, *The Concept of Jacksonian Democracy: New York as a Test Case* (Princeton: Princeton University Press, 1961), 72, 73.

24. *Autobiography*, 56; Seward to Frances Seward, January 12, 1831, in *Autobiography*, 166. Westward expansion was the lodestar of the Democratic Party generally, but Seward saw it in terms of commerce rather than land ownership. Frederick Merk, *Manifest Destiny and Mission in American History* (New York: Knopf, 1963), 41ff.

25. *Autobiography*, 57; Seward letter, quoted in *New York Evening Post*, February 17, 1858.

26. *Autobiography*, 74.

27. Stahr, *Seward*, 29–30; Seward to Frances Seward, January 16, 1831, in *Autobiography*, 168.

28. Seward, Address to the Senate, February 16, 1833, in *Autobiography*, 228. Nelson was appointed to the US Supreme Court in 1845 by President John Tyler, the fourth choice to fill a vacancy left by Smith Thompson, also of New York. See Peter Charles Hoffer, Williamjames Hull Hoffer, and N. E. H. Hull, *The Supreme Court: An Essential History*, 2nd ed. (Lawrence: University Press of Kansas, 2018), 86.

29. Stahr, *Seward*, 35–37, 38, 46, 47; Seward to Nelson Beardsley, June 21, 1835, in *Autobiography*, 269; Frederick Seward, *Reminiscences*, 15; Swaine, *Cravath*, 1:61–66.

30. Joel H. Silbey, *Martin Van Buren and the Emergence of Popular Politics* (Lanham, MD: Rowman and Littlefield, 2002), 141: Martin Van Buren, Seward (and Weed's nemesis) called the Seward victory a "tornado." Swaine, *Cravath*, 1:62, 66; Obed Edson, *History of Chautauqua County* (Boston, MA: Fergusson, 1894), 344; Stahr, *Seward*, 50–53. The Holland Company lawsuits, in which Seward was involved, were complex, involving equity (a trust) and legal issues, and would continue for twenty years. See Schermerhorn v. Talman 14 N.Y. 93 (1856); Paul Demund Evans, *The Holland Land Company* (Buffalo: Buffalo Historical Society, 1924), 424–427. Theoretically, notes that Seward took of his consultations with his clients regarding these affairs remain protected by client-attorney privilege. Swidler and Berlin v. U.S., 524 U.S. 399 (1998).

31. Swaine, *Cravath*, 1:67. This in-house study of the forerunners of one of New York City's largest and most prestigious law firms gives the best account of Seward's practice in the 1830s.

32. Frederick Seward, "The Virginia Requisition," in *Autobiography*, 420; Seward to Hopkins, September 30, 1839, in Baker, ed., *Works*, 2:452.

33. Joseph Story, *Commentaries on the Conflict of Laws, Foreign and Domestic* . . . (Boston: Hilliard and Gray, 1834), 517, 518, 520–521.

34. Seward to Hopkins, October 24, 1839, in Baker, ed., *Works*, 2:457; Hopkins quoted *Seward at Washington*, 1:437; Pacific Employers Ins. Co. v. Industrial Accident Comm'n, 306 U.S. 493, 502 (1939).

35. Seward to Henry Hopkins, September 16, 1839, Baker, ed., *Works* 2:451, 452, 453; Leslie M. Harris, *In the Shadow of Slavery, African Americans in New York City, 1626–1863* (Chicago: University of Chicago Press, 2003), 126–127.

36. Seward to Henry Hopkins, October 24, 1839, in Baker, ed., *Works*, 2:458, 459, 460.

37. Seward to Thomas Gilmer, November 9, 1840, in Baker, ed., *Works*, 2:470.

38. Seward to Thomas Gilmer, November 9, 1840, in Baker, ed., *Works*, 2:479. Most of the academic discussion of rendition or extradition (of fugitives from one country to another) concerns criminal fugitives escaping from one country to another. See, e.g., Christopher L. Blakesley, "The Practice of Extradition from Antiquity to Modern Frances and the United States, A Brief History," *Boston College International and Comparative Law Review* 4 (1981), 39–60.

39. Calhoun was vice president of the United States when he undertook to defend South Carolina's nullification of the tariff of 1828. The key to his argument was his belief that the Constitution created a "union of the states" rather than a union of the people of the states. His "Exposition and Protest" was written anonymously, but everyone knew that he was its author. John Niven, *John C. Calhoun and the Price of Union, A Biography* (Baton Rouge: Louisiana State University Press, 1988), 137ff.

40. Seward to Thomas Gilmer, November 10, 1840; Seward to John M. Patton, March 25, 1841; Seward to Patton, April 6, 1841, Seward to John Rutherford, June 8, 1841, Seward to Rutherford, November 8, 1841 in Baker, ed., *Works* 2:489–509, 516. Seward similarly refused to return one Alanson Greenman to Georgia when requested, said Greenman allegedly concealing a runaway slave. The state framed the indictment for larceny (stealing two blankets, presumably to conceal the more serious offense, but the indictment revealed what Greenman had allegedly done with the blankets—hide the slave). Seward to Charles J. M'Donald, June 15, 1841, July 14, 1841, October 12, 1841, October 26, 1841, December 27, 1841, in Baker, ed. *Works*, 2:519–546.

41. Seward to Jarvis N. Lake, August 19, 1844, in Baker, ed., *Works*, 3:403. Seward was well aware that he needed support from New York antislavery politicians. This meant keeping good relations with both the abolitionists and the Liberty Party men, while not joining either camp. See, e.g., Richard H. Sewell, *Ballots for Freedom: Anti-Slavery Politics in the United States, 1837–1860* (New York: Norton, 1980), 63, 124.

42. Seward, *Natural History of New York*, 3, in Baker, ed., *Works*, 2:9–10.

43. *Autobiography*, 465, 490, 529, 546, 547; Stephen J. Valone, "William Henry Seward, the Virginia Controversy, and the Anti-Slavery Movement, 1839–1841," *Journal of Afro-Americans in New York Life and History* 31 (2007), 75–76; Van Deusen, *Seward*, 65–67.

44. *Notes on New York* (1842) in Baker, ed., *Works*, 2:22–28, 37–38, 40; Seward to the Chautauqua Convention, March 31, 1846, in Baker, ed., *Works*, 3:407. The analogy to Martin Luther King's famous August 28, 1963 "I Have a Dream" speech is intentional on my part.

45. *Autobiography*, 587, 588; Philip Klein, "Prison Methods in New York" (PhD diss., Columbia University, 1920), 312; Ian Bartrum, "The Political Origins of Secular Public Education: The New York School Controversy 1840–1842," *New York Law School Journal of Law and Liberty* 3 (2008), 267–348. The trial by jury law was rendered moot by Prigg v. Pennsylvania (1842) 41 U.S. 539, striking down a similar Pennsylvania law. H. Robert Baker, *Prigg v. Pennsylvania: Slavery, the Supreme Court, and the Ambivalent Constitution* (Lawrence: University Press of Kansas, 2012), 171–172.

46. *Autobiography*, 596.

47. *Autobiography*, 477–478; Peter J. Coleman, *Debtors and Creditors in America, Insolvency, Imprisonment for Debt, and Bankruptcy 1607–1900* (Washington, DC: Beard, 1999), 129. Full reform of the code of pleading, doing away with separate suits in law and equity, and the end of the fee system were the work of David Dudley Field. Henry Field, *The Life of David Dudley Field* (New York: Scribners, 1898), 46–50.

48. Harold Schechter, *Killer Colt: Murder, Disgrace, and the Making of an American Legend* (New York: Random House, 2010), 68–70, 283; Charles McCurdy, *The Anti-Rent Era in New York Law and Politics, 1839–1865* (Chapel Hill: University of North Carolina Press, 2001), 21–22, 33.

2. "Harboring and Concealing a Weary and Fainting Slave"

1. Extraditions, boxes 62–66, Seward Papers, University of Rochester Library Collections; Seward to Christopher Morgan, November 12, 1842, *Autobiography*, 627; Seward to Thurlow Weed, February 14, 1843, *Autobiography*, 649; Patricia C. Johnson, "'I Could Not Be Well or Happy at Home . . . When Called to the Councils of My Country': Politics and the Seward Family," *University of Rochester River Campus Library Bulletin* 31 (1978), https://rbscp.lib.rochester.edu/1018.

2. Erastus Root to Thurlow Weed, September 10, 1843, in Harriet A. Weed, ed., *Autobiography of Thurlow Weed* (Boston: Houghton, Mifflin, 1884), 554. On his attitude toward legal practice, *Autobiography*, 162, 252. Seward's legal papers, box 86, folders 13–18, for the rest of 1843, do not contain evidence of a busy lawyer. By March 1844, box 90, folder 2, shows the legal business had picked up again, but does not show a busy practice. Seward Papers, University of Rochester Library Collections. The published cases of the New York Court of Appeals rarely listed Seward, nor did the rough draft of the clerk of the court, housed at the New York State Archives.

3. Frederic Bancroft, *The Life of William H. Seward* (New York: Harper, 1900), 171; Seward to Frances Seward, December 7, 1842, *Autobiography*, 638. Rough Minutes Series, clerk of the Commission of Appeals, 1847–1861, New York State Archives, Albany NY; cases included Schemerhorn v. American Life Insurance, 14 Barber 113 (1856) and Schemerhorn v. Talman 14 N.Y. 93 (1856), (repayment of bonds on the western New York lands); Weed v. Foster and Stimson, 11 Barber 203 (1851) (arising out of Seward's term as governor); and Schneider v. McFarland, 4 Barber 139 (1848) (land ownership).

4. Seward to Frances Seward, October 18, 1846, *Seward at Washington*, 1:32; Seward to Frances Seward, October 16, 1847, *Seward at Washington*, 1:56.

5. *Autobiography*, 75, 646, 650; Seward to Weed, January 13, 1843, *Autobiography*, 647; Van Deusen, *Seward*, 21, 88. He owed over 60,000 dollars to private creditors, including Blatchford, the bond to the America Life Company was at least 150,000 dollars, and the total, over 200,000 was almost a crushing load.

6. Seward to Frances Seward, October 22, 1844, *Autobiography*, 730; Seward to Frances Seward, May 23, 1843, *Autobiography*, 659; Cornelius Cox, recollection of Seward, in *Autobiography*, 705, 707.

7. Cox, recollection, in *Autobiography*, 707; Henry W. Scott, *The Courts of the State of New York* (New York: Wilson, 1909), 321; William James, "The Present Dilemma in Philosophy," in *William James, Writings, 1902–1910* (New York: Penguin, 1987), 491.

8. Jackson, "County-Seat Lawyer," 497. On criticism of lawyering in the antebellum era, see, e.g., Maxwell Bloomfield, "Lawyers and Public Criticism: Challenge and Response in Nineteenth-Century America," *American Journal of Legal History* 15 (1971), 269–277. His need for conviviality would, in future days, be one reason why he got along so well personally with members of the Senate whose politics he deplored.

9. Greeley on lost votes: *Albany Log Cabin*, November 9, 1840, 3. For more on the Cooper-Greeley episode, which was not just about freedom of the press, see Robert C. Williams, *Horace Greeley, Champion of American Freedom* (New York: New York University Press, 2006), 62. Cooper was litigious, particularly concerning his work. See Wayne Franklin, *James Fenimore Cooper, The Later Years* (New Haven: Yale University Press, 2017), 215–220, 245–247.

10. Seward's argument for Greeley quoted in *Autobiography* 741, 742; Greeley quoted in *Autobiography* 510; Cooper v. Greeley and McElrath, New York Supreme Court, 1 Denio 347 (1845), opinion reprinted in *New York Tribune* August 7, 1845. Seward's defense echoed the themes of James Madison's Virginia Resolves of 1798 and the Supreme Court in New York Times v. Sullivan, 376 U.S. 254 (1964).

11. 1 Denio at 13, 17 (Seward for the defense); 27 (Jewett, J.).

12. Edward Jewett, "Freeborn Jewett," History Society of the New York Courts, http://nycourts.gov/HISTORY/legal-history-new-york/legal-history-eras-04/history-era-04-jewett.html; Francis Bergan, *The History of the New York Court of Appeals, 1847–1932* (New York: Columbia University Press, 1985), 3.

13. *Autobiography*, 483 (pardons). He did not pardon John C. Colt, convicted in the 1842 murder trial of Samuel Adams, a printer, despite pleas from Colt's well-placed friends and family. The gruesome details of the murder and the subsequent attempt to conceal the crime influenced Seward. Schechter, *Killer Colt*, 283.

14. R v M'Naghten (1843) 8 E.R. 718; (1843) 10 Cl. & F. 200; Carl Elliott, *The Rules of Insanity: Moral Responsibility and the Mentally Ill Offender* (Albany: State University of New York Press, 1996), 10–11; Kenneth J. Weiss and Neha Gupta, "America's First M'Naghten Defense," *Journal of the American Academy of Psychiatry and the Law* 46, no. 4 (December 2018), 503–512. But not the first judge. In Commonwealth v. Rogers, 48 Mass. 500, 501 (1844) (Shaw, C.J.), Chief Justice Lemuel Shaw of the Supreme Judicial Court of Massachusetts found Abner Rogers not guilty by reason of "irresistible impulse" in his murder of the prison warden. "In order to constitute a crime, a person

must have intelligence and capacity enough to have a criminal intent and purpose; and if his reason and mental powers are either so deficient that he has no will, no conscience or controlling mental power, or if, through the overwhelming violence of mental disease, his intellectual power is for the time obliterated, he is not a responsible moral agent, and is not punishable for criminal acts."

15. Marc Bloustein, "A Short History of the New York State Court System," Historical Society of the Courts of the State of New York, http://www.nycourts.gov/history/legal-history-new-york/documents/History_Short-History-NY-Courts.pdf.

16. *Report of the Trial of Henry Wyatt* (Auburn: J.C. Derby, 1846), 16.

17. *Trial of Henry Wyatt*, 11, 12, 13, 16, Seward to Weed, May 26, 1846, *Autobiography*, 810.

18. *Trial of Henry Wyatt*, 26, 27–28, 29.

19. Andrew W. Arpey, *The William Freeman Murder Trial: Insanity, Politics, and Race* (Syracuse, NY: Syracuse University Press, 2004), focuses on the racist attitudes of local people. Stahr, *Seward*, 99–105, focuses on Seward's refusal to recognize inherent racial inferiority. Robin Bernstein's forthcoming "The Trials of William Freeman" is a more imaginative probing of Freeman's early life, including the argument that he was falsely accused of stealing a horse, and for that convicted and incarcerated at the Auburn penitentiary where he was tortured. https://pma.cornell.edu/content/performance-encounters-black-childhood-trial-tragedy-william-freeman-lecture-and-walking. Wright was born in Pennsylvania but practiced law in Auburn. A Quaker and an abolitionist, his fame was overshadowed by his wife, Martha, who was an advocate of women's rights as well as abolition. See Sharon H. Penney, *A Very Dangerous Woman, Martha Wright and Women's Rights* (Amherst: University of Massachusetts Press, 2004), 35–36ff.

20. *Argument of William Seward in Defense of William Freeman, on His Trial for Murder*, at Auburn, July 21, and 22 (Auburn, NY: Oliphant, 1846), n.p.

21. Even those judges who had personal compunctions against favoring slavery were trapped by existing statutes and Constitutional provisions. They swallowed hard and ruled for the slave owners. See Robert Cover, *Justice Accused: Antislavery and the Judicial Process* (New Haven: Yale University Press, 1975), 131–148. But not always. See, e.g., U.S. v. Schooner Amistad, 40 U.S. 518 (1841).

22. In general, on Prigg, see H. Robert Baker, *Prigg v. Pennsylvania: Slavery, the Supreme Court, and the Ambivalent Constitution* (Lawrence: University Press of Kansas, 2012), and Paul Finkelman, "Story Telling on the Supreme Court," *Supreme Court Review* 1994 (1994), 247–294.

23. Prigg v. Pennsylvania 41 U. S. 539, 611 (Story, J.).

24. 41 U. S. at 612 (Story, J.); Seward, *Autobiography*, 600.

25. 41 U. S. at 632 (Taney, C. J.); 41 U. S. at 656, 657 (Daniel, J.).

26. 42 U.S. at 668, 669 (McLean, J.).

27. McLean to Chase, December 19, 1846, in John H. Niven, ed. *The Papers of Salmon P. Chase: Correspondence, 1823–1857* (Kent, OH: Kent State University Press, 1994), 2:137. Note that this is different from defending Blacks accused of being runaways. So-called constitutional abolitionists like John Jay II and Richard Henry Dana were members of the bar who offered their services in such cases.

28. Salmon P. Chase, "Reclamation of Fugitives from Service," *Argument in . . . Wharton Jones v. John Van Zandt, submitted to the December 1846 term of the US Supreme*

Court (Cincinnati: Donogh, 1847), 14, 19; Seward to Frances Seward, January 14, 1847, *Seward at Washington,* 1:34. On Seward and Chase, Seward to Lewis Tappan, 1847, in *Seward at Washington,* 1: 41; Seward to Chase, February 18, 1847, *Chase Correspondence,* 2:141; Stahr, *Seward,* 104; John Niven, *Salmon Chase, A Biography* (New York: Oxford University Press, 1995), 78–86, covers the early stages of the case.

29. Jones v. Van Zandt, 46 U.S. 215 (1847); Cover, *Justice Accused,* 170–174, 226–237.

30. The idea that slavery warped hospitality was not unique to Seward. It was a theme in Northern antebellum fiction. See Rebecca Wiltberger Wiggins, "Meeting at the Threshold: Slavery's Influence on Hospitality and Black Personhood in Late-Antebellum American Literature" (PhD diss., University of Kentucky, 2018).

31. Paul Finkelman, ed., *Slavery in the Courtroom* (Union, NJ: Lawbook Exchange, 1998), 72–73. Chase did not go to Washington, but Seward was in Washington in January 1847.

32. *Argument for the Defendant by William H. Seward, on the Law of Congress Concerning the Recapture of Fugitive Slaves* (New York: Weed and Parsons, 1847), 7.

33. Seward, *Argument,* 3.

34. Seward, Argument, 12.

35. Seward, Argument, 12. As it happened, Van Zandt died before the court confirmed his debt to Wharton Jones; Frederick J. Blue, *Salmon P. Chase, A Life in Politics* (Kent, OH: Kent State University Press, 1987), 38; Niven, *Chase,* 73 remarks that Van Zandt's heirs had to pay the fine.

36. Seward, *Argument,* 13, 15, 17.

37. Seward, *Argument,* 22, 23.

38. Seward, *Argument,* 23–24. Well, not quite free—various attempts to reintroduce slavery came very close to success. No one could buy or sell slaves in the state, but slavery itself was not illegal until an 1841 statute, and slaves could still be transported through the state with or by their masters. By 1849, many "black laws" restricting the rights of free persons of color were repealed; still, southern parts of Ohio were resistant to the drive to stiffen antislavery laws. Matthew Salafia, *Slavery's Borderland: Freedom and Bondage along the Ohio River* (Philadelphia: University of Pennsylvania Press, 2013), 220–222.

39. Seward, *Argument,* 25. The personal liberty law usually associated with northern state resistance to the Fugitive Slave Act of 1850 actually anteceded it by many decades. The Pennsylvania anti-kidnaping law of 1820 was one of these; that was the law challenged in *Prigg.* Thomas D. Morris, *Free Men All, The Personal Liberty Laws of the North, 1780–1860* (Baltimore: Johns Hopkins University Press, 1974), 94ff.

40. Francis Lieber, *Legal and Political Hermeneutics* (Boston: Little, Brown, 1839), vii, viii, 53, 57–58. Lieber hated slavery and inveighed against it yet owned slaves for the over two decades he lived and taught in Columbia, South Carolina. He did not fully embrace abolitionism even when he returned to teach at Columbia College in New York City in 1856. Hartmut Keil, "Francis Lieber's Attitudes on Race, Slavery, and Abolition," *Journal of American Ethnic History* 28 (2008), 13–33; Frank Freidel, "Francis Lieber, Charles Sumner, and Slavery" *Journal of Southern History* 9 (1943), 75–93.

41. Seward, *Argument,* 29–30. A copy of Lieber, *Essays on Property and Labor* (1841) in Seward's library was inscribed William H. Seward. Seward Family Digital Archive, https://sewardproject.org/seward-book-list/public/holdings/64646. For abolitionist writing on the Rendition Clause, see Sean Wilentz, *No Property in Man: Slavery and*

Anti-Slavery at the Nation's Founding (Cambridge, MA: Harvard University Press, 2018), 225–228.

42. Seward, *Argument*, 32, 33, 36, 38.

43. Note that Chase had never mentioned hospitality, or what Van Zandt owed to Andrew, as a fellow member of the community.

44. Seward, *Argument*, 18.

45. Seward, *Argument*, 18.

46. Seward, *Argument*, 14–15.

47. Seward to Chase, February 18, 1847, *Chase Papers, Correspondence*, 2:141. On the judge as Hercules, see Ronald Dworkin, *Taking Rights Seriously* (London, UK: Duckworth, 1977), 132–133. There was another voice in Seward's head, to be sure—Frances remained a consistent and insistent critic of slavery. See, e.g., Frances Seward to Lizette Worden [her sister], February 10, 1850, Seward Family papers, Seward Family Digital Archive, University of Rochester: "If I feel provoked with southern people for their persever[ance] in wrong my indignation is mixed with pity that they have been made by education unable to distinguish wrong from right—But for a northern man who advocates slavery my contempt is unmitigated." She shared these opinions with William; e.g., Frances Seward to Henry Seward, June 14, 1852, Seward Family Papers, Seward Family Digital Archive, University of Rochester. "I sat up after all had returned last night to read Dr [William Ellery] Channing on Slavery—It is full of true and beautiful sentiments," primarily religious objections to slavery.

48. Popular opinion on slavery in the 1840s did not favor abolition, but Free Soil proponents and the Liberty Party were slowly gaining ground. Eric Foner, *The Fiery Trial, Abraham Lincoln and Slavery* (New York: Norton, 2010), 41–42. Leonard L. Richards, *The Slave Power: The Free North and Southern Domination, 1780–1860* (Baton Rouge: Louisiana State University Press, 2000), 140, 164.

49. 46 U.S. 215, 225 (Woodbury, J.). Woodbury was engaging in what today would be called "textualism"—basing the decision on the plain text of the statute. "We see nothing, then, in the facts here, or in the instruction of the judge on them, secundum subjectam materiam, which shows this case not to have been, as the jury found it to be, one within the manifest design of the statute against harbouring and concealing persons who were fugitives from labor, after notice, or full knowledge of their character." 46 U. S. 215, 227. But the statute was itself unclear on the nature of "notice"—a slender threat upon which to hang Van Zandt's defense.

50. Bill Loomis, "The Great Railroad Conspiracy," http://www.hsmichigan.org/wp-content/uploads/2013/08/Railroad; Ronald P. Formisano, *The Birth of Mass Political Parties, Michigan, 1827–1861* (Princeton: Princeton University Press, 1971), 280.

51. Seward to Frances Seward, August 20, 1851; Seward to Frances Seward, September 4, 1851, *Seward at Washington*, 1:167.

52. Argument of William H. Seward in Defense of Abel Fitch and Others, September 11, 12, and 14, 1851 (Detroit: T. C. Leland, 1851), 3, 4.

53. U.S. v. Marigold, 50 U.S. 560 (1850); 13 (Seward argument).

54. Propeller Genesee Chief v. Fitzhugh, 53 U.S. 443 (1852).

55. Seward to James Renwick, October 1839, *Autobiography*, 443. Adam Mossoff, "The Rise and Fall of the First American Patent Thicket: The Sewing Machine War of the 1850s," *Arizona Law Review* 53 (2011), 171–194.

56. Frederick Seward on James Wilson, *Autobiography*, 670–671; Seward admitted to practice, Seward to Frances Seward, January 8, 1846, *Autobiography*, 773; Wilson v. Simpson, 50 U. S. 109 (1850); Stahr, *Seward*, 92.

57. Buck v. Hermance, 1 Blatchford 398 (N. D. NY) (1849) (the battling stove patent case); Troy Iron and Nail Factory v. Corning, 55 U.S. 193 (1853); *Seward at Washington*, 1:235, 239; *Autobiography*, 143; Seward, "Annual Message," 1839, in Baker, ed., *Works*, 2:192.

58. Foote v. Silsby, 9 F. Cas 373, 380 (N.D. New York) (1849) (Nelson, J); Silsby v. Foote, 55 U.S. 218 (1853); Silsby v. Foote 61 U.S. 378 (1858); W. J. Wesseler, "Elisha Foote," *Journal of the Patent Office Society* 9 (1920), 437–439.

59. Seward to Frances Seward, January 30, 1848, *Seward at Washington*, 1:63; McCormick v. Seymour, 15 F. Cas. 1329 (1854); Herbert N. Casson, *Cyrus Hall McCormick, His Life and His Work* (Chicago: McClurg, 1909), 91–93.

60. In these cases, I cannot see any of the cagey slippery side of Seward that political opponents decried. He simply tried to fulfill his duties to the client as counsel and pleader. There were legal questions as well in patent infringement cases, including an accounting of the receipts of the infringer that were due to the patent holder. But the suit for abridgment did not have to establish a legal right to the patent before the equitable remedy applied. John Norton Pomeroy, *A Treatise on Equitable Remedies* (San Francisco: Bancroft-Whitney, 1905), 972, sec. 566. The rules have changed greatly since that time, but Pomeroy was the gold standard then.

61. Daniel Webster and Henry Clay both had active appellate practices in federal courts during their Senate tenures; see Peter Charles Hoffer, *Daniel Webster and the Unfinished Constitution* (Lawrence: University Press of Kansas, 2020), 125, 140; Robert V. Remini, *Henry Clay, Statesman for the Union* (New York: Norton, 1991), 624.

62. Wiswall v. Sampson, 55 U.S. 52 (1853); Troy Nail and Iron v. Corning, 55 U.S. 193 (1853); Huff v. Hutchinson, 55 U.S. 586 (1853). The purpose of diversity is to prevent an out-of-state party to a suit from the bias of judges or jurors in a state court proceeding. It was part of the Judiciary Act of 1789. The provision was and remains controversial, and over the years has been modified to require complete diversity and to raise the monetary minimum at stake. See Peter Charles Hoffer, Williamjames Hull Hoffer, and N. H. E. Hull, *The Federal Courts: An Essential History* (New York: Oxford University Press, 2016), 37.

63. *Argument of William H. Seward, in The Albany Bridge Case, Before The United States Circuit Court, Held at The City of New York in September, 1858* (Albany, 1859).

64. Charles River Bridge v. Warren Bridge, 46 U. S. 420 (1837); Pennsylvania v. Wheeling and Belmont Bridge Company, 52 U. S. 421 (1855). For Webster's argument in Gibbons, see Hoffer, *Webster*, 73–93.

65. Jeremiah S. Black, "The Character of Mr. Seward, A Reply to C. F. Adams Sr." [1874], in *Essays and Speeches of Jeremiah S. Black*, ed. Chauncey F. Black (New York: Appleton, 1886), 136. As outcoming secretary of state, Black had to sign Seward's appointment to the post—one that Black would have been happy to occupy himself.

3. "There Is a Higher Law Than the Constitution"

1. *Autobiography*, 60–64.

2. William H. Seward, *The Life and Public Services of John Quincy Adams*, 2nd ed. (New York: Saxton, Barker, 1860), xi. On Seward as Adams's disciple, see Richard Immerman,

Empire for Liberty: A History of American Imperialism (Princeton: Princeton University Press, 2010), 16, 105.

3. *Autobiography*, 671–672, 771; *Seward at Washington*, 1:44; Seward, *The Life and Public Services of John Quincy Adams*, 45; 378; 390. On Adams and abolitionism, see Hoffer, *Gag Rule,*, 87 (antislavery petitions gag rule would die, but not by his hand).

4. By contrast, "The Seward House on 33 South Street was a stop on the Underground Railroad—a secret network of safe houses in which Conductors like Harriet Tubman led runaway slaves, or "Passengers," to freedom. These dangerous journeys took place by night and on foot, so freedom seekers had to travel light. In this module, learn about what precious few things Passengers would carry with them on their flight to freedom." Seward House Museum, "Hands on History," https://sewardhouse.org/education/hands-history. It has been argued that female abolitionists saw their program not in legalistic terms, but in religious terms, sometimes incorporating lawlessness. See, e.g., Elizabeth B. Clark, "Religion, Rights, and Difference in the Early Woman's Rights Movement," *Wisconsin Women's Law Journal* 29 (1987), 29–57.

5. This does not mean that everyone or indeed anyone was listening. Rachel A. Shelden, *Washington Brotherhood: Politics, Social Life, and the Coming of the Civil War* (Chapel Hill: University of North Carolina Press, 2015), 27.

6. *New York Tribune*, March 19, 1850, 1; Gideon Welles, *Diary of Gideon Welles* (Boston: Houghton Mifflin, 1911), 1:205.

7. Sean Wilenz, *The Rise of American Democracy, Jefferson to Lincoln* (New York: Norton, 2005), xxi–xxii, 629–630.

8. Seward's views, *Seward at Washington*, 1:57; Lincoln's views, Michael Burlingame, *Lincoln, A Life* (Baltimore: Johns Hopkins University Press, 2008), 1: 278.

9. Robert Kagan, *Dangerous Nation* (New York: Knopf, 2007), 249–250; Michael F. Holt, *The Rise and Fall of the American Whig Party: Jacksonian Politics and the Onset of the Civil War* (New York: Oxford University Press, 1999), 300.

10. Seward to Frances Seward, January 1848, *Seward at Washington*, 1:60–61; Seward to Weed, August 31, 1848, *Seward at Washington*, 1:77; Seward campaign talks, *Seward at Washington*, 1:86; Seward's rule for debate [1850]: *Seward at Washington*, 1:121.

11. Zachary Taylor, Inaugural Address, March 5, 1849, https://avalon.law.yale.edu/19th_century/taylor.asp; Stahr, *Seward*, 118–119.

12. Stahr, *Seward*, 120–121; Herman Belz, "Popular Sovereignty, The Right of Revolution, and California Statehood," in *The California Republic*, ed. Brian P. Janiskee and Ken Masugi (Lanham, MD: Rowman and Littlefield, 2004), 12–26.

13. California State Constitution of 1849, https://www.sos.ca.gov/archives/collections/constitutions/1849/.

14. George Edward Carter links Seward's higher language to the work of William Lloyd Garrison and other immediatist abolitionists. George Edward Carter, "The Use of the Doctrine of Higher Law in the American Anti-Slavery Crusade, 1830–1860" (PhD diss., University of Oregon, 1970), 177–196. But Seward was not one of these, and I argue that the basis for his notion was not radical abolitionism but relational rights. As he explained himself in a letter to Frances in the first days of his US Senate service, on March 8, 1849, he told the members "that I was uncompromising in my opposition to slavery, but at the same time calmly firm in my intention to abide by the Union and to practice the necessary moderation to save the Union and to accomplish

whatever was attainable." Seward Family Papers, Seward Family Digital Archive, University of Rochester. On the events of that day, see Stahr, *Seward*, 116–132. On Seward's views: Manisha Sinha, *The Slave's Cause: A History of Abolitionism* (New Haven: Yale University Press, 2016), 491–492; on Clay's compromise: Robert Remini, *Henry Clay: Statesman for the Union* (New York: Norton, 1991), 732–737; on the Calhoun and Webster speeches: Hoffer, *Gag-Rule*, 66–85. Once he was a senator, Seward paid for the printing of his speeches. *Seward at Washington*, 1:162. Prior to that, he depended on Weed or Greeley to print and disseminate his speeches.

15. Flat, hoarse voice: Taylor, *Seward*, 81. Seward prepared notes for his Senate speeches then wrote drafts. He spoke rather than read, like an attorney in court addressing the bench. The notes are preserved in the Seward papers, drawer 32, folders 58, 60, 67, 106–112, University of Rochester Library. Greeley's *New York Tribune*, March 12, had the galleries full. Frederick Seward recalled that "no crowd filled the galleries, and there was but a slim attendance of senators" (*Reminiscences*, 77). More members of the House of Representatives crossed over to the Senate chamber to hear the speech than senators remained to listen. Greeley's motives were suspect, but perhaps Frederick's memory was equally unreliable. Seward, Speech in the Senate, March 11, 1850, in Baker, ed., *Works*, 1:56. Seward's "higher law" speech deserves far more attention than it has gotten in recent historical studies, compared, for example, to Abraham Lincoln's "house divided" speech. See, e.g., Avery Craven, *The Coming of the Civil War* (Chicago: University of Chicago Press, 1957), 340; Eric Foner, *Fiery Trial*, 102.

16. Was Seward a white supremacist? Yes. This was true of most of the Conscience Whigs and the Republicans. See Michael F. Holt, *The Political Crisis of the 1850s* (New York: Wiley, 1978), 188; James A. Rawley, *Race and Politics: Bleeding Kansas and the Coming of the Civil War* (Lincoln: University of Nebraska Press, 1969), 256; and George M. Frederickson, *The Arrogance of Race: Historical Perspectives on Slavery, Racism, and Social Inequality* (Hanover, NH: University Press of New England, 1988), 60. But it was possible to be a white supremacist and still argue long and hard for the legal and civil rights of Blacks. Lincoln, in his first debate with Stephen Douglas, on August 21, 1858, conceded, "I, as well as judge Douglas, am in favor of the race to which I belong having the superior position. I have never said anything to the contrary, but I hold that, not withstanding all this, there is no reason in the world why the negro is not entitled to all the natural rights enumerated in the Declaration of Independence, the right to life, liberty, and the pursuit of happiness. . . . I agree with judge Douglas he is not my equal in many respects . . . perhaps not in moral or intellectual endowment. But in the right to eat the bread . . . which his own hand earns, he is my equal and the equal of . . . every living man." Lincoln, First Debate with Douglas, August 22, 1858, reprinted in Stephen Berry, ed., *A House Dividing: The Lincoln Douglas Debates of 1858* (New York: Oxford University Press, 2016), 19. On biformities in American life, see Michael Kammen, *People of Paradox: An Inquiry Concerning the Origins of American Civilization* (New York: Knopf, 1972).

17. Seward, Speech of March 11, 1850, in Baker, ed., *Works*, 1:57.

18. Seward, Speech of March 11, 1850, in Baker, ed., *Works*, 1:60–61; capitalization per the published version of the speech that Seward printed and distributed.

19. Seward, Speech of March 11, 1850, in Baker, ed., *Works*, 1:62–63. Seward may have been referring to Senator Calhoun's idea of "concurrent majority," in which a

minority of the states or the interests therein could block a majority of states or the people from acting. It was a negative theory of constitutionalism. See Lawrence M. Anderson, *Federalism, Secession, and the American State: Divided, We Secede* (New York: Routledge, 2013), 37, 38.

20. Seward, Speech of March 11, 1850, in Baker, ed., *Works*, 1:65–66.

21. Seward, Speech of March 11, 1850, in Baker, ed., *Works*, 1:67–68; Seward to Frances Seward, February 15, 1831, *Autobiography*, 181.

22. Seward to Frances Seward, January 31, 1831, *Autobiography*, 176.

23. Seward to Roscoe Conkling, quoted in Van Deusen, *Seward*, 120.

24. Seward, Speech of March 11, 1850, in Baker, ed., *Works*, 1:72–73.

25. Seward, Speech of March 11, 1850, in Baker, ed., *Works*, 1:72–73.

26. Seward, Speech of March 11, 1850, in Baker, ed., *Works*, 1:74. Seward had long argued and here continued to argue that the principles of hospitality required that southerners remained part of the political community. See Seward to William Jay and Gerritt Smith, October 22, 1838, in Baker, ed., *Works*, 1: 431.

27. Seward, Speech of March 11, 1850, in Baker, ed., *Works*, 1: 73

28. Seward, Speech of March 11, 1850, in Baker, ed., *Works*, 1:74–75. One might read Seward's reference to higher law as abolitionist rhetoric. His critics later certainly assumed that it placed him in their camp. Steven Lubet, *Fugitive Justice: Runaways, Rescuers, and Slavery on Trial* (Cambridge: Harvard University Press, 2011), 320, 322; R. L. Dabney, "Memoir of a Narrative received of Col. John B. Baldwin, of Staunton, Touching the Origin of the War" [March 1865], *Southern Historical Society Papers* 1 (1876), 458. But Seward was not an abolitionist. See Jane Pease, "The Road to the Higher Law," *New York History* 40 (1959), 117–136. Seward's opponents in the Whig Party explicitly rejected his relational rights language. See, e.g., Benjamin Robbins Curtis, speaking at Faneuil Hall in Boston, on November 26, 1850, "With rights of fugitive slaves, I firmly believe Massachusetts has nothing to do. It is enough for us that they have no right to be here. Our peace and safety they have no right to invade; whether they come as fugitives. . . . this is our soil sacred to our peace." *Proceedings of the Constitutional Meeting at Faneuil Hall, November 26, 1850* (Boston: Beals and Green, 1850), 18. Curtis, a lawyer, was a commissioner under the Fugitive Slave Act of 1850 charged with returning runaways to their masters who, later sitting on the Supreme Court, dissented in *Dred Scott v. Sandford* (1857). Nor did advocates of fugitives' rights use relational rights jurisprudence. Generally, see Earl M. Maltz, *Fugitive Slave on Trial: The Anthony Burns Case and Abolitionist Outrage* (Lawrence: University Press of Kansas, 2010).

29. Mark E. Neely, Jr., *Lincoln and the Triumph of the Nation: Constitutional Conflict in the American Civil War* (Chapel Hill: University of North Carolina Press, 2011), 51.

30. Seward, Speech of March 11, 1850, in Baker, ed., *Works*, 1:75.

31. Seward, Speech of March 11, 1850, in Baker, ed., *Works*, 1:75. There were plausible arguments that the Union was dissoluble. See, e.g., Forrest McDonald, *Novus Ordo Seclorum: The Intellectual Origins of the Constitution* (Lawrence: University Press of Kansas, 1985), 281; Cynthia Nicoletti, *Secession on Trial: The Treason Prosecution of Jefferson Davis* (New York: Cambridge University Press, 2017), 84–120.

32. Seward would revisit these points in his October 25, 1858 "Irresistible Conflict" speech and come to a different conclusion. On slavery's spread, see Edward Baptist, *The Half Has Never Been Told: Slavery and the Making of American Capitalism* (New

York: Basic, 2014), 33–34, 125–126; Robert H. Gudmestad, *A Troublesome Commerce: The Transformation of the Interstate Slave* Trade (Baton Rouge: Louisiana State University Press, 2002), 210–211; Walter Johnson, *Soul by Soul: Life Inside the Antebellum Slave Market* (Cambridge: Harvard University Press, 2000); 104–105; Thomas D. Morris, *Southern Slavery and the Law, 1619–1860* (Chapel Hill: University of North Carolina Press, 2004), 65; Adam Rothman, *Slave Country: American Expansion and the Origins of the Deep South* (Cambridge, MA: Harvard University Press, 2005), 49.

33. Seward, Speech of March 11, 1850, Baker, ed., *Works*, 1:79. The reference to the Carpathian Mountains was inspired by Seward's strong support of Louis Kossuth, the Hungarian politician exiled by the Austro-Hungarian imperial government.

34. Seward, Speech of March 11, 1850, Baker, ed., *Works*, 1:79.

35. Seward, Speech of March 11, 1850, Baker, ed., *Works*, 1:79.

36. Seward, Speech of March 11, 1850, Baker, ed., *Works*, 1:88, 89.

37. Weed's response: Stahr, *Seward*, 126.

38. Frederick Seward, *Reminiscences*, 78; Thomas Pratt, quoted in Frederic Bancroft, *The Life of William H. Seward* (New York: Harpers, 1900), 1:255–256.

39. Seward, Speech of July 2, 1850, in Baker, ed., *Works*, 1: 100

40. 9 Stat. 462 (1850).

41. The full story appears in Angela F. Murphy, *The Jerry Rescue: The Fugitive Slave Law, Northern Rights, and the American Sectional Crisis* (New York: Oxford University Press, 2016), 132–133 (Seward goes bail for Smith). There is some surmise that this episode was the reason why Frances opened the Seward House as a stop on the underground railroad.

42. Leonard L. Richards, *Gentlemen of Property and Standing, Anti-Abolitionist Mobs in Jacksonian America* (New York: Oxford University Press, 1970); David Grimsted, *American Mobbing, 1828–1861, Toward Civil War* (New York: Oxford University Press, 1998), 76; Robert H. Churchill, *The Underground Railroad and the Geography of Violence in Antebellum America* (New York: Cambridge University Press, 2020), 180–198.

43. See, e.g., Alice Felt Tyler, *Freedom's Ferment: Phases of American Social History, to 1860* (Minneapolis: University of Minnesota Press, 1944), 166–224.

44. Seward to Christopher Morgan, January 11, 1851, *Seward at Washington*, 1:161; Frederick Seward, *Reminiscences*, 108.

45. Michael F. Holt, *Franklin Pierce* (New York: Times Books, 2010), 10–11, 124; Frederic Bancroft, *The Life of William H. Seward* (New York: Harper, 1900), 1:304.

46. Seward to Frances Seward, January 4, 1854; Seward to Thurlow Weed, January 13, 1854; Letter to the New York meeting against the compromise, February 1854; *Seward at Washington* 1:216, 217, 218, 220; Alice Elizabeth Malavasic, *The F-Street Mess: How Southern Senators Rewrote the Kansas-Nebraska Act* (Chapel Hill: University of North Carolina Press, 2017), 140–141, 151–152; Wade quoted in John R. Wunder and Joann M. Ross, "'The Eclipse of the Sun': The Kansas Nebraska Act in Historical Perspective" in *The Kansas-Nebraska Act of 1854* (Lincoln: University of Nebraska Press, 2008), 1. For Wade's view of slavery, see James Oakes, *The Scorpion's Sting: Antislavery and the Coming of the Civil War* (New York: Norton, 2014), 48 (Wade acknowledged that the Constitution forbade the federal government from abolishing slavery where it existed).

47. Seward, "Freedom and Public Faith" Speech of February 17, 1854, in Baker, ed., *Works*, 4:438, 439.

48. Seward to Theodore Parker, March 12, 1854, in *Seward at Washington*, 1:232.

49. Williamjames Hull Hoffer, *The Caning of Charles Sumner: Honor, Idealism, and the Origins of the Civil War* (Baltimore: Johns Hopkins University Press, 2010), 7–35, *Seward at Washington*, 1:272. Frances Seward had come to admire Sumner, and visited with him just before his Crime Against Kansas speech. Frances Miller Seward to Lazette Worden, December 25, 1851, "Charles Sumner was here yesterday I met him in the office—I like him exceedingly & so would you I think—he is frank & fearless & sincere—very well looking and gentlemanly in his deportment." Frances Miller Seward to Lazette Worden, April 26, 1856, "Charles Sumner dined with Henry yesterday—I saw him after dinner—He is to speak on the Kansas question next week or the week after." Seward Family Papers, Seward Family Digital Archive, University of Rochester.

4. "An Irrepressible Conflict between Opposing and Enduring Forces"

1. William E. Gienapp, *The Origins of the Republican Party, 1852–1856* (New York: Oxford University Press, 1987), 82–84, 86, 308–309; Stahr, *Seward*, 155–157; Seward, Speech of October 12, 1855, in *Seward at Washington*, 1:256.

2. Seward, "Freedom in Kansas," Speech of March 3, 1858, in US Senate, Baker, ed., *Works* 4:586.

3. The case is fully traced in Don E. Fehrenbacher, *The Dred Scott Case: Its Significance in American Law and Politics* (New York: Oxford University Press, 1990). The original documents for the first federal (circuit) court case can be found in the Kansas City NARA archive. These are described in Peter Charles Hoffer, Williamjames Hull Hoffer, and N. E. H. Hull, *The Federal Courts: An Essential History* (New York: Oxford University Press, 2016), 135–138.

4. Seward, Speech of March 3, 1858, in Baker, ed., *Works*, 4: 587; Fehrenbacher, *The Dred Scott Case*, 473–474; Dred Scott v. Sandford, 60 U.S. 393 (1857). Lincoln interpreted Taney as saying that in his "House Divided" speech of June 16, 1858. "Such a decision is all that slavery now lacks of being alike lawful in all the States. Welcome, or unwelcome, such decision *is* probably coming, and will soon be upon us, unless the power of the present political dynasty shall be met and overthrown. We shall *lie down* pleasantly dreaming that the people of *Missouri* are on the verge of making their State *free*; and we shall *awake* to the *reality*, instead, that the *Supreme* Court has made *Illinois* a *slave* State." See also John Stauffer, *Giants: The Parallel Lives of Frederick Douglas and Abraham Lincoln* (New York: Hachette, 2008), 197, 292.

5. Stahr, *Seward*, 170–171; Kenneth M. Stampp, *America in 1857: A Nation on the Brink* (New York: Oxford University Press, 1990), 295.

6. Taylor, *Seward*, 106–107; *Seward at Washington*, 1:351. Kenneth M. Stampp dismisses these addresses as "occasional flings at the South" meant to appease Northern antislavery opinion. *And the War Came*, 19.

7. Seward, Speech at Cleveland, Ohio, October 26, 1848, in Baker, ed., *Works*, 3:293, 295; *Seward at Washington*, 1:85–86.

8. William H. Seward, Address at Rochester, New York, October 25, 1858, "The Irrepressible Conflict." *New York Evening Journal*, 1.

9. Seward, "Irrepressible Conflict," 1.

10. George Fitzhugh, *Cannibals All!, or, Slaves without Masters* (Richmond, VA: Morris, 1857), xiii, 371; Thomas E. Schneider, *Lincoln's Defense of Politics: The Public Man and His Opponents in the Crisis over Slavery* (Columbia: University of Missouri Press, 2006), 10, 54–55.

11. Seward, "Irrepressible Conflict," 1.

12. Seward, "Irrepressible Conflict," 1. Herbert Butterfield, *The Whig Interpretation of History* (New York: Norton, [1931] 1965), 11, is eerily similar to Seward's approach.

13. Seward, "Irrepressible Conflict," 1.

14. Seward, "Irrepressible Conflict," 1.

15. Seward, "Irrepressible Conflict," 1.

16. Seward, "Irrepressible Conflict," 1.

17. Seward, "Irrepressible Conflict," 1.

18. Seward, "Irrepressible Conflict," 2.

19. Seward, "Irrepressible Conflict," 2.

20. Fitzhugh, *Cannibals All!,* 368; "Republican principles" Speech of Hon. Abraham Lincoln, of Illinois, at the Republican State Convention, June 16, 1858," reprinted in *New-York Tribune,* June 24, 1858, 3.

21. Seward, "Irrepressible Conflict," 2.

22. Seward, "Irrepressible Conflict," 2. Seward to Theodore Parker, November 19, 1858, Seward Papers, University of Rochester.

23. Seward, "Irrepressible Conflict," 2

24. Seward, "Irrepressible Conflict," 2, 3.

25. Seward, "Irrepressible Conflict," 3.

26. Seward, "Irrepressible Conflict," 3. If this sounds familiar, it was repeated almost verbatim by Lincoln in his Cooper Union address two years later. See Hoffer, *Uncivil Warriors,* 39. On the uses of the Declaration of Independence by the antislavery forces, see Dwight Dumond, *Antislavery Origins of the Civil War in the United States* (Ann Arbor: University of Michigan Press, 1939), 73; and Oakes, *The Scorpion's Sting,* 84–89. For the southern version of the framers' thinking, see Michael O'Brien, *Intellectual Life and the American South, 1810–1860* (Chapel Hill: University of North Carolina Press, 2012), 192.

27. Seward, "Irrepressible Conflict" 3.

28. Seward, "Irrepressible Conflict" 3.

29. Seward, "Irrepressible Conflict" 3. Of the profitability of slavery there is no doubt. On this, see Baptist, *Half Has Never Been Told,* 414; and Robert W. Fogel and Stanley L. Engerman, *Time on the Cross: The Economics of American Negro Slavery* (New York: Norton, 1974) 1:225.

30. David Brion Davis, *The Problem of Slavery in the Age of Emancipation* (New York: Random House, 2014), 218–219; James Henry Hammond's Senate speech, on March 4, 1858, is discussed by Samantha Maziarz, "Mudsill Theory," in *Class in America: An Encyclopedia,* ed. Robert Weir (Westport, CT; Greenwood, 2017), 549–550.

31. Seward, "Irrepressible Conflict," 3.

32. Seward, "Irrepressible Conflict," pp. 3–4. On the so-called Ostend Manifesto of 1854, see Michael Todd Landis, *Northern Men with Southern Loyalties: The Democratic Party and the Sectional Crisis* (Ithaca: Cornell University Press, 2014), 94–95. On the movement to reopen the Atlantic slave trade, see Sinha, *The Slave's Cause,* 363ff.

33. Seward, "Irrepressible Conflict," 4.
34. Seward, "Irrepressible Conflict," 4.
35. Seward, "Irrepressible Conflict," 4.
36. Seward, "Irrepressible Conflict," 4, 5.
37. Seward, "Irrepressible Conflict," 4, 5.
38. Stahr, *Seward*, 177, surmises that some of Seward's supporters wanted him to absent himself from the scene lest he further inflame sectional passions and cost himself the nomination. Seward, "The State of the Country" Speech to the Senate on the admission of Kansas, February 29, 1860, in Baker, ed., *Works*, 4:619, 628, 632–633.
39. Seward, "Annual Message to the State Legislature of January 1, 1839," in Baker, ed., *Works*, 2:191. "Free legal professionals," that is, those counsel for the abolitionists or the alleged runaway slaves in the antebellum era, are discussed in Peter Karsten, "Revisiting the Critiques of Those who Upheld the Fugitive Slave Acts in the 1840s and 1850s," *American Journal of Legal History* 58 (2018), 291–325.

5. "I Am to Engage in Conducting a War against a Portion of the American People"

1. Michael S. Green, *Lincoln and The Election of 1860* (Carbondale: Southern Illinois University Press, 2011), 41–65; Stahr, *Seward*, 182–209; Goodwin, *Team of Rivals*, 75, 263.
2. On Lincoln and secession, see David Donald, *Lincoln Reconsidered: Essays on the Civil War Era* (New York: Knopf, 1955), 129–130; Hoffer, *Uncivil Warriors*, 20–47; Stephen A. Channing, *Crisis of Fear: Secession in South Carolina* (New York: Norton, 1974), 265–291.
3. Seward to Lincoln, December 26, 1860, *Seward at Washington*, 1:484. On the proposed compromise, see Daniel W. Crofts, *Reluctant Confederates: Upper South Unionists in the Secession Crisis* (Chapel Hill: University of North Carolina Press, 1989), 199.
4. Taylor, *Seward*, 142–144: the staff was forty-two, only a few of whom were diplomats, and some of whom were southern sympathizers. George F. Kennan, *American Diplomacy* (Chicago: University of Chicago Press, 1951), 46; U.S. Department of State, Duties of the Secretary of State, https://www.state.gov/duties-of-the-secretary-of-state and https://history.state.gov/departmenthistory/people/; William P. Mahoney, "The Lawyer as Diplomat," *American Bar Association Journal* 53 (1967), 46–47. My sense from the literature is that lawyers/diplomats are not always regarded highly.
5. Goodwin, *Team of Rivals*, 280, 283–284, explores the choice but does not link it to country lawyering.
6. Jean H. Baker, *James Buchanan* (New York: Henry Holt, 2004), 128–139; Stahr, *Seward*, 222; Goodwin, *Team of Rivals*, 296–300.
7. Seward, "The State of the Union" January 12, 1861, in Baker, ed., *Works* 4:651.
8. Seward, "The State of the Union" January 12, 1861, in Baker, ed., *Works* 4:652.
9. Seward, "The State of the Union" January 12, 1861, in Baker, ed., *Works* 4:662, 663; Stahr, *Seward*, 225; Goodwin, *Team of Rivals*, 300–301, quoting northern newspaper accounts. Not everyone was favorably impressed. Radical abolitionist Wendell Phillips accused Seward of leading "a hellish crew, whose Sermon on the Mount was the slave clause of the Constitution." Wendell Phillips, "The Argument for Disunion" January 20, 1861, in Louis Filler, ed., *Wendell Phillips on Civil Rights and Freedom* (New

York: Hill and Wang, 2965), 117. For a parallel argument about the primacy of the Constitution in the secession crisis see Michael F. Conlin, *The Constitutional Origins of the Civil War* (Cambridge, UK: Cambridge University Press, 2019).

10. Seward, "The State of the Union" Speech in the Senate, January 30, 1861, in Baker, ed. *Works*, 4:670, 672.

11. For two different judgments of the role that Seward played in the months between the election and the inauguration, see Michael Robinson, "William Henry Seward and the Onset of the Secession Crisis," *Civil War History* 59 (2013), 32–66 and Stampp, *And the War Came*, 20.

12. Seward to Frances Seward, January 13, 1861, *Seward at Washington*, 1:496; Stahr, *Seward*, 225–236, 243–244; Van Deusen, *Seward*, 246–251.

13. Stahr, *Seward*, 327. Dorothy Wickenden, *The Agitators: Three Friends Who Fought for Abolition and Women's Rights* (New York: Scribner's, 2021), 136, suggests that Frances's retreat to Auburn was a form of protest, an "internal rebellion steadily gathering force" during the ten years in Washington, against Seward's moderation on the slavery issue.

14. *Seward at Washington* 1:492; Albany Bridge Case, 69 U.S. 403 (1865).

15. There is no documentary evidence from that time that Seward was the moving force behind the project, but it may be inferred. Aaron W. Mars, "Chapter Two: The Civil War Origins of the FRUS Series," A History of the *Foreign Relations of the United States* Series, https://history.state.gov/historicaldocuments/frus-history/chapter-2; Richard W. Leopold, "The Foreign Relations Series: A Centennial Estimate," *Journal of American History* 49 (1963), 597.

16. On the idea of a "law office cabinet," see Daniel W. Stowell, "Abraham Lincoln: Lawyer, Leader, President," in *Lincoln, the Law, and Presidential Leadership*, ed. Charles M. Hubbard (Carbondale: Southern Illinois University Press, 2015), 24, and Hoffer, *Uncivil Warriors*, 49–50. Speed quoted in Victor B. Howard, *Black Liberation in Kentucky, Emancipation and Freedom, 1862–1884* (Lexington: University of Kentucky Press, 2015), 88. Other descriptions from Hoffer, *Uncivil Warriors*, 49–52.

17. Frederick Seward, *Reminiscences*, 147 (Lincoln relies on Seward in foreign affairs).

18. Lincoln quoted in Goodwin, *Team of Rivals*, 319; Don E. Fehrenbacher and Virginia Fehrenbacher, eds., *Recollected Words of Abraham Lincoln* (Palo Alto, CA: Stanford University Press, 1996), 243; Ronald C. White, Jr., *A. Lincoln: A Biography* (New York: Random House, 2009), 355 (Cameron choice).

19. Goodwin, *Team of Rivals*, 324–326; Lincoln, "Address at Cooper Institute," February 27, 1860, in *Collected Works of Abraham Lincoln*, ed. Roy P. Basler (New Brunswick, NJ: Rutgers University Press, 1954), 3:523. On the address in context, see Harold Holzer, *Lincoln at Cooper Union: The Speech that Made Abraham Lincoln President* (New York: Simon and Schuster, 2004), 249–284.

20. Goodwin, *Team of Rivals*, 326. Lincoln, "First Inaugural Address—Final Version," March 4, 1861, in Basler, ed., *Collected Works*, 4:262–271. The reference to a lawless invasion surely meant John Brown's raid at Harper's Ferry, but it was federal territory, not Virginia's. My account is taken from my *Uncivil Warriors*, 41–46.

21. Seward's proposed revisions are in Abraham Lincoln, "First Inaugural Address—First Edition and Revisions," in Basler, ed., *Collected Works*, 4:261–262.

22. Stahr, *Seward*, 253.

23. Stahr, *Seward*, 254, 258; Charles Francis Adams, *An Autobiography* (Cambridge, MA: Houghton Mifflin, 1916), 73. Seward visited with Adams when the former stayed in Quincy, Massachusetts, in the Summer of 1860. George E. Baker, "Memoir of Seward," in Baker, ed., *Works*, 4:83.

24. Martin Duberman, *Charles Francis Adams, 1807–1886* (Stanford: Stanford University Press, 1960), 236–237, 251, 253, 256.

25. Commissioners to Mr. Seward, March 12, 1861, https://avalon.law.yale.edu/19th_century/csa_c031261.asp; William J. Cooper, *We Have the War upon Us, The Onset of the Civil War, November 1860–April 1861* (New York: Knopf, 2012), 222–225.

26. Don H. Doyle, *The Cause of All Nations: An International History of the American Civil War* (New York: Basic Books, 2014), 4. Seward's penchant for loose conversation did not always further this aim. See, e.g., Thurlow Weed defending Seward from the accusation of demeaning Britain during a dinner party: Thurlow Weed, "To the Editor of the [London] Times, December 12, 1862," in *Selections from the Newspapers Articles of Thurlow Weed* (Albany, NY: Weed and Parsons, 1877), 104–108.

27. Thornton Kirkland Lothrop, *William Henry Seward* (Boston: Houghton Mifflin, 1899), 310–311. See also Jack L. Goldsmith and Eric A. Posner, *The Limits of International Law* (New York: Oxford University Press, 2005), 48, accusing Seward of manipulating "customary" international law to fit national aims.

28. Goodwin, *Team of Rivals*, 334–344.

29. Seward to Frances Seward, March 16, 1861, *Seward at Washington*, 1:530; Seward to Lincoln, March 15, 1861; Chase to Lincoln, March 16, 1861, Lincoln Papers, LC.

30. Horace Greeley to William Henry Seward, June 16, 1860, *New York Saturday Press*, 4. On "April Fools letter," see Patrick Sowle, "A Reappraisal of Seward's Memorandum of April 1, 1861, to Lincoln," *Journal of Southern History* 33 (1967), 234–239; Garry Wills, "Henry Adams on Lincoln," in *Lincoln Revisited: New Insights from the Lincoln Forum*, ed. John Y. Simon, Harold Holzer, and Dawn Vogel (New York: Fordham University Press, 2009), 306. Frederick Seward recalled that his father's handwriting was "almost illegible, and he actually copied the document and hand-carried it to Lincoln." Frederick Seward, *Autobiography*, 149.

31. Abraham Lincoln to William H. Seward, April 1, 1861, in Basler, ed., *Collected Works*, 4:317–318.

32. Abraham Lincoln to William H. Seward, April 1, 1861, in Basler, ed., *Collected Works*, 4:317–318; Donald Stoker, *Grand Design: Strategy and the U.S. Civil War* (New York: Oxford University Press, 2010), 38; Allan Peskin, *Winfield Scott and the Profession of Arms* (Kent, OH: Kent State University Press, 2003), 236, 238–239.

33. Stephen C. Neff, *Justice in Blue and Gray: A Legal History of the Civil War* (Cambridge: Harvard University Press, 2010), 40–44. John C. Fremont, military governor of Missouri at the start of the war, declared martial law and under it freed the slaves. Lincoln countermanded both orders and removed Fremont when he refused to rescind the emancipation order. In 1864, because of the almost continuous operation of Confederate marauders, martial law was declared over the entire state of Kentucky. Martial law was sometimes declared in localities when draft resistance broke out. There as in southern Illinois, Ohio, and Indiana, state courts did little to restrain the imposition of martial law by Union commanders.

34. Crofts, *Reluctant Confederates*, 300; Emory M. Thomas, *The Dogs of War, 1861* (New York: Oxford University Press, 2011), 49; Kevin Peraino, *Lincoln in the World: The Making of a Statesman and the Dawn of American Power* (New York: Random House, 2013), 112; Doyle, *The Cause of All Nations*, 63–65.

35. Abraham Lincoln to William H. Seward, April 1, 1861, in Basler, ed., *Collected Works*, 4:318.

36. Van Deusen, *Seward*, 289–290; Mark E. Neely, Jr., *The Fate of Liberty: Abraham Lincoln and Civil Liberties* (New York: Oxford University Press, 1991), 10–11, 18–20, 28; Stahr, *Seward*, 287–288. But Seward's role is questioned in Noah Feldman, *The Broken Constitution: Lincoln, Slavery, and the Refounding of America* (New York: Farrar, Straus and Giroux, 2021), 188.

37. William C. Davis, *Jefferson Davis, The Man and His Hour* (Baton Rouge: University of Louisiana Press, 1996), 43, 61, 87; John Carl Parrish, *George Wallace Jones* (Iowa City: State Historical Society of Iowa, 1912), 241–245.

38. Jones v. Seward, 1864 N.Y. Misc. LEXIS 27 ** (1863).

39. Seward to Charles Francis Adams, April 10, 1861, no. 39, Message of the President to Congress, 2nd Sess., 37th Cong., https://history.state.gov/historicaldocuments/frus1861/d39.

40. Seward to Charles Francis Adams, April 10, 1861.

41. Seward to Charles Francis Adams, April 10, 1861; Charles Francis Adams [son], *Charles Francis Adams* (Boston: Houghton Mifflin, 1900), 195.

42. Seward to Charles Francis Adams, April 10, 1861.

43. Seward to Charles Francis Adams, April 10, 1861.

44. Seward to Charles Francis Adams, April 10, 1861.

45. See, e.g., the argument in Hoffer, *Uncivil Warriors*, 52–55.

46. Seward to Charles Francis Adams, April 10, 1861.

47. Seward to Charles Francis Adams, April 10, 1861.

48. Stahr, *Seward*, 291; Seward to Charles Francis Adams, May 21, 1861, no. 46, Message of President Lincoln to 2nd Sess., 37th Congress, https://history.state.gov/historicaldocuments/frus1861/d46.

49. But like his entry into patent law, Seward was not only learning, he was mastering diplomatic techniques of intrigue. See Stephen P. Randolph, "William Seward and the Diplomacy of the Civil War," *Oxford Research Encyclopedia of American History*, https://doi.org/10.1093/acrefore/9780199329175.013.751.

50. Seward to Charles Francis Adams, May 21, 1861.

51. Seward to Charles Francis Adams, May 21, 1861.

52. Seward to Charles Francis Adams, May 21, 1861.

53. Seward to Charles Francis Adams, May 21, 1861. On the blockade, see James M. McPherson, *The War on the Waters, The Union and Confederate Navies, 1861–1865* (Chapel Hill: University of North Carolina Press, 2012), 20–21. On the legality of the blockade and the Prize Cases that followed, see Hoffer, *Uncivil Warriors*, 94–116, and the Prize Cases, 67 U.S. 635 (1862).

54. Seward to Adams, May 21, 1861.

55. Seward to Adams, June 19, 1861, no. 55; Seward to Adams, July 21, 1861, no. 61; Seward to Adams, September 11, 1861, no. 81; Message of President Lincoln to

2nd Sess., 37th Congress, https://history.state.gov/historicaldocuments/frus1861/; Jones, *Blue and Gray Diplomacy*, 192–202.

56. Seward to Adams, August 17, 1861, no. 70; Seward to Lord Lyons, October 14, 1861, no. 97, Message of President Lincoln to 2nd Sess., 37th Congress, https://history.state.gov/historicaldocuments/frus1861; Christopher Dickey, *Our Man in Charleston, Britain's Secret Agent in the Civil War South* (New York: Crown, 2016), 280–284; *The War of the Rebellion*, Ser. II, vol. 2 (Washington, DC: Government Printing Office, 1897), 644.

57. Duberman, *Adams*, 273; Seward to Adams, August 17, 1861, no. 70; Seward to Lord Lyons, October 14, 1861, no. 97, Message of President Lincoln to 2nd Sess., 37th Congress, https://history.state.gov/historicaldocuments/frus1861; Dickey, *Our Man in Charleston*, 280–284; *The War of the Rebellion*, Ser. II, vol. 2 (Washington, DC: Government Printing Office, 1897), 644; Norman Ferris, *The* Trent *Affair: A Diplomatic Crisis* (Knoxville, TN: University of Tennessee Press, 1977), 124.

58. Duberman, *Adams*, 280–281. The entire incident is traced in Ferris, *The* Trent *Affair*.

59. Ferris, *The* Trent *Affair*, 33; *New York Times*, November 18, 1861, 1; Van Deusen, *Seward*, 309; Frederick Seward to Frances Seward, November 23, 1861, quoted in Stahr, *Seward*, 309.

60. On Wheaton, see *Oxford Handbook of the History of International Law* (Oxford: Oxford University Press, 2012), 1134–1135.

61. Henry Wheaton, *Elements of International Law*, 6th ed. (Boston, 1855), 29–30, 30, cxcii.

62. Wheaton, *International Law*, 31, 86, 95.

63. Wheaton, *International Law*, 147–148.

64. Wheaton, *International Law*, 97, 98, 106, 108.

65. Wheaton, *International Law*, 248–249.

66. Wheaton, *International Law*, 392, 394, 409, 411, 448, 458, 460.

67. Wheaton, *International Law*, 491, 492, 493, 494.

68. Doyle, *The Cause of All Nations*, 47–48.

69. Van Deusen, *Seward*, 311–312; Wheaton, *International Law*, 503–504; Ferris, *The* Trent *Affair*, 109ff.

70. Stahr, *Seward*, 312–323 (Seward's efforts were superb); Ferris, *The* Trent *Affair*, 182–183; Lyons's moderation had another source—he knew that Seward's agents had intercepted and detained Ruston Maury, a southern carrying letters from Confederate officials traveling under a British passport. Ferris, *The* Trent *Affair*, 124. Exposure would have embarrassed her majesty's government.

71. Seward quoted in *Seward at Washington*, 2: 24–25.

72. The insight that American foreign relations are legalistic comes from Benjamin Coates, *Legalist Empire: International Law and American Foreign Relations in the Early Twentieth Century* (New York: Oxford University Press, 2016), 2, although Coates associates the legalism with the progressive era. Seward's approach shows that legalism in our diplomacy appeared much earlier.

73. Seward to Lyons, December 26, 1861, quoted in Ferris, *The* Trent *Affair*, 182–183.

74. Seward to Charles Francis Adams, January 31, 1862, no. 171, Papers Relating to Foreign Affairs, Accompanying the Annual Message of the President to the 3rd. Sess.,

37th Cong., https://history.state.gov/historicaldocuments/frus1862/d10; Howard Jones, *Blue and Gray Diplomacy: A History of Union and Confederate Foreign Relations* (Chapel Hill: University of North Carolina Press, 2010), 110–111, 114–115; Van Deusen, *Seward*, 352–360.

75. Lyons-Seward Treaty of 1862 (12 Stat. 1225); A. Taylor Milne, "The Lyons-Seward Treaty of 1862," *American Historical Review* 38 (1933), 511–525.

76. Warren F. Spencer, *The Confederate Navy in Europe* (Athens: University of Georgia Press, 1983), 216; Robert Thorpe, *Mersey Built: The Role of the Merseyside in the American Civil War* (Wilmington, DE: Vernon, 2018), 170–175; Seward to Adams, July 29, 1863, no. 667, Papers Relating to Foreign Affairs, Accompanying the Annual Message of the President, 1st. Sess, 38th Cong., pt. 1, https://history.state.gov/historicaldocuments/frus1863p1/d252.

6. "To the Arbitrament of Courts of Law and to the Councils of Legislation"

1. Lincoln had always hated slavery but had not made slavery a major public issue until the Dred Scott decision in 1857 and the debates with Stephen Douglas in 1858. Stephen Berry, *A House Dividing: The Lincoln Douglas Debates of 1858* (New York: Oxford University Press, 2016), 9; Orville Vernon Burton, *The Age of Lincoln* (New York: Hill and Wang, 2007), 113. Foner, *Fiery Trial*, 64–65, argues that the Kansas-Nebraska Act of 1854 was a turning point in Lincoln's attention to the slave issue.

2. On the importance of the border states, see, e.g., William E. Gienapp, *Abraham Lincoln and Civil War: A Biography* (New York: Oxford University Press, 2002), 85. On Seward falling in line with Lincoln, see, e.g., Goodwin, *Team of Rivals*, 468.

3. William E. Gienapp, *The Origins of the Republican Party, 1852–1856* (New York: Oxford University Press, 1987), 191.

4. Seward, "The National Idea" Speech in Chicago, October 3, 1860, in Baker, ed., *Works*, 4:351, 356.

5. Seward to Lincoln, April 1, 1861, in Basler, ed., *Works of Abraham Lincoln*, 4:317; Seward to William L. Dayton, April 22, 1861, in Baker, ed., *Works*, 5:225, 227; Seward to Adams, February 22, 1862, in Baker, ed., *Works*, 5:313.

6. Stahr, *Seward*, 341–347; Seward to Adams, November 30, 1862, no. 8, Papers relating to Foreign Affairs, Accompanying the Annual Message of the President to the 1st Sess., 38th Cong., pt I, https://history.state.gov/historicaldocuments/frus1863p1/d8; James Oakes, *Freedom National: The Destruction of Slavery in the United States* (New York: Norton, 2013), 217ff.; Eric Foner, *Fiery Trial*, 219, 220, 231.

7. Leonard L. Richards, *Who Freed the Slaves?* (Chicago: University of Chicago Press, 2015), 29ff., is an effective brief for the crucial role of Ashley in the ending of slavery; see also Robert F. Horowitz, *The Great Impeacher: A Political Biography of James M. Ashley* (New York: Columbia University Press, 1973), 92–95. On Hale and the other proponents of further congressional action, see Oakes, *Freedom National*, 431–440 and Richard H. Sewell, *John P. Hale and the Politics of Abolition* (Cambridge, MA: Harvard University Press, 1965), 211–212.

8. Richards, *Who Freed the Slaves?*, 132–133 (battle within the Republican Party); 154–185 (Democrats versus Republicans); 118–119, 186–187, 193–194 (lining up votes).

9. Lincoln, Address at Gettysburg, November 19, 1863 in Basler, ed., *Papers*, 7:23; Garry Wills, *Lincoln at Gettysburg* (New York: Simon and Schuster, 1992), 31–32 (Seward influence on Lincoln's remarks); Richards, *Who Freed the Slaves?*, 204–213; Foner, *Fiery Trial*, 258–261.

10. Seward, Remarks at Gettysburg, November 18, 1863, *New York Times*, November 21, 1863, 1.

11. Michael Vorenberg, *Final Freedom: The Civil War, the Abolition of Slavery, and the Thirteenth Amendment* (New York: Cambridge University Press, 2001), 91–92.

12. See Peter Charles Hoffer, *John Quincy Adams and the Gag Rule, 1835–1850* (Baltimore: Johns Hopkins University Press, 2017).

13. James F. Wilson, *A Free Constitution, Speech . . . Delivered in the House of Representatives March 19, 1864* (Washington, DC: W. H. Moore, 1864), 1–7, 9. On the idea that the Preamble to the federal Constitution should be read as self-enabling, see Hoffer, *For Ourselves and Our Posterity*, 150–152.

14. Carl Sandburg, *Abraham Lincoln: The War Years* (New York: Harcourt, 1939), 2:558; Richards, *Who Freed the Slaves?*, 44.

15. Vorenberg, *Final Freedom*, 97–98; Patricia Ann Reid, "Between Slavery and Freedom" (PhD diss., University of Iowa, 2006), 123–124; Norman B. Ferris, "Reverdy Johnson," in *Great American Lawyers, An Encyclopedia*, ed. John R. Vile (Santa Barbara, CA: ABC-CLIO, 2001), 1:409–410.

16. George Ticknor Curtis quoted in Bernard Christian Steiner, *Life of Reverdy Johnson* (Baltimore: Norman, Remington, 1914), 38; Reverdy Johnson, *Speech . . . in Support of the Resolution to Amend the Constitution so as to Abolish Slavery*, April 5, 1864 (Washington, DC: n.p., 1864), 1. On the "old Constitution," see Hoffer, *Uncivil Warriors*, 2, 3, 136, 149, 153.

17. Johnson, *Speech*, 3, 4, 5.

18. Johnson, *Speech*, 12.

19. Johnson was never an advocate of slavery and never owned slaves, but he believed that slavery was legal under the Constitution. Steiner, *The Life of Reverdy Johnson*, 32.

20. Johnson, *Speech*, 18–19; Vorenberg, *Final Freedom*, 97.

21. Vorenberg, *Final Freedom*, 106. On enforcement clause and enumerated powers, see Timothy S. Huebner, *Liberty and Union: The Civil War Era and American Constitutionalism* (Lawrence: University Press of Kansas, 2016), 329.

22. Stahr, *Seward*, 353–360.

23. Seward, "On the Fall of Atlanta," September 3, 1864, in Baker, ed., *Works*, 5:503.

24. Paul D. Escott, *"What Shall We Do with the Negro": Lincoln, White Racism, and Civil War America* (Charlottesville: University of Virginia Press, 2009), 122–123; Stahr, *Seward*, 401. Arkansas had had two governments, one Union and one Confederate. The Union government altered the state constitution to end slavery in 1864. West Virginia entered the Union in 1863, with a constitution barring slavery. Maryland ended slavery in 1864 by a referendum and an amendment to its constitution. Tennessee slaves were freed in October 1864 by executive order of military governor Andrew Johnson. Missouri ended slavery by a state-wide ordinance in January 1865. Slavery ended in those portions of Louisiana still in rebellion as a result of the Emancipation Proclamation on January 1, 1863. A constitutional convention in 1864 confirmed their freedom, although much of the state remained in confederate hands until the end of the war.

25. Seward, "The Great Issues" Speech at Auburn, New York, September 3, 1864, printed as a broadside, https://ia800604.us.archive.org/12/items/greatissuesspeec00sewa/greatissuesspeec00sewa.pdf.

26. Seward, "The Great Issues" Speech.

27. Seward, "The Great Issues" Speech. He was convincing enough, and New York went for Lincoln with a slim margin of 6,000 votes.

28. Mark E. Neely, Jr., *Lincoln and the Democrats, The Politics of Opposition in the Civil War* (Cambridge, UK: Cambridge University Press, 2017), 114–120.

29. Vorenberg, *Final Freedom*, 42, 155–156, 182–183; La Wanda Cox and John Cox, *Politics, Principle, and Prejudice, 1865–1866, the Dilemma of Reconstruction America* (New York: Free Press, 1963), 1–30.

30. Lincoln, Fourth Message to Congress, December 6, 1864, in Basler, ed., *Collected Works*, 8:149.

31. Abraham Lincoln to the Senate, December 6, 1864, https://millercenter.org/the-presidency/presidential-speeches/december-6-1864-fourth-annual-message.

32. Abraham Lincoln to the Senate, December 6, 1864.

33. Abraham Lincoln to the Senate, December 6, 1864; Stahr, *Seward*, 414 J. W. Schuckers, *The Life and Public Services of Salmon Portland Chase* (New York: Appleton, 1874), 514; Vorenberg, *Final Freedom*, 176–179.

34. Lincoln, "Second Inaugural Address," March 4, 1865, in Basler, ed., *Collected Works*, 8:333.

35. Vorenberg, *Final Freedom*, 130, 131, 134, 135, 180–187; Paul D. Escott, *Lincoln's Dilemma: Blair, Sumner, and the Republican Struggle over Racism and Equality in the Civil War Era* (Charlottesville: University of Virginia Press, 2014), 182–183; David E. Long, *The Jewel of Liberty, Abraham Lincoln's Election Victory and the End of Slavery* (Mechanicsburg, PA: Stackpole, 1994), 153–177.

36. See, e.g., Seward "Advent of the Republican Party" Speech at Albany, October 12, 1855, in Baker, ed., *Works*, 4:228; Speech at Buffalo, October 18, 1855, in Baker, ed., *Works*, 4:247; Speech at Detroit, October 2, 1855, in Baker, ed., *Works*, 4:257.

37. Seward, Speech at Cooper Institution, February 22, 1866, in Baker, ed., *Works*, 5:530, 531, 532, 533, 538. Note the word restoration, far less radical than reconstruction. Stahr, *Seward*, 449. Seward was not out of line with Lincoln, who was "never at ease" using the word "reconstruction," always qualifying it. Allen Guelzo, *Reconstruction: A Concise History* (New York: Oxford University Press, 2018), 2. Seward was one of the three members of Johnson's cabinet who remained after the latter vetoed Republican reconstruction legislation. Michael Les Benedict, *The Impeachment and Trial of Andrew Johnson* (New York: Norton, 1973), 15. In the cabinet, Seward had argued for a military trial for Jefferson Davis, and was believed by Davis's legal council to hate Davis with a passion. Nicoletti, *Secession on Trial*, 71–72.

7. "The Union Has Been Rescued from All Its Perils"

1. Stahr, *Seward*, 422–426.

2. Stahr, *Seward*, 427, 435–440; Van Deusen, *Seward*, 413–417; Taylor, *Seward*, 243–249. Although all three accounts are based on the same primary sources, they vary in detail.

3. Hans Trefousse, *Andrew Johnson: A Biography* (New York: Norton, 1989), 257 (Seward role in Johnson's vice presidency).

4. Seward to Surgeon General Joseph Barnes, June 1865, *Seward at Washington*, 2:284; E. L. Godkin, *The Nation*, February 2, 1871, p. 1; Stahr, *Seward*, 387, 414, 446; *Seward at Washington*, 2:283 (Lincoln and Seward reconstruction program); Eric Foner, *Reconstruction: America's Unfinished Revolution, 1863–1877* (New York: Harper and Row, 1988), 191, 219, 247; John Hope Franklin, *Reconstruction After the Civil War* (Chicago: University of Chicago Press, 1961), 28; Kenneth Stampp, *The Era of Reconstruction, 1865–1877* (New York: Knopf, 1966), 59, quoting Cox and Cox, *Politics*, 222.

5. James Morton Callahan, "The Evolution of Seward's Mexican Policy," *West Virginia University Studies in American History* 1 (1909), 133; Stahr, *Seward*, 464–465; Van Deusen, *Seward*, 488. Jeff Ludwig agrees with Joseph A. Fry, *Lincoln, Seward, and US Foreign Relations in the Civil War Era* (Lexington: University of Kentucky Press, 2019), 161, that Seward was one of the greatest US secretaries of state. He certainly was an empire builder. Whether his achievements match those of Jefferson, John Quincy Adams, and Daniel Webster, who preceded him, and Charles Evans Hughes, Dean Acheson, Henry Kissinger, and Colin Powell is a matter for other scholars to debate.

6. See, e.g., Ernest N. Paolino, *The Foundations of American Empire: William Henry Seward and US Foreign Policy* (Ithaca: Cornell University Press, 1973), 11ff.

7. Seward, Speech at Detroit, September 4, 1860, in Baker, ed., *Works*, 4:310–311. On dual sovereignty and ratification, see Pauline Maier, *Ratification: The People Debate the Constitution, 1787–1788* (New York: Simon & Schuster, 2010), 109–110 (James Wilson at Pennsylvania ratification convention); James Madison, Federalist No. 15, in Clinton Rossiter, ed., *The Federalist Papers* (New York: Penguin, 1961), 109; Madison, Federalist No. 39, in Rossiter, ed., *The Federalist Papers*, 245.

8. Thomas A. Bailey, *A Diplomatic History of the American People* (New York: Appleton Crofts Century, 1958), 371–372; Bailey, "Why the United States Purchased Alaska," *Pacific Historical Review* 3 (1934): 39–49; Stahr, *Seward*, 482–491; Van Deusen, *Seward*, 535–548. Lee Farrow's account, *Seward's Folly: A New Look at the Alaska Purchase* (Chicago: University of Chicago Press, 2016), locates the purchase in its international context, perhaps where Seward truly saw it. Seward was an avid continentalist. Farrow, *Seward's Folly*, 23ff. The epithet, Seward's folly, appeared first in 1880, although Frederick Seward recalled its earlier use. Stahr, *Seward*, 487–488.

9. Charles Francis Adams Jr. to Charles Francis Adams, June 29, 1867, quoted in Stahr, *Seward*, 493; Mark Wahlgren Summers, *The Ordeal of the Reunion: A New History of Reconstruction* (Chapel Hill: University of North Carolina Press, 2014), 208–210.

10. *Seward at Washington*, 2:243 (speech on Sherman's victory); *Seward at Washington*, 2:320–321 (Cooper Institute speech); *Seward at Washington*, 2:464 (speech on return from the west, March 1870); Van Deusen, *Seward*, 550 ("dreaded retirement"); Stahr, *Seward*, 472 (whistle stop talks), 491 (talk at Chapel Hill); Harold Lewis Lawson, "The Speaking of William Henry Seward, 1845–1861" (PhD diss., Ohio State University, 1967), 314.

11. Stahr, *Seward*, 509; Hans Trefousse, *Andrew Johnson: A Biography*, 242, 289; David O. Stewart, *Impeached: The Trial of President Andrew Johnson* (New York: Simon & Schuster, 2010), 59–61, 240–249; Seward, *The Situation and the Duty, Speech at Auburn, October 31, 1868* (Washington, DC: Philip and Solomons, 1868), 18.

12. Although those who met him were shocked by his facial scars, they were impressed by his quickness of perception and soundness of mind. Jeff Ludwig to the author, December 7, 2021.

13. Seward Address at Auburn, October 31, 1868, in Baker, ed., *Works*, 5:554.

14. Seward to Frances Seward, December 7, 1842, *Autobiography*, 638–639; Stahr, *Seward*, 542; Van Deusen, *Seward*, 562; Taylor, *Seward*, 294.

15. Seward, "Irrepressible Conflict," 5; On slavery and dispossession of Indian lands in the Revolutionary War, see Robert G. Parkinson, *The Common Cause: Creating Nation and Race in the American Revolution* (Chapel Hill: University of North Carolina Press, 2016), 185–263.

16. Foner, *Reconstruction*, 364–379.

17. Autobiography, 58, 59.

18. Seward, Speech at Sitka, August 12, 1869 (Washington, DC: Chapman, 1879) 5, 10; removal of statues (and misquoted text of speech): Steve Langdon, "Why the William Henry Seward Statues Should Be Removed," *Anchorage Times*, July 27, 2020. On the Awa'Uq massacre of 1784, see John Enders, "Probable Site of Alaskan Massacre Explored" August 16, 1992, *Los Angeles Times*. The Seward "shame" totem pole was first erected in Saxman, Alaska, in the 1880s to shame Seward for discourtesy to a Tongass Village elder, and has most recently been restored in 2017, https://alaskahistoricalsociety.org/about-ahs/special-projects/150treaty/150th-resource-library/new-articles/the-seward-shame-pole-countering-alaskas-sesquicentennial/.

19. Richard Milward, *Table-Talk: Being the Discourses of John Selden* (London: Dent, [1689] 1906), 72; Elliott Visconsi, "Seldenism," in Lorna Hutson, ed., *Oxford Handbook of English Law and Literature, 1500–1700* (Oxford: Oxford University Press, 2017), 380–389; Oliver Wendell Holmes, *The Autocrat of the Breakfast-Table, Every Man His Own Boswell* (Boston: Philips, Sampson, 1858), 16; Seward Family Digital Archive, Seward Family books, https://sewardproject.org/seward-book-list/public/holdings/64031.

20. "Table Talk," *Seward at Washington*, 2:471, 472, 474, 476.

21. Burlingame-Seward Treaty of 1868 was almost immediately under attack from leading Democrats, and was substantially abandoned in the Chinese Exclusion Acts of 1882. See Earl M. Maltz, "The Federal Government and the Problem of Chinese Rights in the Era of the Fourteenth Amendment," *Harvard Journal of Law & Public Policy* 17 (1994), 223–252.

Conclusion

1. On Seward as a radical, see Frederick Bancroft, *The Life of William H. Seward* (New York: Harper, 1899), 1:263; Arthur C. Cole, *The Irrepressible Conflict, 1850–1865* (New York: Harper, 1934); Eric Foner, *Free Soil, Free Labor, Free Men: The Ideology of the Republican Party Before the Civil War* (New York: Oxford University Press, 1970), 211. For Seward as a conservative, Allan Nevins, *The Emergence of Lincoln* (New York: Scriber, 1950), 2:300. For Seward as a flexible adherent of the idea of progress, see Major L. Wilson, "The Repressible Conflict: Seward's Concept of Progress and the Free Soil Movement," *Journal of Southern History* 37 (1971), 533–567. For Seward as a moralist motivated by and limited by the assumptions of antebellum individualistic voluntarism, see Ronald G. Walters, *The Antislavery Appeal: American Abolitionism After 1830* (Baltimore, MD: Johns Hopkins University

Press, 1976). Even in formal logic there are proofs of the inevitability of incompleteness. Surely one could find many inconsistencies in Seward's thought, but that does not mean he was illogical. To conclude that he was a slippery character who said or wrote whatever the time, place, and issue required is simply unfair.

2. C. Vann Woodward, *The Strange Career of Jim Crow* (New York: Oxford University Press, 1955), 31–32.

3. Seward, "The True Basis of American Independence," Address to the American Institute, October 20, 1853, in Baker, ed., *Works*, 4:150, 153; Seward, 1844, quoted in *Autobiography*, 697. No one has attributed this liberal or democratic jurisprudence to Seward, but it still echoes in the legal academy. See, e.g., Robert Cover, "The Supreme Court, 1982 Term—Foreword: Nomos and Narrative," *Harvard Law Review* 97 (1983), 25: "the Constitution must compete with natural law, the Declaration of Independence, the Articles of Confederation, and the Revolution itself for primacy in the narrative tradition."

4. The concept of utilitarian law—the greatest happiness or good for the greatest number—is usually associated with Jeremy Bentham, *An Introduction to the Principles of Morals and Legislation* (London: T. Payne, 1789), iii. I can only find one reference to Bentham in Seward's writings, in his "Remarks at Cherry Valley Centennial, 1840": "what could have been . . . the science of law before Montesquieu, Pufendorf, Blackstone, and Bentham." That seems to be a boilerplate reference, however. *Autobiography*, 489. A more modern version is Barry Friedman, *The Will of the People: How Public Opinion Has Influenced the Supreme Court and Shaped the Meaning of the Constitution* (New York: Farrar, Straus and Giroux, 2009), 367–369.

5. Gordon Wood, *Empire of Liberty, A History of the Early Republic, 1789–1815* (New York: Oxford University Press, 2009), 16, 718; Robert Rantoul Jr., Oration at Scituate, July 4, 1836, in Luther Hamilton, ed., *Memoirs, Speeches, and Writings of Robert Rantoul, Jr.* (Boston: Jewett, 1854), 282; Perry Miller, *The Legal Mind in America, From Independence to the Civil War* (Cambridge, MA: Harvard University Press, 1962), pt. 3.

6. Michael Kammen, *People of Paradox: an Inquiry Concerning the Origins of American Civilization* (New York: Knopf, 1972), 190–193, 214–215; Edmund S. Morgan, *American Slavery, American Freedom* (New York: Norton, 1975), 338–339; David Waldstreicher, *Slavery's Constitution, From Revolution to Ratification* (New York: Hill and Wang, 2010), 108–109. But see Sean Wilentz and James Oakes, With a Reply by Nicholas Guyatt, "No Property in Man, an Exchange," *New York Review of Books*, June 27, 2019. In a curiosity of changing historical interests over time—Kammen's Pulitzer Prize-winning study discoursed on all manner of biformities, but relegated slavery to a few pages, and the index did not mention the word. As I write, slavery is a centerpiece in the study of colonial and early national America.

7. Robert A. Dahl, *How Democratic Is the American Constitution?*, 2nd ed. (New Haven: Yale University Press, 2003), 68; Michael Klarman, *The Framers' Coup: The Making of the Federal Constitution* (New York: Oxford University Press, 2016), 622; Seward, "Election of Mayors, Speech in the New York State Senate, April 22, 1831, in Baker, ed. *Works*, 1:11.

8. Peter J. Galie, *The New York State Constitution* (New York: Oxford University Press, 2011), 10; David A. Bateman, *Disenfranchising Democracy: Constructing the Electorate in The United States, the United Kingdom, and France* (Cambridge, UK: Cambridge University Press, 2018), 131–132, 139.

9. Mark Neely Jr., *Lincoln and the Triumph of the Nation* (Chapel Hill: University of North Carolina Press, 114–115; but see Michael Les Benedict, *The Blessings of Liberty*, 3rd ed. (Lanham, MD: Rowman and Littlefield, 2017), 163–167 (northern opposition to the spread of slavery).

10. Seward, "Development of the American People," Address to Phi Beta Kappa, Yale College, July 26, 1854, in Baker, ed., *Works*, 4:176. On instrumentalism in law, see Morton Horwitz, *The Transformation of American Law, 1780–1860* (Cambridge: Harvard University Press, 1977), 23.

11. Karl Llewellyn, *The Bramble Bush* (New York: Oxford University Press, [1930] 2008), 174.

12. Charles Francis Adams, *An Address on the Life, Character and Services of William Henry. Seward*, delivered to the New York State Legislature, April 18, 1873 (New York: Weed, Parsons, 1873), 15, 72; Claude Lévi-Strauss, *The Savage Mind* (Chicago: University of Chicago Press, 1966), 21, 22. It is not by chance, then, that Karl Llewellyn, whose jurisprudential contributions were broad but not entirely coherent, was also a bricoleur. See N. E. H. Hull, *Roscoe Pound and Karl Llewellyn, Searching for An American Jurisprudence* (Chicago: University of Chicago Press, 1996), 8, 9, 10. What is missing from this bricolage is religion.

13. Daniel Walker Howe, *The Political Culture of the American Whigs* (New York: Oxford University Press, 1979), 198–209. Howe, about the only historian who takes Seward's thinking seriously, finds a somewhat different combination of attributes in Seward's thinking: Seward was a modernizer in most matters, a believer in mind over matter, and a champion of universal education. His thinking was not novel, but very much in the Whig tradition. Howe does not emphasize in any way Seward's legalism, nor the influence of his law practice on his politics, however.

14. For the notion that the meaning of an author's ideas depends on what the author is doing, and that thinking and acting together rest on events in a time and place, see Quentin Skinner, *The Foundations of Modern Political Thought 1: The Renaissance* (Cambridge, UK: Cambridge University Press, 1978), xiii–xiv. On equity, see, e.g., Peter Charles Hoffer, *The Law's Conscience: Equitable Constitutionalism in America* (Chapel Hill: University of North Carolina Press, 1990), 8, 213; on win-win, see Roger Fisher and William L. Ury, *Getting to Yes*, 2nd ed. (New York: Houghton Mifflin Harcourt, 1991).

15. The "civic humanism" school of the founders is best reflected in the work of J. G. A. Pocock, Gordon Wood, and Lance Banning. The key concept is that a republic can only exist in a climate of civic virtue that requires the sacrifice of private interest for the public good and the disinterestedness of republican leaders. See, e.g., Pocock, *The Machiavellian Moment: Florentine Political Thought and the Atlantic Republican Tradition* (Princeton: Princeton University Press, 1975), 462ff.; Gordon Wood, *The Creation of the American Republic* (Chapel Hill: University of North Carolina Press, 1969), 68, 96; Lance Banning, *The Jeffersonian Persuasion: Evolution of a Party Ideology* (Ithaca: Cornell University Press, 1978), 46, 82.

16. Mark W. Summers, *Corruption and the Crisis of the Union, 1849–1860* (New York: Oxford University Press, 1989); Summers, *The Ordeal of the Reunion*, 273–297; Richard White, *The Republic for Which it Stands: The United States During Reconstruction and the Gilded Age, 1865–1896* (New York: Oxford University Press, 2017), 118ff.

17. See, e.g., Taylor, *Seward*, 204–205. On Sumner's law practice, David Donald, *Charles Sumner and the Coming of the Civil War* (New York: Knopf, 196), 69.

18. Seward to E. J. Fowle, August 26, 1848, in Baker, ed., *Works*, 3:413. Historians have sometimes accepted the verdict of Seward's critics that he was more militant than he was. In the light of the limits of country lawyering, this is a serious misunderstanding. See, e.g., David M. Potter, *The Impending Crisis, 1848–1861* (New York: Harper and Row, 1976), 139 (Seward a "militant" antislavery man), 172 ("antislavery man in the same way as Chase and Seward").

19. Seward to William Jay and Gerritt Smith, October 22, 1838, in Baker, ed., *Works*, 3:428.

20. Seward to Jay and Smith, October 22, 1838, in Baker, ed., *Works*, 3:430.

21. An exception to my lament about the lack of lasting impact of Seward's philosophy of law is its (admittedly pale) influence on Thomas M. Cooley's treatises on state and federal constitutional law. Cooley, who grew up and studied law in New York state a generation after Seward, and even corresponded briefly with the older man, was an advocate of what today would be called libertarian jurisprudence. Seward believed in the state taking an active role in the economy; Cooley opposed that, but their view of the importance of good law was similar. Cooley, *A Treatise on Constitutional Limitations Which Rest upon the Legislative Power of the States of the American Union* (Boston: Little, Brown, 1871).

22. Ralph Waldo Emerson, "Self-Reliance," in *Essays* (Boston: Munro, 1841), 19.

23. Close, but not completely aligned, is John Rawls's idea of fairness within communities. See Rawls, *A Theory of Justice* (Cambridge: Harvard University Press, 1971), 17, 31–32. Seward was not interested in the "good" or the "moral" in an abstract sense.

INDEX